# Bookbinding in America

# BOOKBINDING IN AMERICA

## *THREE ESSAYS*

EARLY AMERICAN BOOKBINDING BY HAND
By *HANNAH DUSTIN FRENCH* of *Wellesley College Library*

THE RISE OF AMERICAN EDITION BINDING
By *JOSEPH W. ROGERS* of *The Library of Congress*
*Formerly of Milwaukee Public Library*

ON THE REBINDING OF OLD BOOKS
By *HELLMUT LEHMANN-HAUPT*
*EDITOR*

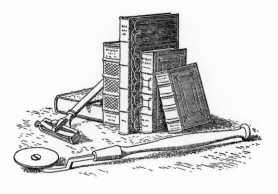

*R. R. BOWKER COMPANY*
NEW YORK AND LONDON
1967

# Foreword

AMONG the men and women who bound books for our ancestors in Colonial times and in the days of the young Republic there were some of great talent and skill. But we know only a few of them by name and not many bindings have survived. These precious specimens of colonial design and craftsmanship are scattered through many libraries, private and public, where they have remained often unobserved and unidentified. Miss Hannah Dustin French, of the Wellesley College Library, has made a thorough search for them and has collected a unique record. She found names of binders, biographical data, business records on one side. On the other side she searched out the bindings. Some of these had been previously described, others have never before been published. A few of them were signed by their makers, some contained evidence of their origin, others did not. From these varied sources of miscellaneous information Miss French succeeded in presenting a coherent and vivid picture of early American bookbinding. She has described the workshop, the tools and materials of the old master binders and has been able to ascribe surviving examples to definite ateliers, establishing valuable criteria for the dating and identifying of historical American bindings. She has discovered certain workshops established by craftsmen immigrated from Europe and has taught us how to distinguish their work from the older native schools.

The first results of her studies were accepted in 1939 as a Master's Essay in the Book Arts field at the School of Library Service, Columbia University. Their inclusion in this volume marks their first appearance in print.

The profound influence of the machine age upon any aspect of our society and culture is turning the eyes of many

thoughtful men and women to the beginnings of this development. The history of American bookbinding in the
nineteenth century shows, within its realm, a very true reflection and a very prompt reaction to these great and universal changes. Bookbinding, the successive manipulation
of a great many, minutely interwoven steps, each of them
sanctioned by up to fifteen centuries of experience, turned,
almost over night, from an ancient craft to a modern industry.

It is the story of this development which is told by Mr.
Joseph W. Rogers, of the Milwaukee Public Library, in the
second part of this book. His account is an almost unbroken
record of American technical achievement, showing how
the young Republic's great dependence upon other countries changed in the course of the nineteenth century and
how it gave way gradually to a distinct leadership in the
graphic arts industry.

The story of how bookbinding turned from a craft to an
industry, besides symbolizing mechanical achievement, has,
however, yet another significance. Bookbinding by machine
became the main factor in the development of publishers'
binding and that in turn had a deep influence upon publishing methods and practices. Bibliographers, collectors, and
librarians, in recent years have begun to pay much attention
to these practices. The whole complex of questions which
concern the definition of first editions, sequence of impressions, and priority of issue hinges, to a very large extent, on
binding practices. A good deal of attention has been paid,
in the recent past to English publishers' binding cloth and
there has been some investigation of the underlying technical developments. Mr. Rogers' essay is the first thorough
study of the crucial American side of this evolution, and it
contains the first study of American publishers' binding
cloth.

There is no doubt that the very complicated picture of nineteenth-century inventions and changes in the graphic arts will receive a great deal of attention from all those interested in the study and appreciation of bookmaking, and by bibliographers and collectors. Mr. Rogers' essay is therefore a very timely contribution. One convincing example of the value of his study is the third essay in this volume, which deals with the rebinding of old volumes. Several years ago the editor of this book sat down to the task of recording, for the benefit of the many who are constantly seeking advice in these matters, some of his observations and recommendations for the care and preservation of valuable old volumes. This task turned out to be insoluble without a close analysis of current bookbinding practices in this country, and particularly in the library binding field—and that, almost at once, revealed the necessity for a study of the historical and technical background of contemporary conditions.

It was fortunate that Mr. Rogers assumed the responsibility for such an analysis. His findings, accepted as a Master's Essay at Columbia University Library School in 1937, were first printed in abbreviated form, in the Gutenberg Yearbook of 1938. His article, although none too accessible in that form, was hailed by competent critics as a contribution of genuine merit and originality. It was obviously desirable that it should be published in this country, in expanded and fully documented form.

The third part of this book will be of particular interest to all those who in one way or another are concerned with old and valuable volumes, be they in a private collection or an institutional library. There are many factors tending to shorten the lives of the fine old bindings in the libraries of this country and many influences unfavorable to their preservation and fitting replacement when necessary. The question of how best to preserve and protect against future destruction the many precious relics of the past is of great importance. For a successful solution of these problems we depend upon the experience and the understanding of collectors and librarians as well as upon the sympathy and the skill of the modern bookbinder. I have attempted, in the third part of this book, to examine the current rebinding practices, to show where they are at fault and to demonstrate ways and means of solving the various difficulties. Although these pages contain certain definite practical suggestions, this essay is not primarily to be read as a technical manual. Rather, it is a discussion of the ethics and aesthetics of rebinding.

In the preparation of this book the three authors have enjoyed the assistance and advice of not a few experts in the various fields with which this volume is concerned.

Miss French wishes to express her gratitude to the many owners and curators of collections which contain early American bookbindings. She is particularly indebted to Mr. Lawrence C. Wroth, Miss Ruth Shepard Granniss, Mr. Clarence S. Brigham, Mr. Robert W. G. Vail, Mr. Valta Parma, Mr. Thomas J. Holmes, Miss Elinor Gregory, Mr. Zoltan Haraszti; and to Mr. Allyn Forbes, Miss Lucy Eugenia Osborne, Miss Elizabeth Steer, Dr. Victor H. Paltsits, Mrs. Betty Carson Tyson, Dr. Samuel Woodhouse and Mrs. Harry M. Bland.

Mr. Rogers owes a debt of gratitude to the many men now active in various phases of edition binding who gave him assistance by letter or interview. He has acknowledged their help in the text and footnotes of his essay. Their co-operation has been most valuable. He also wishes to thank Mr. David M. Glixon, the Editor of *Bookbinding and Bookproduction,* for the loan of catalogs and machine illustrations issued by manufacturers of bookbinding machines; and Mr. Harry Miller Lydenberg, for permission to photograph early

American edition bindings on the shelves of the New York Public Library.

My own indebtedness is perhaps largest to various book-binders, both individuals and firms, who have taught me to appreciate their work and to understand some of their difficulties. Mr. Pelham Barr, Executive Director of the Library Binding Institute, has given valuable assistance in looking over my manuscript and in offering detailed and concrete suggestions. I also wish to thank Mr. Ernst F. Detterer and Mrs. Gertrude L. Woodward for the photographs of material in the Newberry Library in Chicago; Mr. George A. Hathaway for his guidance in the matter of parchment and vellum, and the late Dr. Theodore W. Koch for the University of Pittsburgh book oil formula. I am also grateful to the staff of Columbia University Library, particularly to Dr. Mary A. Bennett, Miss Marianne von Dobeneck and Mr. Walter E. Hering for the preparation of photographs, and to Miss Bertha M. Frick and Mr. Martin K. Howes for valuable editorial assistance.

Our combined thanks are due to Columbia University which offered opportunity and facilities for our studies, and to Mr. Fred Anthoensen, our publisher.

H. L.-H.

*Low Memorial Library,*
*April* 8, 1941.

# Foreword to the 1967 Reprint

TWENTY-FIVE years ago *Bookbinding in America* was published by the Southworth-Anthoensen Press, and later taken over by the R. R. Bowker Company. The book has long been out-of-print and copies have been practically unobtainable for many years.[1]

A large number of new publications dealing with many aspects of the history and technique of bookbinding, as well as with care and repair, have appeared in the last quarter century. Nevertheless, there has been distinct evidence of continuing demand for *Bookbinding in America,* which could only be explained by the fact that the book contains a good deal of information and ideas not repeated, expanded, or superseded by any of these later publications.

For this reason, the R. R. Bowker Company decided to reprint *Bookbinding in America* rather than to publish a new, revised edition. However, in order to "update" the book where this seemed desirable, the original editor and authors of the volume were each asked to add a brief supplement, reporting new developments and listing new publications in their respective fields. It is hoped that these supplements, found at the end of each of the three parts, will be welcomed by the future readers of this volume.

H. L.-H.

*September 5, 1966.*

---

[1] For the bibliographically minded I should explain that the copies issued directly from the Southworth-Anthoensen Press (now the Anthoensen Press) in Portland, Maine, were bound in black half-cloth, the sides covered with an attractive hand-made paste paper by Veronica Ruzicka. The copies sold by the R. R. Bowker Company were bound in a similar black cloth back of a more marked texture, and with plain green paper sides.

# Contents

## PART TWO

### THE RISE OF AMERICAN EDITION BINDING
#### By Joseph W. Rogers

*Contents*

# List of Illustrations

*PART I*

Early American Bookbinding by Hand

1636-1820

*By HANNAH D. FRENCH*

# Early American Bookbinding by Hand
## 1636-1820

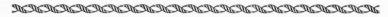

## CHAPTER I

### *INTRODUCTION*

THE art of binding books in leather had reached a high stage of development in the Middle Ages and the Renaissance. No fundamentally new principles have been introduced into the craft between the sixteenth century and the beginning of the nineteenth. There have, of course, been certain changes in technique and in the choice of materials. But these changes are not nearly so obvious as those which can be observed in the ornamentation or finishing of bookbindings. These final touches of decoration and their underlying principle have been emphasized by the historians of the art of bookbinding, with little regard for the fundamental technical processes involved. We are beginning to realize today that no discussion of ornamental leather bindings can be complete without an understanding of the methods by which these volumes came to be bound: the materials chosen, the techniques employed, and the decoration applied.

Simplicity and durability characterized the leather-bound volumes of the fifteenth century. They were thick folios and required heavy wooden covers. Some kind of leather skin was used as a covering for the wooden boards, and the signatures of the book were sewed around leather thongs before these were pegged into the covers. Paste and glue were the only additional materials needed. A single craftsman undertook all the steps involved: folding the sheets, arranging them in their proper sequence, sewing them on thongs, attaching the board covers to the book, putting on the leather covering and decorating it with small stamps impressed in blind. In time certain changes occurred, such as the substitution of pasteboard for wooden covers, the replacement of leather thongs by hempen cords, and the shaping of the book by a process of rounding and backing to keep the back from caving in. All these, however, were merely refinements which gradually developed out of a traditional and well-established method of bookbinding.

Decoration was important, and it is significant that the early craftsmen were not content with purely utilitarian covers, but took added pains to introduce an element of beauty. We know, from Goldschmidt's careful study of mediaeval binding,[1] that ornamentation was achieved at the beginning of the fifteenth century, by small blind-impressed stamps of animals, flowers, and leaves, which were replaced towards the close of the century, when the annual output of books had become much greater, by the roll and the panel stamps, as labor-saving devices. The manner of their disposition early became representative of various localities, and certain individual patterns came to be associated with given countries. From that time onward style has been studied as characteristic of a period, a nation, or an individual.

Bookbinding history has been told either by brief historical sketches that survey the work of individual craftsmen in separate countries, or by detailed monographs that consider the work of limited periods or of single individuals within a country. The lacunae are numerous. The history of bookbinding in France has been told and, to a far more limited extent, that of England. There is no single continuous history of English bookbinding, but there are numerous monographic studies which cover their limited areas well. We know the work of the English seventeenth century through that of Samuel Mearne and the eighteenth

[1] E. P. Goldschmidt, *Gothic & Renaissance Bookbindings*, 2 vols. (London: Benn, 1928).

through that of Roger Payne, but of the less ambitious work of their periods little notice has been taken.

Up to this point there has been no one study of American bookbinding which has attempted fully to trace the history and conditions of hand bookbinding in this country. The reason for this can be put no better than it has been, in the catalogue of an exhibition held at The Grolier Club in 1902:[2]

The history of bookbinding in America has received little or no attention, chiefly, probably, because of a lack of collected material from which to write it. A few bindings have been found with designs made from small tools, and some stamped and roulette patterns; and early examples of mosaic work, even, are known, having timid designs executed in their leather; but an enthusiastic bibliophile is yet to be found willing to undertake the collection and description of the examples of this one of the American crafts.

The writer goes on to say that American bookbinders need to be aware of the tradition of design in their craft and to have access to examples in libraries and museums. Such examples for study would form the basis for original work. This brief reference, hidden in the middle of a catalogue of mosaic bindings which listed only one American example bound before 1820, is interesting in its unexpectedness and in its apt interpretation of the need for such a history. In 1902, the year of the publication of The Grolier Club Catalogue, the appearance of William Loring Andrews' study of American bookbinding,[3] with its generous collection of plates, did much to introduce the subject and call attention to a field worthy of investigation. Much the same thing is true of a volume published the following year, in 1903, by Henri Pène Du Bois on the American bindings in Mr. Poor's collection, carefully printed and

[2] *Mosaic Bookbindings, a Catalogue of an Exhibition* (New York: The Grolier Club, January 23-February 22, 1902), 53 p. Reference on pp. 46-48.

[3] W. L. Andrews, *Bibliopegy in the United States* (New York: Dodd, Mead, 1902), 130 p.

illustrated at the Marion Press.[4] The earlier interest of The Grolier Club was followed in 1907 by a definite contribution in an interesting exhibition and the publication of a *Catalogue of Ornamental Leather Bookbindings*.[5] The importance of this brochure was greatly enhanced by the introduction written by Henry W. Kent. After 1907, however, it was nearly twenty years before mention of the subject reappeared, this time in the final pages of Meiric K. Dutton's *Historical Sketch*.[6] Since then, an increase of interest is indicated by the study of Ratcliff and Ranger, two seventeenth-century bookbinders in Boston, made two years later by Thomas J. Holmes,[7] and by a chapter in Wroth's *The Colonial Printer*.[8]

I have undertaken in these pages to trace the history and conditions of hand bookbinding in America during the years 1636 to 1820; so far as possible to discover the centers of activity and the names and origins of the binders, as well as the kind of work they did; to identify specific bindings with their makers; to show the relationship between native and immigrant craftsmen; and to indicate the forces which led to the adoption of machinery. The difficulties have been manifold, and at times the obstacles have seemed all but insurmountable. Original bindings are scattered over a wide geographical area, are not segregated in individual collections, and have often been repaired. Some collections of Americana have been badly defaced by library labels and stamps; and others have been wholly or partly rebound in

[4] Henri Pène Du Bois, *American Bookbindings in the Library of Henry William Poor* (Jamaica, N. Y.: Marion Press, 1903), 77 p.

[5] *Catalogue of Ornamental Leather Bookbindings Executed in America Prior to 1850*, exhibited at The Grolier Club, 1907, 107 p. (Hereafter referred to as Grolier Club Catalogue.)

[6] M. K. Dutton, *Historical Sketch of Bookbinding as an Art* (Norwood, Mass.: Holliston Mills, 1926), 128 p.

[7] T. J. Holmes, 'The Bookbindings of John Ratcliff and Edmund Ranger, Seventeenth Century Boston Bookbinders,' *Proceedings of American Antiquarian Society*, n. s., XXXVIII, 31-50; XXXIX, 291-306.

[8] L. C. Wroth, *The Colonial Printer* (2d ed., Portland: The Southworth-Anthoensen Press, 1938), 368 p.

the modern style, probably in the innocent belief that it improved the appearance of the books, and not for utilitarian reasons only. It must be remembered that fine or extra binding was a fetish in the late nineteenth century, and primitive bindings were replaced by shining morocco and gilt with a fine disregard for the dignity and appropriateness of the originals. Whatever the motive, however, artistic or utilitarian, the result is simple destruction. I have been successful to a surprising degree, however, in locating examples of early decorated bindings which seem to be the work of American binders; have seen and handled a considerable number; and obtained many names of individual craftsmen. Printed and manuscript sources were extremely helpful as far as they went, and my gratitude to those who have pointed the way is profound.

It would be sheer presumption on my part to assume that I have been able to piece together anything approaching a definitive history of American bookbinding from its earliest undertaking until 1820. It is with no little trepidation that I set down what I have discovered in this neglected and unorganized field, knowing full well that the proportion of the known to the unknown is still alarmingly small, and that many questions have been raised but not answered. Incomplete as my work must necessarily be with the materials at hand, it will have done much towards fulfilling its purpose if it opens the field a little further and points out areas requiring further and more detailed investigation.

# CHAPTER II

## *BOOKBINDING IN THE COLONIAL PERIOD*
### (1636-1783)

THE early settlers in the American colonies, with the problem of a wilderness to conquer, were thrown on their own resources and forced to face conditions more nearly like those of the Middle Ages than those of the seventeenth-century England they had left behind. Much has been written of the harsh and stern reality of the practical side of their lives, but only within recent years has there been any emphasis laid upon the creative and imaginative aspect, and the arts and crafts which expressed it. We have been too prone to dwell on the physical hardships and to think of our Puritan forebears as wholly engaged in the endless felling of trees and fighting of Indians. Doubtless many of them used up their lives in just such occupations. And yet, after a series of tercentenary celebrations such as the founding of Massachusetts Bay Colony, that of Harvard College, and that of the Cambridge Press, we have become increasingly aware of our intellectual heritage. Cultivation of the mind was apparent not only in those early civilizing influences of a college and a press, but in the constant demand for books which caused them to be imported from abroad, by both private individuals and booksellers. The number of books in colonial libraries astonishes us. Then too, with the discovery of the work of Edward Taylor, the unknown poet of the seventeenth century, our ancient belief in the arid and non-creative New England mind is severely shaken.

Art for its own sake could not exist in the earliest primitive surroundings, but the cultivation of the arts and crafts could and did. Our early craftsman could turn out useful objects of a robust and vigorous beauty. Samuel Eliot Morison hints at this in *The Puritan Pronaos* when he speaks of the Puritan's plain style in letters, not a plainness that was striven for as an end in itself, but that was the highest expression of art of which he was capable. The New Englander did not consciously sacrifice art. 'In architecture and silverware this is perfectly evident, as you may see for yourself by visiting the New England rooms in some of our modern museums of fine arts. . . .'[1] What of the early American craft of bookbinding?

Bookbinding was one of the very early crafts to be practised in this country, but where the first book was bound and what it was like we do not know. A bookbinder, John Sanders by name, took the freeman's oath in Boston in 1636 and purchased a shop for himself there in 1637.[2] Those are the only facts known concerning him or his work. It may seem unusual to find a bookbinder preceding a printer, but the first printer did not come for another year, and the first book from his press to need binding was not printed until 1640. Only recently have the few facts about the first press at Cambridge and the probable importance of John Sanders to that press been pieced together and been presented. George Parker Winship has suggested that Sanders had probably been connected with a printing establishment in England, since printing and binding were closely allied there at the time, and that he would have been of inestimable value in helping the inexperienced printers at Cambridge to make a start.[3]

As in England, so in colonial America the work of binding was carried on, to some extent at least, in the printing office. Isaiah Thomas's *History of Printing in America,* various local records, and early imprints give us the only information available for the colonial period. Contemporary records show that Samuel Green was paid for binding as well as for printing copies of the Indian New Testa-

[1] S. E. Morison, *The Puritan Pronaos: Studies in the Intellectual Life of New England in the Seventeenth Century* (New York: New York University Press, 1936), 281 p. Reference on p. 152.
[2] Grolier Club Catalogue, p. 93.
[3] G. P. Winship, 'Facts and Fancies,' *The Colophon,* n. s., III, No. 4, 534.

ment in 1662,[4] and the inventory of the estate of Marmaduke Johnson, printer, contains the following entry: 'It:
book Bynders Press & tooles 006—00—00.'[5] At an early date
binding was carried on in the bookseller's shop as well. It
is not possible to say with any certainty just when bookbinding passed out of the hands of the printer into those
of the bookseller. It does not seem in keeping with the
well-known versatility of the colonial craftsmen that there
should be some who would confine themselves wholly to
bookbinding, especially as early as 1636. Yet we have only
our lively imaginations to supply additional capacities in
the case of John Sanders and the two or three others who
are known only as seventeenth-century bookbinders in the
local records which mention them. If they worked in printing shops or bookselling establishments we are not told of
it. In occasional instances even in the early eighteenth century, however, a single individual was still printer, bookseller, and bookbinder simultaneously.

In some cases it seems probable that the pursuit of bookbinding as a craft may have led to a bookselling business
instead of the other way about. Typical of this is the case of
Edmund Ranger, whose name first appears in the records
when he was admitted as a freeman in Boston in 1671. He
purchased a house there in 1673 and worked as bookseller,
stationer, and binder until his death late in 1705.[6] His
name occurs in several early imprints of Marmaduke Johnson and Samuel Green. One of the earliest, brought to light
by Douglas McMurtrie,[7] and dated 1672, bears the words
'Printed by M. J. for Edmund Ranger, bookbinder near
the Dock. . . .' A 1673 imprint reads 'Sold by Edmund Ran-

[4] Wroth, op. cit., p. 197.

[5] G. E. Littlefield, *Early Massachusetts Press, 1638-1711*, 2 vols. (Boston:
Club of Odd Volumes, 1907). Reference in II, 263.

[6] G. E. Littlefield, *Early Boston Booksellers, 1642-1711*. (Boston: Club of
Odd Volumes, 1900). 256 p. Reference on pp. 87-88.

[7] D. C. McMurtrie, 'The First American Bookbinder,' *Bookbinding Magazine*, VI, No. 6 (June, 1927), 22.

ger, Bookbinder in Boston' and a Mather imprint of 1678 reads simply 'printed by Samuel Green, and sold by Edmund Ranger of Boston.' The theory that Ranger's selling interest arose from his binding, first advanced by Mr. McMurtrie, is further carried out by Isaiah Thomas's comment that Edmund Ranger 'was a binder; but had some small concern in bookselling.' Ranger's was a representative case, and however it may have come about, we find this association of bookselling and bookbinding the rule after the first quarter of the eighteenth century.

The name of Edmund Ranger is closely linked with that of John Ratcliff, and the two deserve early mention as they are the only two binders of the seventeenth century known in connection with a number of examples of their work. John Ratcliff had come from England to bind the Eliot Indian Bible, printed in 1663, and worked in Boston about twenty years, probably returning to England in 1682.[8] We owe much to Thomas J. Holmes who, aided by his knowledge and training as librarian, bibliographer, and bookbinder, has been able to identify the work of each man on the basis of these slight facts. It is to these examples of known workmanship and countless others of unknown origin that we must go for the greatest part of our knowledge of the materials, technique, and decoration of colonial bindings.

## *Materials*

Ratcliff and Ranger used a variety of materials, for they did both plain and fine binding. The foundation for their covers was pasteboard and the leathers that covered them ranged all the way from undressed calf to imported morocco and included sprinkled sheep, calfskin, and an inferior morocco which might possibly be domestic. For their more ordinary work leather thongs were used for fastening the book to the covers. Their more ambitious examples showed

8 Littlefield, op. cit., p. 95.

the use of gold, both for the tooled decoration and gilding of the edges, marbled lining papers, and silk for embroidered headbands. The bindings of these two early craftsmen serve to show something of the materials, technique, and decoration of a part of the colonial work, but they are not strictly representative of the larger group of early Boston bindings. Typical of these were blind-tooled native sheep or calf covers over wooden boards, with plain end-papers, or sometimes with no end-papers at all. Ratcliff and Ranger produced some blind-tooled calf and sheep bindings, to be sure, but their bindings impress us more for their exceptionally early use of gold tooling on imported morocco, pasteboard covers, and marbled lining papers.

Morocco, or 'Turkey leather' as it was currently called, appears to have been imported from an early date, to judge from the scattered references in various sources. Two English dealers, Robert Boulter and John Ive, who supplied the Boston bookseller John Usher, include it in their invoices. Robert Boulter sent '22 turkey skins 4: 8: —,' and John Ive, on September 8, 1683, sent 'four skins of Blew Turkey Leather 7—6, 01.17.6,' remarking at the end of his invoice that 'Turkey Leather is a very scarce commodity at this time here.'[9] The estate of Michael Perry, Boston bookseller, inventoried in 1700, included '7 Skins Turkey Leather 2 20.'[10] Samuel Sewall was probably speaking of morocco when he mentioned in his diary (1698) that Noyes's election sermon was the first and only book then bound in red leather,[11] and it was a fact worthy of notice when we consider that morocco was scarce in England, and that red morocco was not used to any extent, even in the mother country, until about 1660.

[9] W. C. Ford, *The Boston Book Market, 1679-1900* (Boston: Club of Odd Volumes, 1917), 198 p. References on pp. 89, 114, 120.
[10] Ibid., p. 178.
[11] S. Sewall, 'Diary,' *Collections of the Massachusetts Historical Society,* Ser. 5 (Boston, 1878-1882), vols. V-VII. Reference in I, 485.

Binders who imported these morocco skins may well have imported pasteboard also, since the first paper mill in the colonies was not erected until 1690, in Philadelphia. Morocco and pasteboard were customarily used with marbled lining papers, also imported. Samuel Sewall has left two memoranda of marbled paper ordered from Amsterdam: a ream ordered through Captain Thomas Carter on April 25, 1698, and another ream through Captain Mason, 1700.[12]

Native materials, available from the date of the first printed book in 1640, were more commonly used. It is quite possible that the Bay Psalm Book itself was bound in native calf or vellum.[13] Although books were ordinarily bound in sheep or calf, some appeared in parchment, buck- and doeskin, and possibly sealskin. Leather was manufactured in the colonies from a very early date, and the industry grew rapidly in importance. Soon after 1630 there were tanneries in Virginia and in Lynn, Massachusetts. In 1719 Matthew Cowley, a Philadelphia skinner, advertised 'Buck and Doe skins drest after the best manner and at reasonable rates . . . also white leather,'[14] which must have been a kind of vellum or parchment, or possibly pigskin. If pigskin was used at all it must have been sparingly, for it does not appear in the usual collection of early American bindings. Even parchment and vellum covers are not often seen, but parchment 'considered by the conveyancers, equal to any imported' was being made by Robert Wood in Philadelphia in 1772.[15]

Wood was plentiful where paper and pasteboard were not, and board covers of birch, maple, and oak were used throughout the colonial period, in New England in par-

[12] S. Sewall, 'Letter-book,' *Collections of the Massachusetts Historical Society*, Ser. 6 (Boston, 1886-1888), vols. I-II. References in I, 199, 248.

[13] Wroth, op. cit., p. 197.

[14] T. L. Bishop, *History of American Manufactures from 1608 to 1860*, 2 vols. (Philadelphia: Young, 1864-1866). Reference in I, 447.

[15] Ibid., p. 458.

ticular. These boards were planed very thin until they were no heavier than pasteboard and served their purpose admirably. The slim volumes of sermons, tracts, and controversial pamphlets, which together with the various printings of the Psalm Book made up the bulk of the products of the earliest presses, called for thin covers where the thick folios of the fifteenth century had called for heavy ones. In the parlance of the day these thin covers were known as 'scabboard,' a contraction of 'scaleboard.' Although boards were used in Pennsylvania too, pasteboard came into general use earlier there. Paper manufacturing had flourished since its start in 1690. Benjamin Franklin was supplied with paper and pasteboard in large quantities from the Pennsylvania mills of Thomas Wilcox, and Dewees and William Dewees, Jr. He in turn supplied Philadelphia binders and an occasional New York and Boston craftsman with paper and pasteboard as well as scabboard, milled boards, skins, and gold leaf.[16] Even when pasteboard became readily available, at the close of the eighteenth century and the beginning of the nineteenth, wooden covers were still used for the more ordinary books bound in sheep, or in blue paper sides with sheepskin spines.

## *Technique*

With these simple materials the bookbinder accomplished his work, going through the same processes of folding, gathering, sewing, lacing into covers, covering, and decorating as had his fifteenth-century predecessor. The individual craftsman carried through all processes himself, even though they were combined with the business of bookseller and stationer, and sometimes with printing. Of the ninety booksellers and printers in Boston before the Revolution, thirty undertook binding also and a number did binding primarily.[17] Not only did these people work

16 G. S. Eddy, *Account Books Kept by Benjamin Franklin*, 2 vols. (New York: Columbia University Press, 1928-1929), References in II, *passim.*
17 Bishop, op. cit., I, 191.

at several trades simultaneously, but they bound books plain or gilt according to the specifications of their customers. Only a few confined themselves to plain binding, among them Daniel Kneeland of Boston, son of Samuel Kneeland the printer, who 'began trade as a bookbinder, in plain work, having been bred to binding as well as printing,' and Andrew Bradford in Philadelphia, who printed books, sold pamphlets and school-books, and until 1730 frequently advertised that he also sold 'whalebone, live geese feathers, pickled sturgeon, chocolate, Spanish snuff, etc. and executed Common binding.'[18]

The techniques employed by colonial binders differed considerably, not only between individuals, as we might expect, but even within the work of a single craftsman. The binders may have been capable of following the best procedure of their European predecessors, and some of the immigrant craftsmen who had been apprenticed in Scotland and England did so quite consistently. On the whole, however, the native binders did not hold themselves to any single standard of excellence, but turned out well-executed or crudely-managed covers according to the demands of their customers. In general, the simply decorated calf and sheep bindings, so characteristic of the period, were of two types: those sewn on raised cords, after the manner then approved in England and on the continent and always associated with the most durable bindings; and those sewn on rawhide thongs sunk into grooves to give a smooth flat back. Headbands, if they appeared at all, were made of coarse linen thread. No attempt whatever was made to round the back or fit the covers into grooves.

The work of Ratcliff and Ranger, already referred to, illustrates this range of technique perfectly. Both produced decorated work that must have been labored over long and lovingly, and again the simplest covers which they might

[18] I. Thomas, *History of Printing in America,* 2 vols. (Worcester: Isaiah Thomas, Jr., 1810). Reference in II, 31.

well have been tempted to slight, from lack of time and small remuneration. It may be argued that the really fine craftsman will never deviate from his ideals of workmanship and that it is he who will dictate rather than his customers. Perhaps John Ratcliff's ideals were not so high as they should have been and it was just that, and not force of circumstances, which led him to use all the short cuts in his work. In any case he was poorly paid and, deservedly or undeservedly, suffered from Ranger's competition after the first few years of his sojourn in Boston. When Ratcliff first came over to this country, he was commissioned to bind some copies of the Indian Bible for 2s 6d each. He complained that he could not live in any degree of comfort unless he received 3s 4d or 3s 6d, as he could complete only one book in one day and had to furnish all the materials for binding each one in full leather with clasps.[19] After Ranger's appearance, he bound Samuel Sewall's *Notebook*, now in the Prince Collection in the Boston Public Library, and inscribed with this legend: 'Decemb. 22, 1677. Bound by John Ratcliff. This together with my clasped Book in quarto cost 18d fr Binding.' The clasped book to which Sewall refers would seem to be his *Commonplace Book*, in the Massachusetts Historical Society, which is inscribed: 'Samuel Sewall his Booke. Decemb. 29, 1677. Bound by Jno. Ratcliff.' At least this is a quarto and bears two small brass clasps. Though the sheep covers of these two books were the cheapest material possible, they were tastefully decorated with blind tooling, and Samuel Sewall would seem to have received good value for his 18d, even if the technique employed did not measure up to the highest standards.

Ratcliff's technique was never of the best and was generally inferior to that of his competitor. His bindings were strong, but crudely executed in comparison with those by Ranger. Where Ratcliff used all the short cuts of cheap

[19] Littlefield, op. cit., p. 95.

work, such as sawn-in cords, not all of which were laced into the covers, no headbands, and imperfectly applied ornaments, Ranger could turn out a volume with raised cords each laced into the covers, silk headbands, and gilt edges. To Ratcliff belongs the dubious distinction of introducing to the colonies the vicious practice of stabbing through the inner margins of a book and sewing through the holes, thus making a rigid binding and a book which will not open easily. Sometimes the four rawhide thongs which were laced into the boards were likewise stabbed through the margins at intervals between the sewing stitches. Ratcliff was by no means the only offender, for the same method was still in use in the colonies some twenty years after he had returned to England. In fact, this unfortunate practice has carried down to the present day, with the same unpleasant results. To its great detriment, modern library binding strikingly exemplifies this same technique.

A craftsman's individuality is ordinarily more apparent in the skill and artistry with which he applies his decoration, but it is also manifest in the fashion in which he prepares his volume for those finishing touches. In the case of Ratcliff and Ranger these basic processes are of especial importance, because they used the same general style of ornamentation and the identical tools. Moreover, they both used the same general methods of technique. Even though Ranger could and did use raised cords, he also turned out flat-backed bindings with sawn-in cords. It was the finest detail, such as the careful application of headbands, the neat squares of his covers, the trimming of the leather, and the general solidity of his books, that proved Ranger to be consistently the better workman. Mr. Holmes has depended primarily upon these details of construction, and secondarily upon the skill exhibited in the application of the decoration, in his difficult task of differentiating the work of the two binders.

## Decoration and Style of Bindings

The technique employed throughout the colonial period made for primitive, enduring bindings of a simplicity and crudity truly provincial in comparison with the best European work of the period. If such a comparison is made, however, there are many considerations to be borne in mind. The unfavorable environment of a pioneer country where a greater emphasis upon utility is inevitable; the economic element and the comparative isolation which made a major reliance on ruder native materials readily at hand a necessity; and the absence of royalty or wealthy collectors as patrons are some of the more blatant reasons for the unfairness of such a comparison. If that common pitfall of considering the average work of the newer country with the more elaborate work of the older is avoided, and bindings of similar pretension from both countries are looked at together, even the most hardened critic will have to declare himself impressed by colonial achievement.

The style of decoration on our early colonial bindings showed a natural dependence upon that of the mother country. The so-called 'Cambridge style' was used almost entirely on theological works in England. English bindings in this style were decorated by double panels outlined with a narrow flower roll bordered by double fillets, with fleurons applied at the outer corners. The books were sewn on raised cords also outlined by double fillets. All tooling was done in blind, and the inner and outer panels were sprinkled dark, leaving the middle panel plain. Only the board edges were decorated in gold, and they were ornamented by a bar roll. The material was invariably calf and the lining papers of Dutch marble, while the book edges were stained or sprinkled red to match the worked headbands. Our own style of decoration, though reminiscent of the English panel, showed a number of ingenious adaptations of that described above.

Ornamentation of seventeenth- and early eighteenth-
century colonial panel bindings consisted of simple blind
tooling produced by a narrow roll stamp. Some of the early
examples have a single, narrow floral border rolled lengthwise of the cover and parallel to the spine, within a single
blind fillet line that borders all four sides of the cover

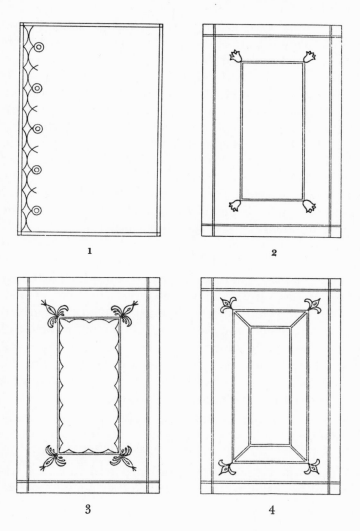

1      2

3      4

(Fig. 1). The majority were decorated with panels formed either by double blind fillet lines (Fig. 2), or by the same fillets bordered with a floral roll and accented by fleurons at the outer corners (Fig. 3). Occasionally the panels were single, but more often double, a panel within a panel, the inner and the outer joined at the four corners either by the double fillet or by the floral roll (Fig. 4). Conventional fleurons were used at the corners, though some Boston bindings show the use of simple, natural tulip stamps. Some form of panel was used throughout the colonies. It occurs constantly on Boston bindings and also in the South. It appears on a copy of Holdsworth's *Muscipula* (Fig. 5) printed by William Parks at Annapolis in 1728, and in its most successful form on a shining calf cover of Cicero's *Cato Major* (Fig. 6) printed at Philadelphia in 1744 by Benjamin Franklin and presented by him to Thomas Clap, the president of Yale College, in 1746. This binding is of the double-panel variety with a conventionalized floral roll around the inner panel, the two joined at the corners by double blind fillets, and the outer corners of the second panel marked by good-sized conventionalized tulips. It is undoubtedly the work of the most accomplished binder Franklin employed at that date, and one of which he might have been justly proud. May it not have been Joseph Goodwin, from England, who had bought pasteboard, marbled paper, parchment, and calfskins from Franklin, and had done considerable binding for him between 1742 and 1746? He must have had the equipment necessary, for the *Pennsylvania Gazette* of February 10, 1746/47, contained a notice inserted by the executors of his estate:

N. B. To be sold by said Lewis Evans, a complete sett of Bookbinder's tools, containing among other things, a vast variety of gilding tools, rollers, and 4 setts of letters.[20]

William and Andrew Bradford departed from the tradition of the panel when one or the other bound *Lex Par-*

20 Eddy, op. cit., II, 60.

*liamentaria* (Fig. 7), reprinted from the London edition of 1716, in a plain, durable, sheep cover ornamented with a cat-tooth rolled border, with a diamond-shaped fleuron in the center, all done in blind.

The spines of early colonial books carried no lettering and no ornamentation other than simple horizontal fillet lines, in blind or gold, to border the cords or to mark their position if they were sunk in to make a flat back. Samuel Willard's *Compleat Body of Divinity*, printed in 1726 by Kneeland and Green, is thought to be the first colonial American book to carry gilt lettering on its spine.[21] It by no means established a custom of lettering, however, for bindings continued to appear without labels or lettering on their backs until well into the nineteenth century. As always, the work of immigrant binders proved an exception to the rule. Their bindings were decorated on the back and carried labels, from the early part of the eighteenth century.

The one convention seldom broken was that of decorating the board edges with a fine, narrow roll design, at first in darkened blind tooling, and later in gilt. As for the covers, calf and sheepskin, sprinkled, provided further ornamentation for most panel bindings. Franklin's Cicero (Fig. 6) is a distinctive example of the practice of sprinkling the inner and outer panels, leaving the middle plain. It shows too the current style of sprinkling the book edges red. Edges were usually red or brown, rarely gilded, and later stained a solid yellow, green, or dark brown.

The use of gold was not widespread before the Revolution. When it was used, it was most often limited to a double gold fillet around the covers, and for a roll to border the cords on the back. Gold tooling had been used by Ranger and Ratcliff, however, in the seventeenth century, and it must have been used by others. The inventory of

[21] Holmes, op. cit., *Proceedings of the American Antiquarian Society*, n. s., XXXVIII, 39.

Michael Perry (1700) included 'four dozen bookes Leafe brass, 3 Setts of Brass Letters and 1 Box of Bk. Binder's Tools.'[22] William Bradford advertised to do 'Binding gilt or plain' in his *Gazette*, soon after 1725.[23] Franklin was billing his customers for gilt bindings in 1733, Newinham 'for binding a Mason Book gilt 4–0,' and Isaac Brown for a 'gilt binding 4–0.'[24] Whether the gilt specified consisted of anything more than simple gold fillet lines it is impossible to say.

No discussion of decoration can be complete without special reference to the Ratcliff and Ranger bindings, distinguished as they are for their individuality and for their early use of gold tooling tastefully applied. Both men used the panel style which later became so popular, in a number of variations and with great success. Ranger was fond of acid-stained leather for its decorative effect and used it in a plain binding with no other ornamentation except a blind-tooled fillet line, and in a more ambitious work, that of the copy of Mather's *Practical Truths* (Fig. 8) in the New York Public Library, in combination with a narrow gold cat-tooth rolled edge and four-petalled fleurons. In this case the acid applied to the brown calfskin has eaten badly into the leather and obscured the original beauty of the binding. Of another copy in the William Gwinn Mather Collection[25] which is gilt only on its spine, board and page edges, Mr. Holmes says, 'It is conceivable that this was the best example of binding, that is, technically the most perfect example of binding, that had been produced in English America until that time.'[26]

Ratcliff made frequent use of the double panel and of another interesting variation seen, for instance, on Samuel

22 Ford, op. cit., p. 317.
23 Wroth, op. cit., p. 203.
24 Eddy, op. cit., I, 41.
25 Now part of MacGregor Jenkins Collection, in the Alderman Library, University of Virginia.
26 Holmes, op. cit., XXXVIII, 40.

Sewall's *Notebook,* where an extra line is drawn within the usual outside border, about one inch from the spine and parallel to it, thus providing a space for six fleurons instead of the usual four. Both binders included the initials of the owners in the decoration of certain examples of their work done in the double-panel style. Their tools, which were identical, probably passed into Ranger's hands when Ratcliff disappeared in 1682, presumably returning to England. One of Ratcliff's most attractive bindings, that on Mather's *Call from Heaven* (Fig. 9), also in the William Gwinn Mather Collection, bears in the center of its cover that same four-petalled fleuron that is on the four corners of the *Practical Truths* in the New York Public Library. The covers of the *Call from Heaven,* which are of olive morocco, are decorated very simply with the characteristic square-dot roll as a border, a spreading three-branch bud and leaf roll somewhat resembling the acorn tool which was so popular in seventeenth-century England, in each corner, and the four-petalled fleuron in the center. The slight ornamentation, so effective in its very simplicity, shows the craftsman's pride in the elegance of the morocco leather, bringing out all its beauty without obscuring it. This is rarely seen in the colonies at that time.

Occasionally a binder attempted to decorate his cover as especially befitted the subject matter of his book. This point is well illustrated by an edition of two funeral sermons owned by the Massachusetts Historical Society. The elaborate decorative title-page of the volume set the tone which the binder has followed. Both sermons were printed by B. Green and sold by Nicholas Boone at his shop and bear an imprint date of 1706. The first, by Samuel Willard, is entitled *The Just Man's Prerogative, a Sermon Preached Privately, Sept. 27, 1706. On a Solemn Occasion: For the Consolation of a Sorrowful Family, Mourning over the Immature DEATH of a Pious SON, viz. Mr. Simeon Stoddard, who was Found Barberously Murdered in Chelsea-Fields near London*

*May 14, 1706;* the second, by Benjamin Wadsworth, is called *Considerations to Prevent Murmuring and Promote Patience in Christians under Afflictive Providences.* To emphasize the solemnity of the occasion, the binder has put on black leather covers and decorated them with a circular medallion containing a skull attended on either side by crossed bones, a simplified version of the title-page ornaments which also included an hourglass and a pick and shovel.

In pleasing contrast to the skull and crossbones we find a lighter side evidenced in the delicate and imaginative design on Joseph Sewall's copy of *Heaven Opened, Or, a Brief and Plain Discovery of the Riches of God's Covenant of Grace,* in the Prince Collection. The fly-leaf bears the inscription: 'Joseph Sewal's Book Anno 1703' and it is pleasant to think that the same Samuel Sewall who commissioned Ratcliff, Ranger, and his son-in-law Samuel Gerrish to do binding for him ordered this binding for his son. The imprint date of 1699 and the inscription of 1703 make it too late for Ratcliff's work, but it is decorated with the same type of panel that he had put on the elder Sewall's *Notebook,* with an extra double blind fillet set in an inch from the spine, parallel to it. In each of the four outer corners a rather large heart-shaped tool has been clearly impressed in blind. Midway of all four edges appears a lacy triangular ornament, which is impressed twice in the center cover to form a diamond. The leather is sprinkled calf and there is elaborate blind-tooled decoration on the board edges and inside the covers.

The simple decorations produced for the most part by roll stamps on the covers, with the backs unornamented except for plain horizontal lines; the primitive techniques of sewing books on rawhide thongs without benefit of headbands, and with no attempt at rounding and backing; the plain native leathers and wooden boards used for covers— all these combined to make American colonial bookbindings solid, substantial, honestly utilitarian, and at the same time decorative, although unassuming. As additional examples of seventeenth-century work are unearthed, it is to be hoped and expected that they will show further evidence of individuality and make it even clearer than it is already that our early colonial craftsmen were more than slavish imitators, making the style which they inherited from the parent country distinctly their own.

The development of a more lavish decoration on colonial bindings turned out by craftsmen who had served their apprenticeship abroad is too interesting to be passed by without some indication of their general characteristics, even though the number of such bindings is proportionately small. From the second quarter of the eighteenth century onward we find occasional examples. Virtually all of those from the shops of binders who had been trained in Scotland and England show the same general type of spine decoration. This consists of crossed fillet lines which break up each panel into triangles, which in turn are filled with small fleurons. Backs thus decorated are used in conjunction with covers ornamented by the customary panel and in a few instances with an unusually elaborate all-over design. Representative of these are the bindings on the copy of its charter in the possession of the College of William and Mary, and on Daniel Horsmanden's *Journal* (Fig. 10), owned by the Library of Congress. Both books seem to be the work of the same craftsman, as the tools used are identical and their disposition is somewhat similar. The morocco covers are decorated with acorns, stars, circles, half circles, straight fillet lines, and the same narrow chain border. The foundation design on the charter is the familiar double panel outlined by the half-circular tool, connected at the corners by a straight-lined fillet. The ground is well covered by the smaller tools. Horsmanden's *Journal* introduces to the colonies a new style which is generally indicative of Scottish work. The basic design is circular rather than rectangular and is well suited to the size of the book it ornaments, as the covers are broader than usual. The large central circle is scalloped and divided into segments by straight fillet lines. The center of the circle is covered by a small circular inlay of red morocco. The straight lines extending inward from the four corners to the outer circumference of the outer circle, decorated on either side by rows of acorns, repeat the identical motive used on the charter. It is tempting to speculate on the identity of the binder of these two books, but as yet there is not sufficient evidence for more than hazarding a guess. The sole clue is the name of William Parks in the imprint of the charter, which was printed by him at Annapolis in 1736. He was a binder as well as a printer and served his apprenticeship in England. Mr. Wroth finds his bindings 'almost the earliest examples of conscious artistic excellence to be met among the books printed and, without question, bound in colonial America.' [27]

Much of the German work of the second half of the eighteenth century showed an opposite tendency, a sobriety even greater than that exhibited in the work of native American binders. For instance, the books bound at the Ephrata Cloister show typical German monastic bindings, almost mediaeval in character. For the most part they were large books, bound solidly in brown calf or cowhide over bevelled oak boards, with brass bosses and clasps. The ornamentation was confined to a few blind lines. Sower's early work was done in the same manner, as the bindings of his successive editions of the German Bible illustrate. In such striking contrast is the Gesang-Buch of 1774 (Fig. 11) that we feel it necessary regretfully to abandon the suggestion that Christopher Sower the second made this dainty binding. Here is an example of peasant art reflected in binding, German in its every detail, from the painted cover design of tulip, heart, and flowers to the embossed gilt edges and flowered end-papers; so much so, in fact, that we must prob-

[27] Wroth, op. cit., p. 209.

ably assume that the book was bound in Germany where by report it was printed.

Ornamentation in colonial America was achieved by means of tools which were in many cases exactly like those used in England and France. For that reason it has been generally assumed that the tools used by American bookbinders have always been imported as they are now. Immigrant craftsmen could bring their tools into the country duty-free and probably did, but that does not solve the problem for the native group. Certainly the existence of tool-makers in the colonies would give the bookbinder, native and immigrant alike, an enlarged scope and greater opportunity for developing an individual style. In 1907 the following tantalizing words appeared in the preface to The Grolier Club *Catalogue of Ornamental Leather Bookbindings Executed in America Prior to 1850:*

Whether tool-makers were to be found in the Colonies is not vouchsafed to us to know, nor when they became a recognized company of workers. . . . Should it happen that with further research it is learned that the early binders' tools were made at home, the results of the tooling will stand even more to the credit of the early workmen than they do at present.[28]

If any workmen were cutting bookbinders' tools at an early date, they were surely not confining themselves to such a specialized occupation. In the days when the binder himself was serving in several capacities, it is only reasonable to suspect the tool-maker of the same practice. The problem becomes one of selecting a similar or allied occupation. If we go back to the fifteenth century again and examine the early history of binding and printing, we find that bookbinders' tools were cut before type was cast, probably in the shop of the engraver. Even the history of the early casting of type points to a connection with the goldsmith's art. There were gold- and silversmiths in this country at the time of the Revolution, as we well know by the classic example of Paul

[28] Grolier Club Catalogue, p. viii.

Revere. It is less generally known that silversmiths were at work as early as the 1720's, and even in the late seventeenth century. We know from the early directories that they existed in no inconsiderable numbers after the war, especially in Philadelphia. It is then with more gratification than surprise that we read of an engraver who included the making of bookbinding tools in a list of his accomplishments. As early as April 18, 1768, the *Pennsylvania Chronicle* carried the following advertisement:

James Smither, Engraver, At the first House in Third Street, from the Cross Keys, Corner of Chestnut-Street, Philadelphia Performs all Manner of Engraving in Gold, Silver, Copper, Steel, and all other Metals—Coats of Arms, and Seals, done in the neatest Manner. Likewise cuts Stamps, Brands, and metal cuts for Printers, and ornamental Tools for Bookbinders. He also ornaments Guns and Pistols, both engraving and inlaying Silver, at the most Reasonable Rates.[29]

This was the very year that the silversmith and lapidary, Abel Buell of Killingworth, Connecticut, was making the first experiments in cutting and casting type. Successful type-casting did not take place for several years. Apparently, the engraving of bookbinders' tools preceded punch-cutting and type-casting in the American colonies as it had in fifteenth-century Europe. What these tools were like we cannot tell, and what degree of skill and creative imagination they showed we shall be able to deduce only gradually as a greater body of work dating from that period is brought together. Specimen books to picture them came much later when firms existed for that specialized business.

## Plain Bindings of the Period

Decorated work has been here described to the exclusion of plain binding simply because it is more interesting in showing the highest achievement of American crafts-

[29] A. C. Prime, [comp.], *The Arts and Crafts in Philadelphia, Maryland and South Carolina. Gleanings from Newspapers,* 2 vols. (Walpole Society, [Topsfield, Mass.], 1929). Reference in I, 27-28.

men, and not because it represents the greatest output of
the colonial binder's shop. As a matter of fact, a good proportion of our early printing was never intended for binding at all. The function of the colonial press was, to a very
high degree, to keep people posted on events of the day,
and quantities of broadsides and newspapers were turned
out for that purpose.

Less ephemeral, perhaps, but still deemed unworthy of
permanent and costly covers were the almanacs and numerous pamphlets of the day, which were usually offered to
their purchasers stitched, with colored paper covers pasted
over the outside sheets. These paper covers were, for the
most part, plain blue in the early eighteenth century,
though marbled paper became the vogue in the years just
preceding the Revolution. Previous to that, marbled paper
was imported; and along with the 'coam' marble which
came from Holland came the Dutch gilt, a tough colored
paper, often green or blue, with figures of animals or of
Biblical heroes stamped in gold upon them.

By the 1770's a goodly number of session laws were half-
bound, with narrow sheepskin spines and corners and marbled paper sides. These paper covers were often waxed and
polished, and their reds and blues have faded under their
smooth surface to a soft rosy red and green-blue that would
seem to us far more lovely to look upon than their pristine
brilliance could ever have been.

Many books, and probably the greatest number, were
bound in full sheep, or more rarely in calf, with no ornamentation whatever. Some examples of the *New England
Primer* have been preserved, despite the hard use they
underwent, in their original sheepskin covers, a mere scrap
of leather drawn on and pasted down without benefit of
the binder's knife either for paring or trimming.

Plain vellum bindings existed, though apparently in no
great profusion. The best examples to be seen are the huge
folio account books preserved in the Pennsylvania Histori-

cal Society, bound plainly but solidly, perhaps in that native vellum Robert Woods was advertising in Philadelphia in 1772 as 'equal to any imported.'

Like the quantities of plain binding turned out in the large centers, almost all of that in the provincial towns was plain, crude, and unornamented. The red leather labels which served as a spot of color in the later period were still unknown; if labels existed at all, they were merely pieces of paper or vellum, carrying handwritten titles and pasted lengthwise of the spine. This fashion of placing the label lengthwise also carried over into the later period when it came to be printed instead of handwritten.

In the provincial workshop the binder was not always skilled, and his interests were divided between bookbinding, bookselling, and notebook ruling. Often he held an official position, too, such as the postmastership of his community. Even if there had been the requisite skill to draw upon, the elements of timeliness and expense were of such importance in the general run of work as to preclude any lingering by a fastidious workman, or the wide use of elegant materials.

Thus we may see that the materials, technique, and style of colonial bindings, decorated or undecorated, have much to tell us of the people who made and used them, as well as of the conditions under which they worked and lived.

### Centers of Activity and Names of Binders

Though bookbinding was carried on extensively in the larger printing centers of Boston, Philadelphia, and New York, it was not limited to these cities. There were binders working in Portsmouth, New Hampshire; in the flourishing towns of Newburyport and Salem, Massachusetts; in New London, Connecticut; Albany, New York; Elizabeth, New Jersey; Bethlehem and Germantown, Pennsylvania; Wilmington, Delaware; Annapolis, Maryland; Williamsburg, Virginia; Charleston, South Carolina; and probably in other communities. Wherever printing was done there was need of a binder, and printing and publishing were not concentrated in the larger centers as they are today. In those early days of slow communication there is no story more thrilling than that of the gradual introduction of the printing press into the distant corners of the colonies.

Names of binders are recorded in great profusion, but they have to be gathered from scattered sources. Occasional scraps of information, relevant and irrelevant, and many approximate dates must be pieced together to present some slight picture of the scene. It is not an easy task and would be all but impossible, were it not for Thomas, McCulloch, The Grolier Club Catalogue, George Simpson Eddy (the editor of *Franklin's Account Books*), and last but not least the long files of early newspapers which often furnish the only record of the colonial craftsmen whose work was advertised in their pages.

The business of advertising was well understood even in colonial days. Eighteenth-century newspapers carried notices of many bookbinders, some of whom showed remarkable ability in setting forth their talents. There was, for example, T. Anderton, who advertised in the *New York Mercury*, December 24, 1764:

> Lately arrived from England and is now at Mr. Charles Gilmore's the Sign of the Orange Tree, in Cannon's wharf, New York. T. Anderton, Bookbinder, letter-case and Pocket-book maker . . . The said T. Anderton performs all bookbinding in its full perfection in all sorts of plain and rich bindings, and rules paper or bill books . . &c (as exact to any pattern) but with greater elegance than if taken from copper plate . . . Gentlemen and Ladies who please to try his abilities may always depend on being well used on the very lowest terms.[30]

Other binders were more modest in their promises, limiting themselves to advertising 'Books neatly new Bound either Plain or Gilt, reasonable.' Whether they succeeded

[30] Grolier Club Catalogue, pp. 99-100.

in turning out the type of bindings they advertised or whether they overstated the case must remain a matter of conjecture until more of their work has been identified.

*Boston.* The greatest activity centered in Boston until the last quarter of the eighteenth century, when Philadelphia became a serious rival in terms of printing output. Throughout the seventeenth century Boston binders had the field to themselves. During that time the names of seven bookbinders are recorded: John Sanders, John Ratcliff and Edmund Ranger, already mentioned, and William Nowell, Thomas Rand, Bartholomew Sprint, and Nicholas Buttolph. Of these Nowell and Rand were entered in 'A list of severall psons returned to ye Countie Courts at severall times not admitted or approved of by ye select men of Boston to be Inhabitants of Ye Towne,' issued by the Boston Record Commissioners, January 29, 1671/72. Such a classification makes it seem unlikely that they were allowed to practise their craft. All we know of Bartholomew Sprint is the fact that he was able to persuade George Pordage, merchant, to become surety for him in 1685. Nicholas Buttolph was a bookbinder, bookseller, and printer, and joined the Ancient and Honourable Artillery Company of Boston in 1692.[31]

In the first half of the eighteenth century a number of native workmen carried on the business of binding. The prominent bookseller, Daniel Henchman, who worked from 1713 to 1761, was said to have carried on bookbinding, and Thomas mentions apprentices who were trained in Henchman's shop, among them Alford Butler, Thomas Hancock, and Samuel Webb. When Wharton and Bowes took over his business after his death in 1761, they continued to bind and sell books, training John Langdon who later sold stationery and carried on binding until the beginning of the Revolution.

31 Grolier Club Catalogue, p. 93.

In the middle of the century a group of immigrant crafts-men appeared. At least six Scottish binders worked in Boston between 1743 and 1769: Walter MacAlpine, his brother William, William Lang, John Hodgson, Andrew Barclay, and John Mein. Thomas mentions only two men as having received their training in England: Charles Harrison, who was working in 1739, and Abraham Ellison, who worked much later, in the years just preceding the Revolution. The work of these immigrant binders was interrupted by the war. John Mein and William MacAlpine, who had pronounced loyalist sympathies, returned to Scotland. Walter MacAlpine 'removed to Connecticut and died there.'[32] The rest disappeared from view.

Boston bookbinders almost never confined themselves to the practice of binding, as explained earlier. Occasionally printers carried on binding in their shops, but more often bookbinding was done in connection with a book-selling and stationery business. By the last quarter of the century binding was combined with notebook and account-book ruling. This combination proved very popular well into the nineteenth century.

*Philadelphia.* The population of eighteenth-century Philadelphia was made up of English, Dutch, Scotch, Irish, and German stock, with bookbinders representing all these nationalities. Their names are fewer and begin to appear later than in Boston, as printing commenced almost fifty years later in Philadelphia. The earliest known binder is William Davies, who was working in 1727 as we know from the imprint on Ellis Pugh's *Salutation to the Britains.* His advertisement in the *Pennsylvania Gazette* of February 3, 1729/30, reads:

All sorts of Books, both new and old, are neatly Bound after the best Manner in Calf or Sheep, and also blank Account Books for Merchants, Shop-keepers and others, in Russet, Vel-

[32] Thomas, *Histroy of Printing* (1810 edition), II, 434.

lum or Parchment, next door to A. Hamilton, Esq. in Chestnut-street, Philadelphia, by W. Davies.[33]

Native-born workmen there were, though it is hard to tell
just how many. Andrew Bradford advertised 'Common
binding' in 1730, and Stephen Potts entered Franklin's
service at about that time. Potts was to work at bookbinding and Meredith at press, both to be taught by Samuel
Keimer who, by his own confession, 'knew neither one nor
t'other.'[34] Just how accomplished Potts, a 'young country-
man . . . of uncommon natural parts, and great wit and
humor,'[35] became we do not know, but he was still working at the craft nineteen years later, in 1749, in a shop of
his own.

Dutch and German binders were at work in the mid-
eighteenth century. Franklin had an account in 1742 with
Mr. Saits, a Dutch bookbinder, and J. Schuppey of Strawberry Alley, at the Sign of the Book. The latter did bookbinding of all sorts in the best manner and also agreed to
teach any gentleman the new improved German and
French languages in evening school '(God willing).'[36]
While it is only suspected that Schuppey received his training in Germany, it is known that G. Christoph Reinhold,
who was working in Philadelphia in 1763, had been apprenticed there.

German binders worked even earlier outside Philadelphia, in Germantown and Bethlehem. The famous Sowers,
father and son, worked at binding from 1738 until 1787.
Christopher Sower the elder is thought to have served his
apprenticeship at the Ephrata Cloister. Although the Sowers
must have kept more than one apprentice busy in their
extensive business of printing and binding, the name of
one only, Zachariah Poulson, has been identified.

33 Eddy, op. cit., I, 43.
34 Ibid., I, 38.
35 Ibid.
36 Ibid., op. cit., II, 115.

English craftsmen were represented in the persons of Joseph Goodwin in 1742, John Anderton in 1768, and William Trickett in 1773. Samuel Dellap was the only binder designated as Irish. Although they have not been positively identified as having received their training in Scotland, the names of Muir and MacGill, appearing in 1753 and 1771 respectively, suggest a Scottish origin. At any rate there was one binder trained in Edinburgh at work in Philadelphia as early as 1769, and that a very important one.

Robert Aitken, printer, bookseller, engraver, and bookbinder, was born in Dalkeith, Scotland. In 1769 he appeared as a bookseller in Philadelphia. That same year he returned to Scotland, presumably to learn binding, since on his return to Philadelphia two years later he added bookbinding to his business of bookselling. In another two years he began to print books also.

Aitken was one of a group of immigrant workmen who appeared in Philadelphia near the outbreak of the Revolution and continued to work after the close of the colonial period. The other members of the group, Samuel Taylor, Caleb Buglass, Robert Bell, and William Woodhouse, had all been associated at Berwick-upon-Tweed, where they had learned their craft. Samuel Taylor seems to have come to Philadelphia first, in 1764, to be followed by Woodhouse, Buglass, and Bell, who had all served as apprentices in his shop in England. Taylor died about 1781, but the others continued to work after the Revolution.

*New York.* Printing was introduced into New York by William Bradford in 1693, eight years after he started printing in Philadelphia. Throughout the colonial period New York lagged behind Boston and Philadelphia as a center of book distribution. For all that, names of at least nineteen different binders have been preserved, commencing with that of William Bradford himself, who advertised regularly in his *Gazette,* first published in 1725, that old books could be 'new Bound, either Plain or Gilt . . . at the Sign of the Bible.'[37] Six other binders were at work in the first half of the eighteenth century. Since the majority of these names have been taken from newspaper advertisements, it is seldom possible to ascertain where the men received their training. Joseph Johnson was the first craftsman to follow bookbinding exclusive of printing or bookselling, so far as we know. He was made a freeman in 1731 and advertised himself in the *New York Weekly Journal,* October 7, 1734, as 'now set up bookbinding for himself as usual.'[38] He had one competitor at least, in Henry De Foreest, who advertised 'Books neatly Bound, Gilded, and Lettered,' in that same journal nine months later.[39] Two binders of the mid-century, John Hyndshaw and T. Anderton, worked only a few years in New York before moving on to a more promising field in Philadelphia.

Two Scottish names, Robert M'Alpine and Malcolm McEwen, appear in the 1740's, at the same time as the Scottish group in Boston. In 1773 George Leedell advertised in the *New York Journal* as 'Bookbinder, late of London,' and two years later, in the same paper, there was notice of a Philip Brooks, 'Book-Binder from Dublin.'[40]

On the whole, these early bookbinders did not travel about very much between cities. Certain names appear in New York as well as in Philadelphia, and one Boston binder, William Green, later established himself in Philadelphia. McCulloch says that Caleb Buglass began bookbinding and selling as a partner of William Green of Boston at No. 9 North Front Street, Philadelphia.[41] The name of William Green appears also in New York in the *Journal*

[37] Grolier Club Catalogue, p. 98.
[38] Ibid.
[39] Ibid., p. 99.
[40] Ibid., p. 100.
[41] "William McCulloch's Additions to Thomas's History of Printing," *Proceedings of the American Antiquarian Society,* n.s. (April, 1921), XXXI, Part 1, 89-247. Reference on p. 219.

of November 16, 1775; apparently he was the exception who worked in all three of the great centers.

*Annapolis.* Although there is no evidence that bookbinding was carried on to the same extent in the South, the quality there made up in large part for the lack of quantity. At least one printer, William Parks of Annapolis (1726), later of Williamsburg (1730), turned out some very creditable work. He advertised more modestly than some as 'one who binds old books very well, and cheap.'[42] He came from England, probably Shropshire, and bound books in the panel style already popular in Boston. His bindings show much greater care in forwarding than those of his Boston contemporaries. The pasteboard covers he used instead of wood, his worked headbands, his use of raised cords rather than sunken leather thongs, and his generally neat workmanship show the contrast between the immigrant and native craftsmanship of the period. In 1742, when Parks was working at Williamsburg, we find that he bought scabboard, leaf gold, milled board (English), Dutch board, skins, embossed paper, and four dozen Catos from Benjamin Franklin in Philadelphia.[43] The item of '4 dozen Catos' brings up again the question of the binder Franklin selected to do the copy which he presented to Thomas Clap, the President of Yale. The book was obviously the work of a binder trained abroad, capable of fine workmanship. The work from William Parks' shop followed high standards and with the additional evidence of the Catos on his account we should be tempted to attribute the binding to him if the tools could be identified with his shop.

It is in Annapolis too that we hear of the visiting binder. An advertisement in the *Maryland Gazette*, May 15, 1760, reads as follows: 'Just imported from London, And to be Sold by Samuel Evans Book Binder, near Mr. Howard's

42 Wroth, op. cit., p. 208.
43 Eddy, op. cit., II, 98.

in Annapolis, a Collection of Books, consisting of History, Law and Physic, together with great Variety of School Books and Stationary. During his stay here, which will be about two months, he will Bind old or new Books in the neatest and most expeditious Manner.' Five years later he was established in New York, according to the *New York Gazette* of April 25, 1765.

*Charleston.* In the last half of the eighteenth century there were two bookbinders from Scotland at work in Charleston. Isaiah Thomas reported Robert Woods there in 1764 and James Taylor as binding and selling books in 1771. Whether or not this was the Robert Woods who was making parchment in Philadelphia in 1772 we do not know.

Incomplete as the picture is, certain facts concerning bookbinders as a group are evident. The influence of immigrant workmen was great, even in Boston where there was strongest evidence of a native school. Philadelphia showed the greatest variety of foreign influence with its English, Irish, German, and Dutch workmen. New York appears to have had a generous proportion of English and Scottish craftsmen if names are any indication. As would be expected, the German influence was most marked in Philadelphia, Germantown, and Ephrata. By far the greatest number of immigrant craftsmen the country over came from Scotland, however. From the middle of the eighteenth century they were at work, scattered through the colonies from Boston to Charleston, South Carolina.

Little has been written about Scottish bookbinding. The casual reference in Brassington's *History of the Art of Bookbinding* to a school of Scottish bookbinders that appeared and disappeared in England about 1730, coupled with the discovery of a school in the colonies immediately after that date, suggests a connection that calls for a further investigation of Scottish bindings, native and immigrant.

The few additional facts brought out since have a very

definite bearing on this inter-connection of Scottish and American bookbinding. Miss Prideaux described a few Scottish bindings in her paper on *English and Scottish Bindings*.[44] There she has reproduced (on page 23) one binding bearing a circular design very similar to that on Horsmanden's *Journal* (Fig. 10), and has referred to additional bindings of the same general type, reproduced in the Burlington Fine Arts Club's Catalogue. A good many years later Mr. George H. Bushnell reiterated Miss Prideaux's theory of the French origin of Scottish binding, deploring as she had, the absence of material from which to make a study. Mr. Bushnell speaks of an 'ornate' school of Scottish binding which flourished from the late seventeenth to the middle of the eighteenth century, exhibiting the most definite style of any period in the annals of Scottish binding.[45] He also appends a list of Scottish binders working from the fifteenth through the eighteenth century. Several names among the 169 of the eighteenth century appear also in the list provided as an appendix to this study. For example, according to the Bushnell list Alexander Christie worked in Edinburgh in 1786. It may well have been this same binder who worked at 3 Rider Street, New York, from 1796 to 1798. It was certainly the same Charles Cleland who worked in Edinburgh in 1786, and appeared three years later in Maiden Lane, New York, since he advertised himself as 'lately from Edinburgh' in the *New York Journal*, November 7, 1792.

### Identification of Bindings

The identification of bindings with their makers is a difficult and hazardous business and must proceed very slowly until more examples of American work can be brought together for comparison. Fortunately, however, certain bindings bear the binder's own inscription or an

[44] S. T. Prideaux, "English and Scottish Bindings of the Last Century," *Bookbinders and Their Craft* (New York: Scribner, 1903), pp. 3-26.

[45] G. H. Bushnell, "Scottish Bookbindings and Bookbinders," *Bookman's Journal*, 3d ser., XV, 78.

owner's inscription which names the binder, giving indisputable proof of American craftsmanship in addition to identification with individual names. There are two types of signature in evidence, the handwritten name and the printed or engraved label. At the moment of writing only a few of each have been discovered, but a careful and systematic search through our collections of Americana would indubitably disclose many more. Helpful as it would be, even a larger group of signed bindings would not completely simplify the matter of identification. It is somewhat disconcerting to find that the craftsmen who signed their work did not do so consistently, and in many cases bindings must be attributed to craftsmen on the basis of comparative study that would include technique and decoration. Even decoration and technique together do not always provide a clear case, inasmuch as binders have been known to exchange tools and to use a variety of techniques. That versatility of the colonial craftsmen which makes them so remarkable makes it that much more difficult to identify the work of individuals.

The earliest method of designating a binder was by the pen and ink inscription, such as helped Mr. Holmes to identify the work of Ratcliff and Ranger. Only one of the bindings he examined bore the name of the binder, however, and the second method, that of careful comparison of technique and decoration, was of the greatest value. A third clue was followed when he found that a binder's name—that of Edmund Ranger—appeared in an imprint. It was not unusual for binders' names to appear in imprints throughout the colonial period, and rightly or wrongly it has been used as evidence that the craftsman so named bound the copies printed for him. In the case of Ratcliff and Ranger it served merely to indicate that there were two bookbinders working in the period and that John Ratcliff, whom Sewall names as his bookbinder, had a competitor in the person of Edmund Ranger.

Thanks to Thomas J. Holmes and William G. Land, we have seventeen bindings attributed to Ratcliff and Ranger, eleven to the former and six to the latter, as follows:[46]

*Bound by John Ratcliff.*

1. Sewall's Commonplace Book. In the Massachusetts Historical Society.

   Inscription inside front cover: 'Samuel Sewall, his Booke, Decemb. 29, 1677. Bound by Jno. Ratcliff.'
   Yellow undressed calf. Blind tooling. Flat spine. Three sawn-in cords. Two small brass clasps. Square-dot roll in double panel. Triple-branch fleuron in corners of inner panel. Blind cat-tooth roll on board edges. Double square-dot fillet to mark position of cords on the back.

2. Call from Heaven, by Increase Mather. Boston, 1679. In the William Gwinn Mather Collection.

   Brown morocco. Gold tooling. Flat spine. Three sawn-in rawhide thongs. Square-dot roll bordering covers and marking position of cords on the back. Triple-branch fleuron in four corners of covers. Four-petalled fleuron in center. Cat-tooth roll on board edges.

3. A Collection of Tracts, by Increase Mather. 1670-1680. In the William Gwinn Mather Collection.

   Black morocco. Blind tooling. Double panel. Three-branch fleuron at inner corners of inner panel and again outside the panel at upper and lower ends.

4. General Laws and Liberties of the Massachusetts Colony . . . Cambridge, 1672. In the American Antiquarian Society.

   Brown calfskin. Blind tooling. Flat spine. Leather thongs stabbed through inner margins. Brass clasps, similar to No. 1, upper missing. Double panel. Fan-shaped fleurons at inner corners of inner panel and conventional fleurons at outer corners, the latter repeated in the center between the initials I and S in gold. Three-branch fleurons at outer center of the inner panel, top and bottom.

5. The Psalms . . . Cambridge, 1651. In the New York Public Library.

   Dark brown sheepskin. Gold tooling. Flat spine. Two sunken cords. Two brass clasps. Single gold fillet and single blind, bordering covers. Small fleuron separating initials F B in gold, on center cover. Double gold fillets marking position of cords on spine.

[46] Holmes, op. cit., *Proceedings of the American Antiquarian Society*, n. s., XXXVIII, 31-50; n. s., XXXIX, 291-306.

6. Book of the General Lawes . . . Cambridge, 1660. In the American Antiquarian Society.

Brown morocco. Blind tooling. Flat spine. Double panels. Fan-shaped tool impressed at inner corners of inner panel. Outside, at corners and center top and bottom, a conventionalized flower with foliage.

7. A Volume of Pamphlets. In the Mather Collection of the American Antiquarian Society.

Russet sheepskin, originally stained black. Blind tooling. Four raised cords, gold-lettered label, of later date than original binding. Double panels connected by diagonal lines at corners. Fan-shaped fleurons at corners of inner panel.

8. Book of General Laws . . . of Connecticut. Cambridge, 1673. In the Connecticut Historical Society.

Calfskin. Blind tooling. Flat spine. Single panel with three-branch fleurons at the corners.

9. Practical Truths, by Increase Mather. Boston, 1682. In the Connecticut Historical Society.

Calfskin. Blind tooling. Three raised cords. Double panels. Five-branch fleuron at outer edges of inner panel. Same fleuron, design pointing downward, just above the center.

10. A Confession of Faith, by the Synod of Boston. Boston, 1680. In the Connecticut Historical Society.

Calfskin. Blind tooling. Flat spine. Sewed on two leather thongs, stabbed through pages. Double, parallel panels. Three-branch fleuron in inside corners of larger rectangle.

11. A Confession of Faith, by the Synod of Boston. Boston, 1680. In the library of Albert C. Bates, Librarian of the Connecticut Historical Society.

Dark brown calfskin. Blind tooling. Flat spine. Single panel, with three-branch fleuron in its corners.

## *Bound by Edmund Ranger.*

1. Practical Truths, by Increase Mather. Boston, 1682. In the William Gwinn Mather Collection.

Sprinkled calf. Gold tooling. Raised cords. Silk headbands. No gold on sides. Full gilt back, gilt roll on board edges and gilt paper edges.

2. Practical Truths, by Increase Mather. Boston, 1682. In the New York Public Library.

Acid-stained calf, badly eaten. Gold tooling. Raised cords. Silk headbands. Half-sheet marble lining papers. Covers bordered by gilt cattooth roll, repeated on board edges. Four-petalled fleuron in gilt in all four corners. All edges gilt.

3. Samuel Sewall's Sermon Notebook. In the Boston Public Library.

   Sprinked sheepskin. Undecorated. Flat back. Three sawn-in rawhide thongs.

4. Volume of Pamphlets. In Mather Collection of American Antiquarian Society.

   Brown sheepskin, sprinkled with black stain. Gold lettering. Blind tooling. Four raised cords. Double panel with two different fleurons at inner and outer corners of inner panel. Fleuron in the center, between gilt initials C M. Worked headbands. Edges stained green.

5. Another Volume of Pamphlets. In the American Antiquarian Society.

   Brown sheepskin, sprinkled with black stain. Blind tooling. Four raised cords. Single panel, outlined by double fillet lines around the covers. A four-petalled fleuron at each corner. Worked headbands. Edges sprinkled green.

6. Covenant-Keeping, by Samuel Willard. Boston, 1682. In the Connecticut Historical Society.

   Calfskin. Blind tooling. Flat spine. Leather thongs stabbed through the inner margins.

To the group of Ratcliff bindings Mr. Wroth has added seven: two copies of the Eliot Indian Bible, owned by J. K. Lilly, Jr., of Indianapolis, and the Harvard College Library, respectively; four copies of Hubbard's *A Narrative of the Indian Wars in New-England*, Boston, 1677, owned by the American Antiquarian Society, the John Carter Brown Library, Goodspeed's Book Shop, and A. S. W. Rosenbach; and a volume of tracts in the Henry E. Huntington Library, No. 551 of the Church Catalogue.[47]

The Prince Collection in the Boston Public Library contains additional bindings which show every evidence of the work of these two men. One volume of Samuel Sewall's *Notebook* is unmistakably the work of John Ratcliff, for Sewall wrote on its fly-leaf: 'Decemb. 22, 1677. Bound by John Ratcliff. This together with my clasped Book in quarto cost 18d fr Binding.' The others resemble this vol-

[47] Wroth, op. cit., p. 204. (The copy owned by Goodspeed's Book Shop is now in the possession of Carroll A. Wilson.)

ume so closely that I should like to assign them tentatively
to the same binder. Unfortunately, two have been rebacked
so that the fine points of their workmanship have been
hopelessly lost. The leather is coarse and of uncertain character, in the first example considered, and is ornamented
with tools blind impressed in the same pattern as that on
Sewall's *Notebook.* This book, the *Institutio Graecae Grammatices Compendaria in Usum Regiae Scholae Westmonasteriensis,*
printed in London in 1656 by Roger Norton, was probably
bound very close to the date of the Sewall binding, as its
title-page is inscribed: 'John Leverett, Septemb. 25, 1677.'
Very likely this was the same John Leverett, then a student
at Harvard, who later became president of the college. The
decoration applied with the familiar square-dot roll and
the three-branched fleuron made a pleasing volume of this
ancient school book even if it was an example of Ratcliff's
cheaper work. There is greater uncertainty as to the binder
of Daniel Gookin's copy of *A Confession of Faith* by the
Synod of Boston. This shows the same general style of ornamentation and the use of the square-dot roll, but the fleuron, though similar to that of the other volumes, is not
identical. It is the same fleuron as that used on the copy of
Samuel Willard's *Covenant-Keeping* in the Massachusetts
Historical Society, which seems to be the work of Ranger,
as does the copy in the keeping of the Connecticut Historical Society. Furthermore, the imprints on both books, 1680
and 1682 respectively, place them in time near the disappearance of Ratcliff. It is disappointing that Ranger, who
did the finer work, appears never to have signed it.

Although it casts no light on the general status of bookbinding and is purely amateurish work, the fifth volume
of Sewall's *Notebook* is not without interest in this consideration of signed bindings. It is inscribed, presumably
in his own hand, 'Bound by Sam. Sewall Sept$^r$ 30, 1697.'

The pen and ink signature was in use as late as 1764, as
Mr. Wroth has discovered what seems to be an edition

binding of the *Votes and Proceedings of the New York Assembly* printed at that date, all signed in pen and ink: 'Bound by Robert McAlpine.'[48]

In the latter half of the eighteenth century, some of the immigrant craftsmen signed their work with engraved and printed labels, a practice which seems never to have been widespread but which became somewhat more extensive in the years after the Revolution. At least two men, Andrew Barclay, one of the Scottish binders in Boston, and Samuel Taylor, the English binder in Philadelphia, used such labels in the 1760's. William Woodhouse had a label, or trade card, which appears in a business book in 1766 when he was in partnership with John Dean: 'W. Woodhouse & J. Dean Bookbinders & Stationers, at the Bible & Crown, the Corner of Front & Chestnut-Streets Philadelphia Makes & sells, all sorts of Stationary Wares.' A few years later a similar trade card appeared to advertise the work of William Trickett, also a Philadelphia binder. Books containing the label of Samuel Taylor (Fig. 12) have not yet come to light, which is a pity; for its elegance and decorativeness lead us to expect fine volumes. As regards Andrew Barclay, we are more fortunate, for we have not only three different versions of his label but three books containing them. The two engraved copies (Fig. 13), owned by Dr. Victor H. Paltsits, are more pictorial than Taylor's and generally more elaborate, although not so carefully executed. A copy of the smaller is found in place inside the cover of a gold-tooled panelled binding of Brady and Tate's *New Version of the Psalms*, and again in a plainer volume of Tillotson's *Sermons*. The first mentioned is owned by the New York Public Library, and the latter by the American Antiquarian Society. Only recently the third version, a printed label decorated with simple typographic ornament, has come to light inside the plain covers of John Mellen's *Fifteen Discourses upon Doctrinal, Connected Subjects,*

[48] Wroth, op. cit., p. 210.

in the possession of the Massachusetts Historical Society. With three labels to draw upon, Andrew Barclay was well equipped to sign his work and must have had a wide patronage.

Binders' names appear in imprints, either as printers and binders or as booksellers and binders. We have already mentioned William Davies, the first bookbinder in Philadelphia. The imprint of Ellis Pugh's *Salutation to the Britains,* containing the earliest known reference to him, reads: 'Phila. Pr. by S. Keimer for W. Davies, Bookbinder in Chestnut Street, 1727.' Here Davies is referred to specifically as a bookbinder. In other cases we supply that information from external evidence, as for William Bradford and William Parks. Ranger was early identified as a binder from imprint information. Even as late as 1765 binders were so mentioned, and we find the name of Thomas Leverett, Boston binder of that period, appearing in the imprint of the 1765 edition of Brady and Tate's version of the Psalms.

Occasionally advertisements at the backs of books contained a printed note announcing terms for binding and a binder's name. Such a note in Blackwell's *Forma Sacra*, printed and sold by William M'Alpine at his Printing-Office in Marlborough-Street, Boston, in 1774, reads as follows: 'N. B. As the above Books are mostly printed and bound by said M'Alpine, he is determined to sell at the lowest Prices, and will warrant all such to be neatly bound, &c.'

By far the greatest number of colonial bindings, however, carry no clue as to who may have made them. The primitive panel bindings of the early eighteenth century, for instance, have not been identified with any single craftsman. They may have come from the Boston shop of Daniel Henchman, who had several apprentices, but that is only a surmise. There is, for example, the small volume of Psalms (Fig. 14) in the Library of Congress, printed in 1729 for J. Phillips, and typically decorated, with a single panel marked by a double blind-tooled line and realistic tulips stamped at the four outer corners. The cover is sheepskin over wooden boards. The back is flat, divided into two panels by double blind fillets. Even in the colonial period there were more elaborate bindings of the same general type, but none more appealing in its simple artistry.

## CHAPTER III

## BOOKBINDING IN THE YOUNG REPUBLIC
### (1783-1820)

WITH the signing of the peace in 1783 the American colonies became politically independent. From that time on, unifying influences were at work and there was a gradual rise of national self-consciousness. A national literature developed slowly. Americans were beginning to realize that they had their own political and intellectual contributions to make. This does not mean, in any sense, that the English cultural background was suddenly ignored and forgotten. Now that the years have given us perspective, we are increasingly aware that the War of Independence was merely a culmination of events and that it brought about a formal separation only after the gradually increasing gulf between England and her colonies had become too wide to bridge. Politically, the estrangement had been increasing in intensity for a long time. Intellectually and artistically, dependence upon the mother country continued long after political bonds were broken. There were other influences than England's at work, however, in the period just after the Revolution. The young Republic was allied to France by a natural sympathy with her political ideas and thought, and by representatives at the French court. Subsequent reception of refugees from the French Revolution led to no inconsiderable infiltration of French style and custom. The study of outside influences upon the arts and crafts, with their own emerging self-consciousness, is a fascinating one, and it is a matter for regret that so few studies of that kind have been made. Clearly the history of each craft, including bookbinding, should reflect certain of these conditions.

It was in this national period, after the War of Independence, that bookbinding came to be carried on more generally as a craft in its own right. Once binding was performed in a separate establishment from bookselling and printing, it assumed a new importance. Of course the history of bookbinding remained closely associated with that of printing, even after the practice of the craft was carried on as a distinct function. Printing and bookselling had flourished in Boston and Philadelphia before the Revolution and there were at the time of its outbreak about fifty presses in the entire British colonies, printing some 461 books a year.[1] By the close of the century, only fifteen years after the signing of the peace, that number had increased four-fold.[2] Printing presses continued to be established in the principal towns and villages; but in this new era printing and bookselling, and with them bookbinding, were becoming more and more centralized in the cities of Philadelphia, Boston, and New York.

By 1783 all materials required for bookmaking were available in the United States. Paper had been manufactured since 1690, when the first mill was established in Philadelphia, and was produced in 1787 by approximately ninety mills throughout the United States, forty-eight of them in Pennsylvania.[3] American-made type was obtainable in quantity in Germantown as early as 1775.[4] Ink had been made in Pennsylvania at an early date in the eighteenth century, though Isaiah Thomas reports that it was not generally available in New England in early times.[5]

By this time Philadelphia had become the foremost printing and publishing center. Boston had held first place until the beginning of the Revolution, after which Philadelphia gained precedence rapidly until it had in 1798

[1] Thomas, 'History of Printing in America, 1874,' *Transactions and Collections of the American Antiquarian Society* (2d ed., Albany: Munsell, 1874), vols. V-VI. Reference in I, 17.

[2] L. C. Wroth, 'Book Production and Distribution from the Beginning to the War Between the States.' In: Lehmann-Haupt, *The Book in America* (New York: R. R. Bowker Company, 1939), p. 99.

[3] Wroth, *The Colonial Printer*, p. 129.

[4] Ibid., p. 105.

[5] Ibid., p. 118.

eighty-eight persons and firms engaged in printing, publishing, and bookselling, in comparison with Boston's forty-one.[6]

With Philadelphia the flourishing center that it was, with all the materials required for printing easily available, it is not surprising that what is now considered the first book made wholly from native materials should have been produced there.[7] *The Impenetrable Secret* was advertised in the *Pennsylvania Mercury* of June 23, 1775, as 'Just Published and Printed with Types, Paper and Ink manufactured in this Province.' No copies survive, ironically enough. It is possible only to speculate upon how it might have been bound and by whom. Materials for bookbinding had been obtainable in America from the earliest practice of the craft, and they had also been imported. Such was the case still, although the evidence at hand indicates an increasing use of native materials. Whereas the earliest craftsmen had imported pasteboard as well as leather, imports were now limited to the latter. Since imported morocco has been found rarely enough on books and only occasionally in the accounts of stock, it seems safe to assume that the usual copy of *The Impenetrable Secret* was bound in native sheep or calf and decorated with simple gold tooling.

## Materials

The materials used at this time were fundamentally the same as the leather, board, and cord of colonial days, except that the use of pasteboard covers had become the rule instead of the exception. Scabboard was still used, but only on school texts and other cheap books covered with paper or undecorated sheepskin; and pack thread was used to the complete exclusion of leather thongs. By the close of the century lining papers were commonly marbled.

[6] Wroth, 'Book Production . . .' In: Lehmann-Haupt, *The Book in America* (New York: R. R. Bowker Company, 1939), p. 99.
[7] Wroth, *The Colonial Printer*, p. 106.

The manuscript records of Isaiah Thomas, in the American Antiquarian Society, give a very good idea of the typical materials used at the close of the eighteenth century. In 1794 Thomas's *Account of Stock* included fourteen bundles of scabboard and eighty hundredweight of pasteboard, while his entries for leather were limited to sheepskins for which he paid 1s 6d or 2s according to the size of the sheep. His later accounts (1802) included red sheepskins at 83½ cents each, a half skin of parchment at 87½ cents, and 18½ dozen English skins at $8.00 a dozen. The price would seem to indicate that the last were sheep also. For native calf he was paying a dollar per skin, and for a buffalo skin six dollars.[8] Morocco was mentioned only twice, both times as an item charged against Joseph Miller, Bookbinder, Worcester. On June 18, 1794, there was a charge 'to morocco ⅓ of a skin 6 (shillings),' and over the period from May 24 to June 25, 1794, this same binder was charged with:

| | |
|---|---|
| 1 quire paper and 1 sheet marble | 2s 2⅔d |
| 5⅜ yds. linen @ 2/6 | 14s ¾d |
| 80 cwt. pasteboard | 6/7 |
| 7 yds. linen | 1/2/2 |
| 44 sheepskins | 4/4s |
| 1 book gold leaf | 4s |
| 1 book Brass ditto | 6d |
| Pasteboard, Morocco, and Rye and Indian | 2/9/6 |

A great variety of decorated papers, marbled, gilt, and block-printed, appear in his accounts also. Of these, only the marbled papers were used extensively as lining papers for leather-bound volumes. The variety is perhaps explained by the fact that Thomas issued a great number of paper-bound books, many of them with decorative covers. In his *Paper Mill Account* of 1794 occurs the following item:

---

[8] Zaehnsdorf notes in his *Art of Bookbinding*, p. 96, 'An imitation russia leather is imported from America, of far greater strength than the real. It is made of buffalo skins, and tanned in the same way as the russia. . . . It is to be had from nearly all leather sellers.'

MESSRS. CALEB AND ELIJAH BURBANK of Sutton, Paper Makers
Aug. 13, 1794      3 Quires marble paper                    12*s*
Aug. 26, 1794      to 200 covering wrappers                 12*s*

Throughout his accounts we find mention of gilt paper, fine chintz, Dutch Blue, Dutch Yellow, Dutch sprinkled 'coam,' Dutch Marble, and Bonnet Paper. 'Bonnet Paper' was stiff pasteboard, used for the frames of bonnets and hats,[9] and not the quaint blocked paper decorated with narrow stripes and sprigs of flowers, used to cover the bandboxes of the period. End-papers decorated with such stripes and sprigs were used, however, as on George Washington's copy of Humphreys' *Miscellaneous Works* in the Boston Athenaeum. It is interesting to observe in this connection that one of the early Salem bookbinders, Isaac Cushing, made bandboxes in addition to binding books.

A change in types of leather was particularly noteworthy at the turn of the century. The plain, durable leathers of the early colonial period had been largely replaced by skins which were not what they seemed, although, as they continued to be tanned with bark, they were still lasting in quality. It was not until mineral salts came to be used in the tanning process that the leather became notably poor and short-lived. The date for deterioration has been set as approximately 1830 for some leathers, while 1860 marks a limit after which nearly all kinds show signs of marked decay.[10] Tree calf and sheep are characteristic after 1800 and remain fairly easy to identify. There were still some sprinkled calf and sheep covers, but there was also a tendency to add further decoration by acid staining, producing the effect of tree calf without its formality of design. When the skins of calves and sheep have been finished as roan, russia, and 'morocco,' as is so often the case, identification of the basic leather becomes rather more difficult.

[9] Elisabeth McClellan, *History of American Costume, 1607-1870* (New York: Tudor, 1937), 661 p. Reference on p. 618.

[10] D. Cockerell, *Bookbinding and the Care of Books* (New York: Appleton, 1908), 342 p. Reference on p. 266.

Roan leather is 'sheep skin tanned in sumach,' dyed and finished like morocco, the difference being its smooth, glossy appearance. Russia originally signified calfskins from Russia, especially treated with birch oil, but came to be imitated elsewhere and finished from horsehides, calf, goat, sheep [and even buffalo skins!]. Originally morocco leather was a product of the Levant, Turkey, and the Mediterranean coast of Africa where it was made from goatskins. The French imitation which developed towards the close of the eighteenth century was made from split calf and especially from sheepskins.[11] Thus sheep might be plain, sprinkled, treed, or stained, or finished as roan, russia, or even morocco.

Imitation morocco leather was first made in this country near the close of the eighteenth century, from sheepskins, imported goatskins artificially grained, and deerskins.[12] It appears from the *Transactions of the Society of Arts in London* for the year 1783 that such a manufacture had been established in England as a direct result of rewards offered by that society, to prepare leather in imitation of 'Turkey' or 'Lisbon' for export to foreign countries. News of this soon reached the United States. *The Pennsylvania Packet and Daily Advertiser* for January 13, 1789, gave news of the investigation to be carried on by a committee appointed by the Pennsylvania Society for the Encouragement of Manufactures and Useful Arts (itself formed in 1787) to inquire into this process, communicated by an Armenian to the London Society.[13] As Philadelphia subsequently became very prominent in the manufacture of morocco, the committee's report was apparently successful and some at least of the morocco bindings of the period may be examples of this domestic morocco, bearing a certain resemblance to roan and very possibly being sheepskin finished in imitation of 'Turkey' leather.

The manufacture of this counterfeit morocco was most

11 *Encyclopaedia Britannica* (9th ed., New York: Scribner, 1882), XIV, 388.
12 Bishop, op. cit., II, 147.
13 Bishop, op. cit., I, 459.

certainly carried on at this time in Massachusetts and is even reported to have been started as early as 1770 by the notorious Lord Timothy Dexter and others at Charlestown. In any case it was manufactured by Elisha Mead in Charlestown in 1796. Quite possibly morocco of his manufacture covers *A Summary of the Principal Evidences for the Truth and Divine Origin of the Christian Revelation,* a small book by Bielby, Lord Bishop of London, printed in its third edition by Samuel Etheridge in Charlestown, for E. and S. Larkin, No. 47 Cornhill, Boston, in 1800, and now in the possession of the American Antiquarian Society. In all probability it was bound by Benjamin Larkin, who worked at bookbinding next door at No. 46 and must have exercised considerable care on this particular volume which bears on the front cover in gold 'American Edition | Presented with | Great Respect to | The Right Reve<sup>nd</sup> Author | By the Publishers.'

In 1800 William Rose, an Englishman who had learned the business in London, began to produce morocco leather at a factory in Lynn and later at Charlestown.[14] The *Boston Gazette* of December 22, 1800, advertises 'a quantity of Morocco Leather for sale at No. 1 Charlestown Long Wharf.' That same year a patent was granted to Jacob Perkins of Boston for polishing and graining morocco.[15] About one quarter of the entire leather output of the United States came from Charlestown.[16] It was not surprising, therefore, that Charlestown and Lynn petitioned for added duties on leather in 1811, at which time eight hundred thousand skins were manufactured annually in the United States, 'equal or superior to' the best foreign product.[17]

The whole manufacture of leather had made such progress that by 1810 tanneries were turning out annually leather valued at twenty million dollars. Quantities of

[14] Bishop, op. cit., II, 84.
[15] Ibid., II, 145.
[16] Ibid., II, 84.
[17] Ibid., II, 170.

American leather were being exported, although some English leather and morocco of superior grade were still imported.[18] The principal centers of manufacture were in Massachusetts, Connecticut, New Jersey, and Pennsylvania. At this time all leather was still bark tanned, with oak in the middle states and in New England with hemlock.[19] Colonel William Edwards, a grandson of the famous Jonathan Edwards, had invented and patented tanning machinery and is believed to have used the first bark-mill run by water, in Northampton. He did much to spread the manufacture by his invention of various mechanical aids and sent leather to the Boston market in 1794.[20]

The United States was now intent on developing its own industries and achieving independence from the foreign markets in every way possible, not the least important being this manufacture of leather. A typical attempt to encourage manufactures and useful arts, and one having a very definite bearing on bookbinding, arose from the resolution passed at the fourth meeting of the American Company of Booksellers, held at New York June 18, 1804. The association had been organized two years before, at the instigation of Mathew Carey, who had in mind the annual literary fairs held at Leipzig and Frankfort. The resolution mentioned premiums, in the form of gold medals, to be offered for the best examples of printing on American paper with American ink, for the best specimen of American-made paper and printing ink, and 'A gold medal of the value of $25 for the best piece of American binding, executed in American leather to be exhibited on a book of American printing of no less than 300 pages . . .'[21]

The following year, at the annual fair held in Newark, New Jersey, a gold medal was awarded to William Swain for the best specimen of binding executed in American

18 Bishop, op. cit., II, 147.   19 Ibid.
20 Bishop, op. cit., I, 442.
21 C. L. Nichols, 'The Literary Fair in the United States,' *Bibliographical Essays: A Tribute to Wilberforce Eames.* (Cambridge: 1924), p. 88.

leather. What book he bound and what materials, technique and ornamentation he used can only be conjectured. Repeated efforts have failed to reveal anything more about Swain beyond his name, address, and occupation. He was working in New York in 1805, first on Reed Street and later on Pearl, which was the heart of the book trade.

What we do have, in the notice of this event, is a manifestation of the current concern with all phases of bookmaking and the encouragement of American manufacture of all materials used for that purpose. More specifically, it emphasizes the need of better binding done with American leather and gives the name of one binder who was presumably more than ordinarily competent and devoted himself entirely to following his craft.

Gold was probably available in Philadelphia before 1820, but we find it advertised twice in a directory for that year:

> Marcus Bull, Gold and Silver Beater, 22 Pear St., will execute orders for Deep and Pale Gold Leaf, Silver Leaf, Deep and pale Gold Powders, Silver Powders & Gold Foil, all of which are of superior quality.

and again:

> John King (from London) Manufacturer of Deep Yellow, Lemon and Pale Gold Leaf of the best quality and on reasonable terms; and maker of Burnish Gold Size, of a very superior quality, equal to the best that can be bought in London, and very cheap; likewise manufacturer of Gold and Silver paper, and Gold and Silver Embossed Borders; from 1-8th of an inch wide to 3 inches do.

Whatever its origin, the gold is still clear and bright on the majority of bindings and was plainly of superior quality.

## Technique

The technique of this period was more consistent than that of the colonial. The flat back, achieved by sawing across the back small grooves into which the bands were sunk, had been introduced into common use in England in the middle of the eighteenth century, probably suggested by the Dutch bindings, themselves in turn influenced by the Islamic bindings of the East. 'Although it was adopted by many of the English and French binders with repugnance, it became fashionable.' [22] American bindings were of that nature with a few exceptions, most of which came from the workshops of binders who had learned their craft in Scotland.

By 1822 bookbinders estimated raised bands at an extra cost, charging one price for false bands, or bands that were merely pasted on and in no sense functional, and twice as much for genuine bands. [23] The backs became rounded, although very slightly, and headbands were an accepted part of the binding. These headbands varied considerably, for they were made of linen thread, silk, wool, or, soon after the turn of the century, muslin or leather. This use of muslin or leather, an expedient resorted to because of increased book production, weakened the structure of the bindings. Like the false bands on the back, the headbands were only stuck on instead of sewed. Their origin as extra cords to give added strength had been entirely forgotten. They had become almost a vestigial structure, no longer serving their essential purpose, and remain so today in the more ambitious machine-bound books, although they have been allowed to disappear completely from the ordinary trade binding. The few headbands in current use serve only to keep the back-strip from tearing when a book is taken from the shelf. In 1822 information concerning headbands was given in the *Price List of the New York Friendly Association of Master Bookbinders*. Worked headbands were

[22] W. S. Brassington, *A History of the Art of Bookbinding, with Some Account of the Books of the Ancients* (London: Stock, 1894). 277 p. Reference on p. 239.
[23] 'Price List of the New York Friendly Association of Master Bookbinders, 1822,' tipped in Library of Congress copy of *The Whole Art of Bookbinding, Containing Valuable Receipts for Sprinkling, Marbling, Colouring, &c.* (Richmond, Va.: Peter Cottom, 1824), 60 p.

to go on all 'super extra' binding and all 'extra Morocco
and Roan gilt.' Cloth headbands were designated for 'Russia and Calf, gilt and plain,' 'Roan plain' and 'Sheep gilt.'

The practice of lacing the book securely into its covers
was slighted in this period of quantity production. The
number of cords used tended to be reduced, with many
books sewed on two cords only. If the usual number of
cords was used, as was prescribed for better work, six cords
to a folio, five to a quarto, and so on, only two or at most
three were laced into the covers, until at last all bands were
simply frayed and pasted down between the pasteboard of
the covers and their lining papers.

Lining papers were nearly all decorative, by far the
greater preponderance marbled, either in the 'coam' pattern mentioned by Isaiah Thomas or, later, in the more
common splash marble. A few highly decorated covers had
plain uncolored end-papers and others plain dark colored
end-papers. The group of books from George Washington's library, in the Boston Athenaeum, show several di-
verse styles, plain white, marbled, plain dark-blue paper
highly burnished, and the striped, sprigged paper previously mentioned.

A group of New York binders working about 1820 introduced plain green and brown end-papers in combination with marbled edges. Various stains had been used for
edges, a plain yellow or a plain brown or green most frequently, as well as the familiar red and brown sprinkle of
the earlier colonial days. Gilding was still infrequent, although the more pretentious volumes carried gold on the
edges to harmonize with the decoration on the covers. In
very rare instances the edges thus gilded were further decorated by a goffered design.

### Decoration and Style of Bindings

The more elaborate style of gold ornamentation used
very generally since the earliest years of the Republic con-

trasted sharply with the first blind-tooled leather bindings turned out from the workshops of the Boston binders in the seventeenth and early eighteenth centuries, as well as with the simple gold tooling of that period. Single line rolls gave way to more decorative rolls which grew consistently broader with the passing of time, until they reached the width of an inch or achieved the effect of even greater width than that by building up a border of several different rolls or the same one repeated. The delicate floral rolls in vogue near the close of the eighteenth century were replaced about 1800 by the more severe classical meander and scroll.

Although there were a few exceptions, it was the general custom to depend entirely upon the use of rolls for cover decoration. Usually the rolls formed a frame around the covers and the centers were left entirely free of ornamentation. Occasionally center designs were used, in the shape of medallions built up of small tools. One pleasing example of this method in its simplest form is to be seen in a roan binding on a copy of *The Christian's Duty* (Fig. 15) in the Library of Congress, printed at Germantown in 1791 by Peter Liebert, who may have bound it himself.[24] In this case a double gold fillet line borders the covers and a small fleuron is used at each corner, the same fleuron being stamped in the center four times to form a larger, four-petalled ornament. In certain examples a cat-tooth roll is used around the outside edge of the covers with larger center designs built up from a number of small tools. One such binding on the Episcopal Prayer Book (Fig. 16) revised for American use and printed by Hall and Sellers in 1786, now in the John Carter Brown Library, shows a center decoration made of four good-sized stamps of acorns, leaves, dots, and curved lines, a cat-tooth rolled border, and tiny marguerites in the four corners. The fine, firm morocco bind-

[24] McCulloch reports that Peter Liebert and his son-in-law bought the sheets of Christopher Sower's *Bible* at auction and completed and bound some copies for sale.

ing on the Mohawk prayer book (Fig. 17) printed in Quebec in 1780, also in the John Carter Brown Library, is a far less elaborate example of the same style. It is bordered by a narrow gold roll containing an acorn, flowers, and leaves, with its corners unmitred and a three-branch naturalistic flower stamped in each corner. The center ornament repeats that same flower, placed slightly below the center, upside-down. This binding is noteworthy also for its five heavy raised cords bordered with the cat-tooth roll and for the smaller flowers with leafy branches which are placed in each panel except the second, which bears instead a brown morocco label. Its solidity of construction, the unusual bulkiness of the cords, and the somewhat haphazard placing of the stamp in the center of the cover suggest a French provincial workshop. If we knew more about French provincial workshops, it might be possible to assign it to its place of binding, perhaps in Quebec, near the printer of the volume.

Several copies of Robert Aitken's *Bible* show decoration by a real artist. As printer of the first complete Bible to bear an American imprint, Aitken's name is familiar in the annals of Americana. No bindings appear with his signature or label to give positive evidence of his workmanship, but there is every reason to believe that he bound a number of the *Bibles* himself. Of the decorated bindings on copies located in the Library of Congress, the British Museum, the New York Public Library, and the John Carter Brown Library, the last mentioned is especially worthy of note (Fig. 18). It is particularly tasteful, with its narrow leafy gold roll as a border and the small realistic flowers in the corners. The tools themselves show off an unusual grace to fine advantage on the soft green morocco they adorn. It was no idle boast of McCulloch's that 'Aitken was . . . a most excellent workman. There was no better finished binding ever done than some of the books executed in his shop.'[25]

25 McCulloch, 'Additions,' p. 105.

Very occasionally, covers were decorated with a border made by the repetition of single small tools. A copy of Watts's *Hymns* (Fig. 19), owned by Mrs. Harry MacNeill Bland of New York, is a very successful example of this unusual style. Notwithstanding its Edinburgh imprint of 1778, it was unquestionably bound in America, since the fly-leaf bears the inscription 'Hannah Boudinot's Book, bound and gilt at Trenton, 1785.' Although it has an outer border of the traditional plain gold fillet roll, repeated three times, it shows a unique treatment in its inner border of single flowers placed regularly around the cover, with their heads pointing toward the center. The tools, although not strictly identical with those of the Aitken *Bible,* show a striking similarity. The easy grace of the flowers on the cover and the elaborately gilt-rolled back are characteristic of Aitken's work. If he did not bind the book himself there is reason to think that William Bradford III, descendant of Philadelphia's first printer, did it. Both binders may very likely have obtained their tools from a common source.

Examples of all-over cover designs were infrequent. Two books from George Washington's library, now in the Boston Athenaeum, were lavishly decorated with rolls and numerous small emblematic tools. Humphreys' *Miscellaneous Works* (Fig. 20), printed in New York in 1790, shows the use of a delicate floral roll across the top and bottom of the covers and an odd collection of crossed flags, bow and arrow, battle axe, drum, swords, viola, and lyre up the sides. The center consists of a black leather inlay bordered with the words 'George Washington Esquire President of the United States of America' and displaying rising suns, stars, and a heart-shaped ornament. On the top corner of this diamond-shaped inlay stands a young eagle. The rest of the cover-ground is filled in with garlands, festoons of leaves and flowers, suns and stars, and a human figure of uncertain symbolism in the lower portion of the cover. With the exception of the center inlay and the symbolic figure, the miscellaneous decoration on this binding is thoroughly uniform in style. Even the emblematic rolls up the side are consistent with the floral rolls they complement, and the style of the ornaments as a whole is delicate and well blended.

The decoration on the other book from Washington's library, *A Collection of the Speeches of the President of the United States* (Fig. 21), is a little less confused, although the space is well filled with stars, medallions, suns, a dove with an olive branch, and vases of flowers. Certain tools are identical with those from Isaiah Thomas's workshop, but others are quite new and make it impossible as yet to attribute this work to any one known shop or binder. Both bindings are quite unrelated to the general style of the period and serve only to make the comparative simplicity of the others more apparent. For all their pretension, however, their general workmanship and type of ornamentation lack the finish of foreign work of the period and mark them as of American origin.

Usually the emphasis of decoration was upon the spine rather than the covers (Fig. 18). Although cords had been sunk to make flat backs, advantage was seldom taken of this new continuous area and the backs continued to be broken up into panels, artificially now, by means of narrow gold rolls. Often the same roll or a narrower one was rolled lengthwise of the spine, on its outer edges, making a rectangular frame for each panel (Fig. 16). Within this framework was stamped a single flower or a bird, a lyre, or a vase, with leafy scrolls at the four corners to set them off. The old familiar treatment of the back, especially popular earlier with the Scottish and English binders, was carried over from colonial binding (Fig. 24). Panels continued to be crossed by broken fillet lines running diagonally from the four corners, with small circles or sunbursts at each corner, and the resulting triangular spaces filled in with stars, fleurons, and scrolls. An all-over gilt effect was sometimes obtained by the repetition of narrow gold rolls in rows placed close together to form a gilt network (Fig. 19).

Lettering on the spine had become common but was by no means the rule before the nineteenth century (Figs. 23 and 24). A roll close to the edge of the inside covers was used in rare cases, but was invariably to be found on the board edges.

I have found only one or two examples treating the spine as a single panel, unhampered by fillet lines, that fall within this period. That style became popular soon after 1820, within the era of gift books and annuals. However, George Washington's copy of the *Transactions of the Society Instituted in the State of New York for the Promotion of Agriculture, Arts, and Manufactures* (Fig. 22), printed in New York by Childs and Swaine in 1792, is undivided into panels on the back, except for the leather label bearing the title. It carries decoration symbolical of the contents in the form of a sheaf of wheat at the top, crossed rakes, and a few stalks of grain beneath the label. The remainder of the spine is taken up by an urn, from which rise festoons of leaves and flowers topped by an eagle. The symbolism is more appropriate to the text here, but the binding lacks simplicity just as does that on Humphreys' *Miscellaneous Works* (Fig. 20). This latter cover is less unusual, being decorated in a large rectangular panel bordered by a Greek meander, flanked by a chain roll and an outer border of a flower scroll inside a narrow dot and triangle roll.

The Isaiah Thomas bindings on Psalm Books and the quarto Bible show the same general characteristics, with one exception. They keep alive the old tradition of a panel, outlined by gold rolls, connected at the corners by a diagonal line which takes the place of the fleurons used in colonial days. The result is a more stereotyped and hardened form of ornamentation.

By 1820 a very distinct new style had evolved, that of gold and blind tooling combined. It was used in Philadelphia

and Boston, but is especially well illustrated in a group of
New York bindings executed by George Champley, who
styled himself 'Fancy Binder' on his ticket. One of his best
bindings is done in smooth tan calf on a duodecimo of John
Langhorne's *Correspondence of Theodosius and Constantia* (Fig.
23), the London edition of 1817, in The Grolier Club Library. The borders on the covers of this small volume are
made of a single gilt line roll inside a wider line roll, also
in gold, within which a quarter-inch stylized gilt flower roll
is run around twice, the second time turned to make a
complementary design against the first. Inside the gilt decoration occurs a simpler blind roll accented with long feath-
ery ornaments, likewise blind, set into the corners. The
spine is divided into five panels by four raised cords. All
panels are decorated with a square flowered stamp that fills
the space, with the exception of the center panel which carries the title. The cords are marked with an azured fillet
line identical with that used on the board edges. The covers
are outlined inside with a narrow gold roll. Lining papers
are plain brown and all edges are marbled. Cloth headbands are stuck on. The plain lining papers are characteristic of Champley, while the use of the central panel for the
title label, instead of the second panel from the top, as is
customary, marks the work of the New York binders of the
period (Figs. 22 and 29).

The few examples of inlaid or mosaic binding which appear in America vary in the skill with which the inlay is
applied, and none of them are very ambitious. The two
already mentioned, Horsmanden's *Journal* (Fig. 10) and
Humphreys' *Miscellaneous Works* (Fig. 20), have rather
crudely managed central pieces. The leather, which has
not been pared very thin, is pasted down and covered with
gilt ornamentation. Neither compares with a much more
elaborate example, Washington's own copy of Royall
Tyler's *Contrast*. This volume is bound in a dark-red
polished morocco inlaid with a green border around the

covers, a tiny green medallion in the center, a green title label on the spine, and eight green bands marking the position of the cords. The spine is heavily gilt, and there are three gilt rolls used as a border on the covers: a cat-tooth roll on the outer edges, a flower roll on the green inlay, and another smaller floral roll inside. The small green medallion in the center is outlined by a decorative gold roll and carries a gilt diamond in the center. William Loring Andrews, who describes and reproduces this binding in his *Bibliopegy in the United States,* says, 'Positive proof that this binding was executed in this country is lacking, but appearances and the circumstantial evidence in the case point to that conclusion.' Appearances certainly point that way for, elaborate as the decoration is, the tools and the manner of their application are quite familiar. The panels of the spine bear crossed fillet lines, the intervening spaces filled in with stars and acorns, in the style widely used since the first half of the eighteenth century. The tools have all appeared before, and the broadest flower roll on the covers occurs again in the Boston Public Library's copy of *Washington's Political Legacies* (Fig. 24), a memorial volume for Mrs. Washington printed for John Russell and John West in Boston in 1800. Its cover of blue polished morocco is effectively bordered by this one flower and ribbon roll. The back is divided into six panels, the second containing a red leather label, all others ornamented by an urn, in gilt; and each panel division is marked with a red inlaid strip, tooled in gold with the Greek key design. Not quite so elaborate as *The Contrast*, the binding was carefully executed and no effort was spared to make it worthy of the occasion. The refinements of polished morocco, inlay, gilt tooling and edges, silk headbands, and marbled lining papers combined to make it extraordinary.

For the most part, inlay was restricted to bands across the spine, similar to those on the copy of *Washington's Political Legacies*. One of the numerous examples of this, the copy of

Brown's *Self-interpreting Bible,* formerly in the Poor Library and now in the Henry E. Huntington Library, contains in the binder's ticket indisputable evidence that it was 'Bound and Sold by Thomas Allen No. 12 Queen Street.' Simpler and less assuming examples occur on Isaiah Thomas's folio *Bible* of 1791, a *Book of Common Prayer* issued by Thomas and Andrews in 1794, and Bielby's *Summary of the Principal Evidences of the Truth and Divine Origins of the Christian Revelation,* printed in Charlestown in 1800 for E. and S. Larkin. Simple as these examples are, they are worthy of notice, for there are comparatively few examples of inlay to be found. They appear to have been more ambitious jobs than most of the binders of the day cared to undertake.

Even the plainest sheep bindings often showed some touches of artistry in the red or black leather labels which carried the title. The variety of decoration on the labels of quantities of late eighteenth-century collections of laws shows the craftsman's concern with beauty and individual expression, and his complete lack of the standardization which was soon to come with the machine. Narrow gold rolls, linear and floral, bordered the gold letters, and were sometimes run around the covers in blind. Even the small label carrying the volume number was similarly ornamented. Robert Aitken again proved himself an artist in the decoration of his label for the *Transactions of the American Philosophical Society.* The title in gilt on red morocco was bordered by two narrow decorative gilt rolls, but the volume number in gold on black morocco was further ornamented by an infinitesimally narrow floral roll put on in a circle around the number, and by four three-petalled flowers with straight stems in each corner, pointing their heads inward toward the circle. Touches of real beauty appeared on the most utilitarian of bindings.

Decoration in the federal period was often applied with tools of domestic origin, as it had been as early as 1768. Throughout the eighteenth century, engravers in Philadelphia advertised a great variety of offices, ranging from the cutting of landscapes and portraits to seals, coats of arms, type metal, and bookbinding tools. In the *Pennsylvania Packet* of January 30, 1795, T. Bingham, Engraver, Chaser etc., From Birmingham, No. 67 Mulberry or Arch street announces that he 'Cuts Letter, Figures or Flowers, for Seals, Dyes, Types, Book-Binding, Chasing and Engraving in General.' [26]

Bookbinders and printers also did engraving. Many of them mention letter-press and copper-plate printing in their advertisements. Robert Aitken, the Philadelphia printer, was an engraver, and it is not completely beyond the range of possibility that he engraved his own tools. If so, he should have been proud of the freedom and graceful naturalism expressed in his flowers and the delicate beauty of his narrow rolls.

Engravers in Boston and New York do not mention bookbinding tools specifically in the miscellaneous lists of their achievements. Perhaps tool engraving is included in 'etc., etc.' which invariably winds up their advertisements. At any rate, the activity flourished in Philadelphia over a long period of time. The 1819 directory for that city includes a prominent advertisement for A. & W. Mason, 'Engravers of brass ornaments for Bookbinding, etc.' Unhappily no early specimen book has been discovered, to be placed next to Binny & Ronaldson's *Type Specimen Book of 1812* (the first American type specimen book). In Nicholson's *Manual of the Art of Bookbinding*, [27] Gaskill, Cooper, and Fry are spoken of as bookbinders' tool-cutters, and specimens of rolls and hand-stamps, as they appeared in their pattern book, are reproduced. There were several Gaskills who worked at bookbinding in Philadelphia during the forties and fifties, and there was a firm known as Gaskill and Copper, calico-engravers and bookbinders, listed in the directory

[26] Prime, *The Arts and Crafts in Philadelphia* ... II, 66.
[27] T. B. Nicholson, *A Manual of the Art of Bookbinding* (Philadelphia: Baird, 1856). 318 p. Reference on pp. 197-198.

for 1837. This firm appeared as bookbinders' tool-cutters and engravers, three years later, and in 1852 added another engraver to the business, changing its name to Gaskill, Copper, and Fry. The specimens which they reproduce are the larger, more showy ornaments of the later style, which contrast unfavorably with those used on bindings before 1820.

Ornamentation was achieved by means of tools which were, for the most part, exactly like those used in England and France. It seems reasonable to suspect, therefore, that many of them were imported before the beginning of the nineteenth century and some even later, by individual binders or a printer who carried on a large binding business of his own. It is impossible to speak with authority of the origin of eighteenth-century tools, as their use was not confined to the boundaries of any one country. For example, we find the same cameo stamp used by Derome in France in the eighteenth century appearing again in contemporary England, and again on bindings executed for Isaiah Thomas in the United States. The same rolls and single stamps of birds, lyre, and vases were used in all three countries also. The French influence was transmitted to England and the United States by many emigrés who settled abroad after the French Revolution.

In the closing years of the eighteenth century the papers of Isaiah Thomas show that he imported type even though it was being made at that time in this country. Boston bookbinders may well have taken advantage of Thomas's large business and bought their tools from him. At one time he and his partners controlled sixteen presses in constant use, seven of them in Worcester, and five bookstores in Massachusetts as well as one in Concord, New Hampshire, one in Albany, New York, and one in Baltimore, Maryland. He was one of the largest book publishers here or abroad and was mentioned in the account of Brissot de Warville's travels in the United States in 1788 as the Didot of this country.[28] He was a printer, bookseller, paper manufacturer, bookbinder, and distributor, all in one. His manuscript account books note dealings with several Boston bookbinders, among them Ebenezer Battelle, David Burns, David West, and Benjamin Larkin, and includes such items as 'bookbinder's press,' skins, gold leaf, marble paper, and 'scab$^d$.' From an account of his own stock (Fig. 25), taken in April, 1796, we find a complete listing of tools. Among other items he had eight sets of lettering tools, identified separately as folio, quarto, octavo, and duodecimo, two sets of figures, and a dozen pallats in which to use them. The gilding tools were lumped as a large assortment of stamps, flowers (seventy-eight stamps), six rollers for binding, two hundred pairs of large clasps, thirty-four gilding tools, and one and a half dozen duodecimo flowers.

The decoration on bindings issued by the smaller shops of individual craftsmen depended no doubt upon fewer tools used in a variety of combinations. No itemized inventories of the tools used at a corresponding period in the small shop have been found. Thomas accounts for bookbinding tools in his shop at Walpole, New Hampshire, in a single item worth forty dollars. A Salem binder mentions 'several handsome gilding rolls' without giving further details.[29] Such detailed information would be not without interest; but pleasing decoration is always more dependent upon the skill and imagination of the craftsman in the use and disposition of his tools than upon the number of stamps employed. It is to be expected that the style of decoration may be characteristic of individual bookbinders, as it is also representative of given binding centers.

Throughout the federal period bindings continued to reflect European styles, particularly current classicism, even though the new national self-consciousness encouraged the use of native materials and eventually brought about an en-

[28] Thomas, *History of Printing* (1874 edition), I, lxxv-lxxvi.
[29] H. S. Tapley, *Salem Imprints, 1768-1825* (Salem: Essex Institute, 1927), 512 p. Reference on p. 209.

larged native business of tool-cutting. The covers of books became more ostentatious, with every emphasis upon materials and decoration at the expense of technique. The sprinkled and tree calf, roan and morocco leathers which were used in the early years of the Republic were more pretentious than the plainer sheep and calf characteristic of the colonial period. The tooling made plentiful use of gold which was procurable in the United States in 1820. End-papers and edges were decorated in a variety of styles, mottled or plain.

Lavish gold decoration applied to flat spines, brighter and showier leathers, and the new colored end-papers all pointed to a new sophistication which contrasts sharply with the simple, primitive, blind-tooled bindings of the early colonial period.

### Centers of Activity and Names of Binders

Now, just as in the colonial period, binders worked chiefly in the printing centers. Work was increasingly concentrated in the three large centers, Boston, Philadelphia, and New York; but it was also done to a limited extent in countless provincial establishments. There were bookbinders in Worcester and Salem, Massachusetts; Albany and Hudson, New York; Newark, New Jersey; Baltimore, Maryland; and Charleston, South Carolina. However, information about them is scarce, except possibly for those in Worcester and Salem.

*Worcester.* Isaiah Thomas carried on bookbinding in Worcester and in several provincial establishments, in connection with printing. It is not clear from his account books with how many binders he was connected, how many worked for him in his shop, and how many worked independently. The binding accounts are included in his paper mill account book and name John Salter as foreman of the mill, with Pitman, Whittemore, and Cunningham lads in the binding room. Like Franklin's accounts, Thomas's do not clearly indicate the exact financial arrangements, and it is difficult to find out whether John Salter paid him two dollars for having a quarto Bible bound in Thomas's shop, or whether Salter himself was a binder by trade, or a combination bookbinder and foreman of the paper mill. Whoever bound the Bible did receive two dollars for his work. Joseph Miller and George Merriam are both entered in the accounts as 'Bookbinders, Worcester': Miller as debtor for a bewildering assortment of materials, eggs, cash, morocco, gold leaf, pasteboard, and 'rye and Indian'; and Merriam as charged with one 8vo *Bible* with *Apocrypha*, November 6, 1794, three children's books, December 3, at 6s, and one sheet of bonnet paper at 1s. Recurrent items for board seem to indicate that Merriam paid Thomas for his living and was in turn paid for his work, by an arrangement similar to that between Franklin and Stephen Potts in the earlier days, when Potts worked as Franklin's binder. The mention of Pitman, Whittemore, and Cunningham as 'lads in the binding room' is followed by a later entry dated May 22, 1794–January 6, 1795, naming Clarke Whittemore as a 'Bookbinder bound to Merriam.' Considerably later, on January 11, 1806, a note appears of 'Books remaining with Clarke Whittemore . . . to bind.' He was then apparently working as a journeyman-binder rather than as an apprentice. By this time, too, Thomas, or his son who succeeded to the business in 1802, had changed his practice of having binding done under his own roof and was sending books out.

Just when bookbinding was given up as a part of the work carried on in the shop cannot be accurately determined. Already in 1794 not all the binding was done at home, for there is an entry for October, 1794, headed 'David Burns, Boston, Bookbinder. To 150 Williams history to bind @ 1/9 . . . 9/2/6.' After Thomas's son took over the business in 1802, there are numerous entries of books given out to various individuals to bind. Most of them went to Justin Hinds, some to P. Merrefield, and twenty-two *Romances of the Forest* to David West, Boston, who received $4.40 for the work that he did. In 1820 there is a reference to Lewis W. Reed (or Mead), bookbinder of Oakham, 'whom I employed for that purpose.'

Worcester was a small town, not far from Boston, important in the printing world simply because Isaiah Thomas was established there. One of the chief branches of his business was located in Boston, however, and he and his wife made frequent trips from Worcester thither. When these trips became too tiresome, they purchased a Boston house at 52 Newbury Street, only a few doors from the printing and bookselling business also on Newbury Street, at Faust's statue, and lived there from 1802 until 1808.[30] Here Thomas patronized personally John Roulstone, the noted Boston bookbinder, who lived at 16 Newbury Street, as we know from a receipted bill in Isaiah Thomas's receipt book: 'Boston, Sept. 5, 1811—Received of Isaiah Thomas, Esq., Twenty Dollars — on account — John Roulstone.' Though there is no clue as to the number of books, or which volumes Roulstone bound, it is clear that he was responsible for some of the work on Thomas's private library.Thus this work cannot all have been done at Thomas's own bindery, as Dr. Nichols, his biographer, has assumed.[31]

*Salem.* In the flourishing seaport of Salem there were a number of binders, whose names are recorded in Tapley's *Salem Imprints.* Seven are mentioned there as working before 1820. One of these, John Dabney, was a prominent citizen who not only carried on bookbinding in 1791 in connection with his circulating library and bookselling business but was also the postmaster of the town. Two others,

[30] A. R. Marble, *From 'prentice to Patron; the Life of Isaiah Thomas* (New York: Appleton-Century, 1935), 326 p. Reference on p. 229.

[31] C. L. Nichols, *Isaiah Thomas, Printer, Writer and Collector* (Boston: Club of Odd Volumes, 1912), 144 p. Reference on p. 29.

Joseph Snelling and Charles Steele, came from Boston. At any rate Joseph Snelling moved to Salem from Boston and did some bookbinding there from 1784 until 1788. Either Salem did not please his taste or there was not sufficient work there, for he was following his craft in Boston again twelve years later, in Governor's Alley. After another two years he had moved to Whitebread Alley, where he remained in business for some time. Thomas had recorded him as a binder working in Boston in 1767, on Fish Street, Corner of Boarded-Alley. Although it does not seem to have been customary for craftsmen to move about from center to center, it was quite the usual thing for them to change their street addresses every few years.

Charles Steele sold books, stationery, and blanks, and bound enough books to require the services of a journeyman bookbinder in 1807. His father, Alexander Steele, had been working at bookbinding in Boston contemporaneously with Joseph Snelling. Little is known of the three other early binders mentioned by Tapley — Brian Macanulty, Isaac Cushing, and Thomas Prince. The first of these had come to Philadelphia from Ireland shortly after the Revolution. There he stayed about nine years, moving to Salem in 1794. Isaac Cushing worked eight years later, at binding books and making bandboxes. Thomas Prince carried on a varied business, advertising in 1806 the manufacture of blank books, paper ruling, printing, drawing and copying charts, and repairing philosophical and mathematical instruments, as well as executing 'plain or elegant bindings in the good old English style.'[32]

Of the nineteenth-century binders in Salem Tapley credits Samuel West with the longest career, from 1807 until 1835, with a two-year vacation from 1819 to 1821. He then advertised his tools for sale, in a list which gives a good idea of the equipment of the provincial bindery. It reads as follows:

[32] Tapley, op. cit., p. 205.

1 Standing Press; 3 Cutting Presses; 2 Shaving Tubs; 1 pair large Shears; 1 set Polishers; several handsome gilding Rolls; 1 set Brass Letters; 1 Brass Type Case; Types; 1 Gilding Cushion; Knife ditto; Backing irons; 1 Iron Stove; 2 Marbling Brushes.[33]

With these handsome gilding rolls Samuel West doubtless turned out bindings quite as elegant as those of his competitor, Thomas Prince.

*Boston.* The real center of activity in New England was Boston. Although that city no longer held precedence over Philadelphia and New York as it had before the Revolution, it was still one of the great centers. The first city directory of 1789 contained the names of only four bookbinders, David West, Alexander Steele, Benjamin Larkin, and Samuel Webb. Of these four, Webb is the only one of whom we have additional evidence as having been at work in the colonial period. Thomas identified him with the old Boston school that had served its apprenticeship in Henchman's shop and said that he carried on bookselling and binding for some time, though not to a great extent.[34]

Only one other craftsman working during this period is definitely known to have received his training in the colonial school. Alford Butler, the second, had been apprenticed to the Scottish binder, William MacAlpine. Butler's father had been a bookbinder before him, one of the earliest apprentices in the shop of Daniel Henchman. His career was cut short by his death in 1742, when he was forty-six. The younger Butler worked longer at binding but not so continuously. After he had served his apprenticeship and bound and sold books for a short time, he gave up his trade in favor of teaching school in Portsmouth, New Hampshire. After nearly twenty years of that experience, he returned to Boston to work at bookbinding as before. The directory of 1807 shows him still at work there.

33 Ibid., p. 209.
34 Thomas, *History of Printing* (1810 edition), II, 436.

The 1820 directory lists about a dozen men, among them John Roulstone, who has already been mentioned as the binder of a part of Isaiah Thomas's private library. John Roulstone worked at various addresses in Boston from 1803 to 1825 and was outstanding for the quality of his work and the length of his career. Very little is known of his forebears, except that his father was apparently a clock maker and his brother a brass founder. It seems likely that he can safely be claimed as a native workman, as there are records to show that the family of Roulstone held property in Boston as far back as 1687.[35]

There is no evidence as to where this later group of binders received its training, and no conclusions can be drawn until their careers have been investigated more fully. Conditions of work were changing rapidly. The old combination of bookseller, binder, and stationer was dying out, as is especially apparent in Boston, where the names of several partnerships and firms devoted wholly to bookbinding appear in the directories after 1803.

*Philadelphia.* The situation in Philadelphia was somewhat different. There the same group of immigrant binders which was at work just before the war continued to work under the Republic. Samuel Taylor, the master binder to whom Buglass, Bell, and Woodhouse had been apprenticed at Berwick-upon-Tweed, was the only one of that group who did not live to see the establishment of the new nation. He had begun bookselling and binding in Philadelphia in 1764 and died about 1781. William Woodhouse, who had set up business in 1765, died about 1795. Caleb Buglass, who came from England to Philadelphia in 1774, died two years after Woodhouse. The name of Mary Buglass, bookbinder, appears in the directories as late as 1819. McCulloch reported that Buglass' widow 'still continues bookbinding and supports herself genteelly. She may also

[35] 'John Dunton's Letters from New England,' *Prince Society Publications* (Boston, 1867), IV, 307-308.

be said to continue the bookselling if her little shop would justify the title.'[36] Perhaps the slightly patronizing tone was deserved in this particular instance; but there was at least one woman at work in Philadelphia capable of doing bookbinding that needed no apologies of any kind.

Jane Aitken succeeded to the business of her father, Robert Aitken, when he died in 1802. Trained in Scotland, he had worked at printing, bookselling, and binding in this country since 1771. For a time his only son had worked with him. The name 'R. Aitken & Son, bookbinders and printers' appears in the Philadelphia directory of 1795. The death of the son occurred some time after that and before the death of his father, in 1802.[37] Jane Aitken may well have taken her brother's place in the workshop, where she must have worked rather closely with her father, or even earlier with her father and brother; else she would not have been able to take over the business in its entirety as she did. Information about her is almost entirely lacking. McCulloch did not notice her at all, but Thomas described her printing as 'well and handsomely executed,' adding that she 'attained much reputation by the productions which issued from her press.'[38] She printed the first English translation of the *Septuagint* in 1808, the *Memoirs of the Philadelphia Society for Promoting Agriculture,* also in 1808, and Thomson's translation of the *Bible* in four volumes, in 1810.

We know even less about her activity as a binder than we know of her work as a printer and her life in general. We can only assume that she learned binding from helping her father in his shop, long before she took over the business herself.

In all probability women did more bookbinding than they were given credit for. It was, in fact, a more womanly occupation than some others in which women of the time

[36] McCulloch, Additions, p. 107.
[37] *Christian Instructor and Western United Presbyterian* (Saturday, May 4, 1878).
[38] Thomas, *History of Printing* (1874 edition), I, 266.

engaged. Leaving aside the question of gentility, it was vastly more suited to feminine skill and strength than a printer's or, for instance, a grocer's trade. Women were listed in directories of the period as grocers, and a few widows as bookbinders. The scarcity of women's names is more logical than it seems, since the directories account only for heads of families and would not include those women who, like Jane Aitken in her earlier career, worked to help the men of the family. Whether there were more women binding books in Philadelphia than elsewhere it is not possible to say, but six are mentioned as engaged in bookbinding there in the first years of the nineteenth century — Mary Buglass, Elizabeth Mintz, and Mrs. Wiley, widows, Jane Aitken, and the widows of Thomas Condie and David Dunlap. No women binders are named in Boston and only three in New York, Eliza Culley, Lydia Furman, and Eliza Gilchrist, widow, dwelling at '6 republican alley.'

The German style in Philadelphia was still represented by David Sower, a descendant of the great Christopher Sower of Germantown, by Zachariah Poulson who had been apprenticed to him, and by Peter Liebert who had purchased part of the stock of the second Christopher Sower at the time of his death in 1784.

While the French tradition is represented by one name only, that of Médéric Louis Élie Moreau de St.Méry, a printer, binder, stationer, and bookseller in 1794, there must have been other French bookbinders at work to account for the tools used and the style which made its appearance after the Revolution.

As there was more printing done in Philadelphia than in Boston, it is to be expected that there would be a greater number of individuals at work there. The count of those designated as bookbinders varies from seven in the earliest directory in 1785 to thirty-eight in that for 1820. For some reason there does not seem to have been the same develop-

ment of firms and partnerships as in Boston. Only names
of individuals are listed, each with a separate address.

*New York.* Some idea of the rapidly growing importance
of New York as a book-trade center during this period can
be gained from the large increase in names of binders listed
in the directories of 1786 and 1820. The first contained one
name, that of Robert Hodge, bookbinder and stationer,
38 Maiden Lane, while the latter included fifty-seven. The
majority of these were bookbinders only, though a few were
still undertaking the dual function of selling and binding.
Between these years the craft was carried on in connection
with bookselling, printing, and a stationer's trade, just as
it was in Boston and Philadelphia. It appears also in combination with a lending library, and even with a grocer's
trade. Yet the bookbinder-grocer was not as strange as the
bookbinder-whalebone-cutter or the bookbinder-bottler,
who worked in Philadelphia in 1801 and 1819 respectively.

Of individual binders practically nothing is known. Robert Hodge was Scottish, and Charles Cleland, who was at
work between 1789 and 1792, advertised himself as 'lately
from Edinburgh.' [39] Others may have come from Scotland.
The list of names suggests a very cosmopolitan group. Beat-
tie, Christie, Delamontayne, De Villiers, Hulsart, Duyckinck, Jansen, Judah, Gomez, M'Donald, M'Queen, Mesier,
Vandyck, and Van Ranst indicate foreign ancestry but not
necessarily foreign birth. Where they received their training has yet to be discovered.

With information about the men all but unobtainable,
it is enlightening to find that Peter Mesier, bookbinder and
stationer of New York, was Alderman in 1814, and that one
New York bookbinder, John Bryce, and two Philadelphia
binders, Benjamin January and James Muir, were included
along with George Washington in the list of subscribers to
Brown's *Self-interpreting Bible,* printed in 1792.

[39] Grolier Club Catalogue, p. 101.

In New York, as in Boston, partnerships and companies began to appear at the turn of the century. Even nine years before, in 1791, Thomas Greenleaf, printer, advertised as follows:

Mr. Greenleaf has engaged a complete binder, gilder, and ruler at an extraordinary salary, and will engage that every one who may be pleased to employ him shall be satisfied, or no pay. . . .[40]

## Identification of Bindings

After 1783 at least a dozen binders signed their work. As in the colonial period they appear not to have marked all examples of their binding. At any rate not more than three or four bindings signed by any one name have thus far come to light. The proportion of unsigned specimens remains very large in the era of the young Republic, even as it was in the earlier period. Names of bookbinders appear in great profusion in the city directories of the late eighteenth century, however. And it remains as much of a challenge to connect typical bindings with their makers in the later period as it was in colonial times when names were relatively few.

*Methods of Identification.* In either period methods of identification remain much the same. The signed binding is easily accepted, as no further proof is needed to supplement the engraved label or the gold-tooled signature. The skeptic may question bindings tentatively attributed to a binder on the basis of imprint information, but in the absence of evidence to the contrary we take the liberty of assigning them to the bookbinder-bookseller or bookbinder-printer so indicated. In the colonial period we had found such imprints as 'Printed by M. J. for Edmund Ranger, bookbinder near the Dock, and Joseph Farnham, near the Red Lion in Boston, 1672.' Now, in the later period, we seldom find the bookbinder mentioned as such on the title-

[40] Grolier Club Catalogue, p. 101.

page. Occasionally a binder's advertisement appears at the back of the book, as it does in *Devout Exercises of the Heart* by the late pious and ingenious Mrs. Elizabeth Rowe, which was printed in an abridged form 'for the use of the pious' by Tiebout & O'Brien for E. Mitchell, bookseller at No. 9 Maiden-Lane. Though Mitchell is mentioned in the imprint only as a bookseller, his work as a binder is recognized in the following statement on the last page of the book:

E. Mitchell has for sale a general assortment of books and stationery. . . . All manner of bookbinding, conducted with elegance and dispatch.

In 1794-1795 E. Mitchell was carrying on bookbinding in his bookseller's shop, just as others had done before him.

In certain cases, such as that of Robert Aitken of Philadelphia, the printer is recognized as the binder wholly from external evidence. In other instances the individual tools and general style point to certain localities or cities. It is necessary to exercise great caution in drawing conclusions from tools and style, in general. Although the work of a few individuals stands out, for the most part throughout the national period technique was well standardized and decoration depended upon the use of stock tools. Certain tools may be ascribed to given centers, but many were used indiscriminately. Even the disposition of ornament tended to become standardized.

*Signed Bindings.* The work which has been signed may be small in quantity as compared with that which has not, but it is extraordinarily interesting, even when it is not necessarily of superior beauty and workmanship. There are a dozen or more binders with signed work now known for the national era, as against two or three in the days of the colonies. Furthermore, the later work may be said to indicate the general style used by the individual craftsman more consistently now that binding was specialized to a higher degree, certain individuals doing the plain work while others advertised themselves as 'fancy-binders.' I have found examples of all degrees of elaboration in a group of twelve signed bindings which I have examined. An 'Etruscan' binding on the *Federalist* in the New York Public Library has already been described in Andrews' *Bibliopegy in the United States*. Langhorne's *Correspondence of Theodosius and Constantia,* bound by Champley, appears as Number 35 in The Grolier Club *Catalogue of Ornamental Leather Bookbindings Executed in America Prior to 1850.* Colden's *Memoir,* bound by Wilson and Nichols, is a very fine specimen of the publisher's extra binding, executed about 1825. One copy is described as Number 46 in The Grolier Club Catalogue, and a similar copy is described and reproduced by Andrews. Five additional examples, possibly bound before 1820, are described in The Grolier Club Catalogue. Brown's *Self-interpreting Bible,* bound by T. Allen, is reproduced in Du Bois' *Library of William Poor.* To supplement the descriptions of the three bindings in The Grolier Club Catalogue, Andrews, and Du Bois, I have made the following list:

1. Bailey, David, binder. Charleston, S. C.
   Bible. O. T. Psalms.
   A Version of the Book of Psalms . . . Charleston: Printed by J. MacIver, 1796.

   Ticket inside upper cover: David Bailey, Bookbinder, from London. Tree calf. Gold tooling. Flat spine. Marbled end-papers. Worked headbands. Spine divided into five panels by floral roll. Circular cameo ornament. Black morocco label. Rolled board edges.
   In Library of Congress.

2. Champley, George, binder. New York, N. Y.
   Goldsmith, Oliver.
   The Vicar of Wakefield.
   n. t. p.

   Ticket inside upper cover: G. Champley. Fancy Binder, 61 Barclay-st., N. York.
   Tan calf. Gold and blind tooling. Flat spine. Dark-green end-papers. Edges marbled. Covers bordered by a blind roll with fleurons at the corners, inside a gold roll. Spine in five panels. Square gold ornaments. Title in center panel. Gilt border inside covers. Gold rolled corners on board edges.
   In Grolier Club Library.

3. Craig and Lea, binders. Wilmington, Del.
   Bible, English, Authorized Version.
   The Holy Bible. Trenton, N. J.: Printed and sold by Isaac Collins, 1791.

   Ticket inside upper cover: Craig & Lea, Stationers & Bookbinders, Wilmington, Delaware.
   Sprinkled sheep. Decorated in panels by a blind-tooled roll. Raised cords. Headbands. Plain end-papers.
   In Library of Congress.

4. ——— Copy 2. Similar binding.
   In American Typefounders' Library.

5. De Silver, Robert, binder. Philadelphia, Pa.
   Barlow, Joel.
   The Columbiad. Phila.: Fry & Kammerer, 1807.

   Ticket inside upper cover: Bound by R. De Silver, No. 110 Walnut Street, Philada.
   Full Etruscan calf. Gilt. Wide raised bands.
   In Chapin Library.

6. ———
   [Puglia, James Ph.]
   The Complete Disappointment, or a Touch at Modern Times: a Comedy in Three Acts, written by Me, Author of the Embargo, &c. Philadelphia: Printed for the Amateurs By .... MDCCCIX.

   Ticket inside upper cover. Bound by R. De Silver, No 110 Walnut Street, Philada.
   Black straight-grained morocco. Gold tooling. Flat spine. Marbled end-papers. No headbands. All edges gilt. Covers bordered by narrow gilt rolls.
   In Harvard College Library.

7. Roulstone, John, binder. Boston, Mass.
   Protestant Episcopal Church.
   Book of Common Prayer. N. Y.: Printed by Hugh Gaine, 1795.

   Signed in gold inside lower cover: Roulstone, J. Binder, Boston.
   Dark-red straight-grained morocco. Blind and gold tooling. Raised cords. Marbled end-papers. Covers bordered by seven narrow rolls, alternating blind and gilt. Diamond-shaped panel in center. Spine in five panels. Square pointillé ornaments. Title in center panel.
   In Pierpont Morgan Library.

8. ——— Copy 2. Identical binding.
   In William L. Clements Library.

9. Seymour, William, binder. Albany, N. Y.
Protestant Episcopal Church.
Book of Common Prayer. N. Y.: Printed and sold by
T. & J. Swords, 1810.

Ticket inside upper cover: William Seymour, Fancy blank book
binder, Albany.
Straight-grained red morocco. Gold and blind tooling. Flat spine.
Marbled end-papers. Covers bordered by gilt and blind rolls. Spine
in five panels, heavily gilt. Lettering in center panel.
In Grolier Club Library.

By far the greatest number of craftsmen who chose to
sign their work did so by pasting a label, often referred to
as a ticket or trade-card, inside the front cover. The engraved labels of Andrew Barclay and Samuel Taylor have
already been described, in connection with their work in
the colonial period. Now, in the national era, we find
'George Champley, Fancy Binder, 61 Barclay-st., N. York;
H. G. Megarey, New York; Robert De Silver, No. 110 Walnut Street, Philada; David Bailey, Book-binder, from London [Charleston, S. C.]; Craig & Lea, Stationers & Bookbinders, Wilmington, Delaware; Benjamin Olds, Newark,
N. J.; and William Seymour, Fancy blank book binder, Albany,' all identifying their bindings in this manner. Sometimes the ticket contained more complete information, like
that in the newspaper advertisements. For example, a Psalm
Book printed in Hudson, New York, contains a ticket reading: 'Bound at Parson's Bindery. Where binding is executed in its various branches. Patent Ruling Done in the
neatest manner. Hudson, N. Y.'; and a plain account book
advertises 'Benjn January, Stationer & Bookbindr in Water
street a few Doors below the Drawbridge Philadelph:
Where all Sorts of Account Books are Made Ruled to any
Pattern. He likewise sells all Sorts of Stationary Wares at
the Lowest Rates.' J. & A. M'Lean of New York do not
quite commit themselves as the actual binders of the Etruscan calf bound volume of the *Federalist* in the New York
Public Library, but they did paste a slip inside the front

cover, 'Printed and bound at Franklin's Head, No. 41 Hanover Square,' which would seem to indicate that the binding was done on the same premises as the printing.

At least one binder has signed his name in gold, inside the back cover of his binding in the fashion now current. This is John Roulstone, who kindly added the identifying word 'Boston' after his name, in two identical bindings of Hugh Gaine's folio *Prayer Book*, printed in 1795 (Fig. 26). The work of this John Roulstone, Boston, deserves special mention, and it is a matter of regret that so few examples of his craftsmanship, and so few details of his life, are known. The bindings which have been identified as his are artistically conceived and beautifully executed, the work of a real artist. The elegance of the dark-red straight-grained morocco covers of the *Book of Common Prayer* is in keeping with the pretentiousness of this first folio edition, designed for a lectern or pulpit. We are not surprised that Roulstone signed this work, but sorry that he did not sign his simpler bindings also. Here we have again the simultaneous use of gold and blind tooling, this time in seven narrow rolls applied alternately in blind and gold, two of them repeated to make a nine-roll border. The diamond-shaped panel shows the use of four additional rolls. Tiny cameo ornaments are set into each corner. The spine is divided into five panels with the title in the center. The remaining panels are decorated by pointillé tools which are entirely new in American bookbindings. Even though there are general resemblances to New York bindings done about 1820 and a following of the same convention, there is a real individuality in this binding which puts it in a class by itself. The rolls used for cover decoration are narrow and delicate at a time when the New York tools were becoming wider and heavier, and the panels on the back are filled by a number of small light dotted tools, in place of the larger square stamps then used by Champley and Megarey. The binding was apparently satisfactory to its maker, for he not only signed but repeated it. There are at least two like bindings, one in the Pierpont Morgan Library, the other in the William L. Clements Library.

John Roulstone's name appears for the first time in the Boston directory of 1803 and continues to appear through 1825. In the twenty-two years during which he practised his craft he must have turned out a large body of work. With proof of his ability and his long experience one is tempted to assign to him other bindings of the period. Two bindings in The Grolier Club Catalogue, Numbers 61 and 66, now in the Henry E. Huntington Library, bear very strong evidences of his workmanship. Both bindings are of straight-grained morocco, Buckminster's *Sermons* in a light green and Harris's *Hymns for the Lord's Supper* in dark blue. Both have borders of gilt and blind fillets and rolls, and both show the use of a number of small tools in the panels on the backs. The *Sermons* carry two rolls and a broken fillet line as does also the *Prayer Book*. The larger roll on the outside of its cover also appears on the *Prayer Book,* and still another roll is common to it and the *Hymns*. It is not by accident that the writer of The Grolier Club Catalogue refers twice to Roger Payne in describing Buckminster's *Sermons,* which is ascribed to the same unknown binder as Harris's *Hymns*. 'At the corners are Roger Payne tools, used twice in each corner, giving a graceful effect; back divided by gold fillets, dotted lines and small meander roll, into compartments decorated in the manner of Roger Payne.' [41] The book is further described as having marbled end-papers, as does the *Prayer Book*. The *Hymns* has purple end-papers, another characteristic of Payne's bindings. It is John Roulstone, then, whom we may call the Roger Payne of America.

*Attributed Bindings.* Of those bindings tentatively attributed to a binder on the basis of imprint information, those

[41] Grolier Club Catalogue, p. 50.

assigned to the Aitkens are the most interesting. Robert
Aitken's *Bible* has already been described (p. 60). His daughter Jane may have bound two volumes: the *Memoirs of the
Philadelphia Society for Promoting Agriculture,* in the Ridgeway
Branch of the Library Company of Philadelphia, which she
certainly printed herself, six years after the death of her father;
and Blair's *Lectures on Rhetoric,* owned by Dr. Samuel Woodhouse, printed by Robert Aitken in 1784 but apparently
bound some years later. Both books are bound in stained
calf, a far cry from the soft green morocco used on his *Bible.*
The technique of the flat spine and sawn-in cords is quite
different; the splashed marble end-papers are of a later date
than the Dutch comb used in the *Bible;* the decoration is
profuse and florid, with urns, weeping willow, birds and
baskets of flowers; and the worked headbands are unusually well done. The *Memoirs* bears the only example of double
worked headbands which I have noticed. Such an unusual
amount of needlework argues for a feminine hand. The
binding on Blair was done for a special customer whose
initials, E. H., are stamped in gold on a circular red label
on the spine. It is lavishly decorated in gilt, with birds,
baskets of flowers, and scrolls, and surely shows what fine
work Jane Aitken could do for an appreciative customer.

Bielby's *Principal Evidences* has already been attributed
to Benjamin Larkin (p. 54), and Watts's *Hymns* to either
Robert Aitken or William Bradford (p. 61).

*Unidentified Bindings.* By far the greater proportion of
bindings made during the federal period remain unidentified, either because there is very little evidence as to who
bound them or because there is none at all. Certain bindings show a style of ornamentation and use of tools so unusual that they cannot be attributed to any given binder
on a basis of comparison, and some at the opposite extreme
resemble the work of several different craftsmen who followed a distinct convention of ornamentation. Those in

the first category frequently contain a Philadelphia imprint and were probably bound there, since the craftsmen of that city seem to have maintained their individuality longer than those elsewhere. Bindings in the second classification are more easily identified with New York, not only on the basis of imprint information, but also because a certain style of ornamentation was common to several binders working there in the first quarter of the nineteenth century.

Among these unidentified bindings four outstanding examples appear to have been executed in Philadelphia: two copies of the *Prayer Book,* printed there by Hall & Sellers in 1786, one now in the John Carter Brown Library (Fig. 16), the other in the Library of Congress (Fig. 27); one copy of Brady and Tate's *New Version of the Psalms,* in the American Antiquarian Society (Fig. 28), printed in Boston in 1774 for Nicholas Bowes; and a copy of Anna Seward's *Memoirs of the Life of Dr. Darwin,* in The Grolier Club Library, printed in Philadelphia in 1804. The copy of the Hall & Sellers *Prayer Book* (Fig. 27) from the Library of Congress was decorated with stamps of the French style, the fleur-de-lys, cat-tooth roll, and pomegranate. No French binder has yet been identified as working in Philadelphia in 1786. However, many emigrés came to Philadelphia at the time of the French Revolution, and some bookbinder may have come, bringing his tools. On the other hand, it is possible that Benjamin Franklin may have introduced these tools when he returned in 1785 from his sojourn in France.

The other copy of the *Prayer Book* also shows French influence in the use of a central medallion and the same cat-tooth roll on its cover (Fig. 16). It is because of its general resemblance to this book that Brady and Tate's *New Version of the Psalms* (Fig. 28) is assumed to be of Philadelphian origin, for all its Boston imprint. Although the imprint date is earlier, the book may have been bound as late as 1784, as it bears on its fly-leaf the inscription: 'S. Whalley, 1784, Boston.' It too has a cover decorated by the cat-tooth roll in combination with a central medallion, in a style which has not appeared on any other Boston bindings examined.

In the last years of the eighteenth century a delicate, circular spider's web ornament appeared on several books printed in Philadelphia, the most important example of which is a copy of the Aitken *Bible* in the Library of Congress. Once the doves, vases, urns, and sunbursts came into use, as they did about 1800, any attempt to identify from ornament becomes quite hopeless.

The fourth example, Anna Seward's *Memoirs*, bears an imprint date of 1804 and is typical of nineteenth-century work. It is elaborately conceived and shows unusual decoration and technique. Sprinkled calf with a plain inner panel had been widely used in the colonial period, but the panels were then rectangular and the tooling in blind. This binding shows a new use of the diamond-shaped panel and gold tooling which is particularly profuse on the spine. Its technique is unusual because of the morocco joint, a refinement of construction which seldom appears in American bindings.

Two bindings, Scott's *Lord of the Isles,* printed in New York in 1818, now owned by the Rosenbach Company, and *The Book of Common Prayer* (Fig. 29) printed in New York in 1820 by Henry I. Megarey and now in the American Antiquarian Society, are difficult to assign to their binders for the second possible reason, because they resemble the work of several different men at work in New York in the first quarter of the nineteenth century. The Scott shows all the conventions of a blind-tooled border inside a gilt one, square insets at the corners of the cover border, square ornaments on the spine, and lettering on two narrow panels equidistant from the top and base of the spine. The inner blind roll and fleurons are identical with those used on Champley's *Vicar of Wakefield.* The geometrical gold roll and the tools used on the spine have not been identified, however, and the inset corners and the style of lettering are equally characteristic of Wilson & Nichols, and of Megarey. It is, therefore, possible to ascribe the binding to the New York school, but not to any one individual.

The second book, although printed by Megarey, who was himself a binder, bears little resemblance to those volumes bearing his ticket which have been described in The Grolier Club Catalogue. It shows conventional treatment of the spine, with its title in the center and square gold ornaments above and below. The cover decoration departs from the convention of blind and gold tooling and shows the use of a single, charming, gold roll design of grapes, leaves, and roses. Its bright gold shows off singularly well against the scarlet roan of the binding.

A few stamps which seem to have originated in Isaiah Thomas's workshop were widely used on Worcester and Boston bindings. Most outstanding of these is a small elliptical cameo stamp of a slender red petalled flower against a gilt background, used singly or as a part of a floral roll in a chain design (Fig. 21). It is identical with one used by Derome in eighteenth-century France. Another narrow, rather graceless roll, containing a small, square flower, decorates a number of Worcester and Boston bindings (Fig. 21). A three-branch, fern-like fleuron, pleasing in its realism, appears on the back of a book printed for David West, one of the Boston binders who traded with Thomas, and again on a New York printed *Book of Common Prayer,* which is ornamented with four additional tools from Thomas's shop.

A large group of unidentified bindings come from two important private collections of the period, those of Isaiah Thomas and George Washington. I have already indicated that the books in the library of Isaiah Thomas were probably bound by a number of different craftsmen, some in Worcester and some in Boston. Which books were bound by whom remains to be discovered. It has been suggested that George Washington may have had his own binder in Philadelphia, where he had volumes from his library 'bound in calf, tooled on the back with emblematical designs.'[42] Probable as this is, the binder's identity has never been revealed. In any case, the decorated bindings in Washington's library show signs of originating in a number of different workshops. Of several volumes now preserved in the Boston Athenaeum, the John Carter Brown Library, the Pennsylvania Historical Society, and the Chapin Library, only three or four display any markedly common characteristics. The *Miscellaneous Works* of David Humphreys (Fig. 20) with its New York imprint has been already described as bearing some of the Thomas ornaments. The other bindings vary in materials used, decoration, general style, and types of end-papers, until it is necessary to assume that the library of Washington, like that of Thomas, contained examples of the work of a number of different, unidentified craftsmen. Many of George Washington's books were indubitably presented to him already bound and need not therefore represent his own taste or the work of his chosen binder.

## Plain Bindings of the Period

Plain bindings were issued in profusion throughout the handcraft period in this country, and no better examples of ordinary, purely utilitarian work are to be found than those from Thomas's shop. It would be a mistake to assume that the majority of early American bookbindings were decorated from the fact that so many have been described in these pages, just as it would be wrong to conclude that Isaiah Thomas, the printer with the greatest quantity output, issued most of his books in decorated covers like those in his personal library. The pressure of output was serious, and Thomas wrote to Mathew Carey in 1792 that he found great difficulty in getting any binding done.

[42] A. S. W. Rosenbach, *The Libraries of the Presidents of the United States* (Worcester: American Antiquarian Society, 1935), p. 4.

A large proportion of the products of his press was school-books which carried no ornamentation whatever. For these he used the most inexpensive and durable materials available. Nearly always the foundation was thin scabboard of birch, maple, or oak. Sometimes the covering was plain sheepskin, decorated only with a red label pasted on the back. Other issues of Thomas's press were chap-books, or 'dozen-books' as he called them in inventories, which consisted of a few stitched pages in plain, marbled, gilt, or chintz paper covers pasted on the end-sheets.

The sums paid out to workmen at that time are too small to account for anything more than plain work and are usually for quantity binding. Sometimes as many as three hundred and twenty books were sent to a single binder at one time. Five sets of Josephus's *Works* in six volumes were bound for five dollars, and many ordinary books were put into covers at a cost of approximately twenty cents. In 1800 Isaiah Thomas, Jr., then in charge of the business, followed the current English practice of offering books in a choice of bindings. He advertised in the *Boston Gazette* of October 20, 1800: 'Artillerist's Pocket Companion 37½¢ half bound & 50¢ neatly bound in leather.' Often Thomas's books were advertised for sale in three different bindings: blue paper, marbled paper, and leather.

A cloth binding was also used in the eighteenth century, although just how early it is impossible to say. Cloth-bound books had been sent over to Boston from England as early as 1772, for on July 21, 1772, Thomas Longman of London addressed a letter to Henry Knox, bookseller of Boston, regarding a shipment of books in canvas bindings.[43] Wherever Thomas may have obtained the idea, he did make use of cloth in the early years of his business at Worcester. His accounts of stock frequently list items of buckram and of linen by the yard, and his account for 1794 mentions '4

[43] Wroth, 'Notes for Bibliophiles,' *New York Herald Tribune* (Feb. 12, 1939).

Doz. Perry's Spellg books. Cloth 15/– 3.0.0.' These books
were actually bound in a very coarse cloth, in appearance
much like canvas. They are not to be confused with cloth
covers frequently sewed on over the leather bindings as a
protective covering. It was perhaps to these calico covers
that the following advertisement in the *Boston Gazette*, November 10, 1800, refers: 'A. Gibson . . . has received by the
Holbrook and other late arrivals, an elegant assortment of
Sprig'd and plain Book Muslin, Book Hdkfs. black, dyed
sprigg'd. . . .' The change from leather to cloth as a binding
material is of first importance in the machine era, and this
earlier use of cloth is significant insofar as it points in that
direction.

## Conditions Leading to Introduction of Machines

There was one very good reason for the weakening of
standards in bookbinding. Quantity output of books had
increased tremendously in the early nineteenth century,
until the total value of books published in 1820 was estimated at two and a half million dollars.[44] The binding of
such numbers of books without benefit of machinery was
soon to become impossible, and industrialization was the
logical outcome.

The printing and publishing center had shifted to New
York and taken with it bookbinding, which had formerly
been a craft and was on its way to becoming a trade. The
majority of the fifty or more persons carrying on bookbinding devoted their entire time to it, in contrast to Christopher Sower, the first, who eighty years earlier was pro-
ficient in twenty-four trades, bookbinding being one.[45] Yet
there were still six or seven who served in the dual capacity
of bookbinder and stationer or bookbinder and bookseller,
continuing to execute binding in all its branches as craftsmen of the old school. Meanwhile, specialization was taking

[44] Bishop, op. cit., II, 260-261.
[45] McCulloch, Additions, p. 147.

place. Women worked at bookfolding, and certain individuals had charge of forwarding as others of finishing. Commercial binding became one thing, decorative another. George Champley styled himself 'Fancy Binder' and decorated his calf and morocco bindings with roll stamps in blind and gold. John Roulstone produced two morocco bindings decorated identically with nine small roll stamps. And within five years Wilson and Nichols produced very fine examples of the publisher's extra binding.

The bookbinders of New York organized themselves in 1822 as the New York Friendly Association of Master Book-Binders, under the presidency of Henry I. Megarey, and issued a list of prices. Bindings were classified as 'Morocco Super Extra,' 'Extra,' and 'Plain,' or 'Calf Super Extra,' 'Roan Extra,' or 'Sheep Gilt,' as the case might be. Careful specifications were written down and terms defined. What had been actual practice for some time was now first crystallized and put into print.

Pressure of production brought about specialization. Changes in technique led directly to the new method of covering a book without attaching the cords by which it is sewn to the covers, but by fraying them and pasting them down between the pasteboard and lining papers. This in turn led to casing, a method of joining the covers to the book by pasting a strip of strong paper to the back of the book and leaving projections on either side to be pasted down between the boards and end-papers. We now recognize casing as the chief difference in construction between hand and edition binding.[46] Following closely upon this change came the introduction of cloth as a new material, and of the panel stamp as a new technique for decoration. The latter innovation made it possible to produce elaborate designs by means of a machine known as the embossing or arming press, with the use of a single plate.

[46] Parts II and III of the present volume contain a detailed discussion of this point.

In fine, the new age of industrialization now entered upon absorbed the entire field of binding. Decorated leather bindings had originally been produced as individual examples from the shops of single craftsmen who performed all the processes of forwarding and finishing. Later they were reproduced in small editions for special purposes. Finally they were reproduced in large editions, each binding stamped identically and mechanically from a single plate. The album and the gift book became the most interesting manifestations of the decorated leather bindings. Meanwhile, the ancient handcraft disappeared from sight, not to reappear until after all the possibilities of machinery and new materials had been explored.

# CHAPTER IV

## *CONCLUSION*

THE history of American bookbinding in restricted periods, in specific localities, and even of individual craftsmen is challenging in what remains to be told. What is immediately striking, in a general survey of the development of the craft, is the close analogy between bookbinding practice in fifteenth-century Europe and colonial America. Similar conditions brought about the same general development in these two regions, so widely separated in point of space and time. During the same century which witnessed the invention of printing, certain changes in bookbinding had occurred. Pasteboard was substituted for wooden board covers, linen cords were used in place of leather thongs, books were shaped by rounding and backing, labels were placed on the backs, and embroidered headbands were introduced. Morocco leather was used in addition to native calfskin, and gold tooling was introduced for decoration. Roll and panel stamps were used to apply the decoration when the increased number of books made such labor-saving devices desirable.

Those same changes took place slowly and in similar sequence in America—only later. The same reasons dictated them. Just as increased production had been the significant factor in Europe, so it was now in America. The changes which resulted with mechanization of bookbinding in the first quarter of the nineteenth century were even greater, in direct proportion to the greater increase in the number of books. Before this pressure became evident, the colonial craftsman in America had himself carried through all the processes of binding, from the first sewing of the sheets to the final application of the tooling, exactly as his fifteenth-century predecessor had done. In the earliest years

he even practised the same economies, using printers' waste-
sheets for making pasteboard covers, sometimes coloring
and marbling them for use as outside covering. Not only
did the primitive conditions of an undeveloped and isolated country force a dependence upon local materials and
prevent a duplication and exact imitation of contemporary
English work; they also led back to that earlier period of
sound craftsmanship and simple decoration.

Decorated leather bookbindings were produced continuously in America throughout the handcraft period.
Through a constant absorption of immigrant craftsmen
and the importation of tools, influences were introduced
from a number of foreign countries, especially Scotland,
England, France, and Germany. The work of immigrant
craftsmen tended to show a greater refinement and skill
than that of the natives, but native-born Americans worked
simultaneously with immigrants in the great printing centers. Furthermore, a style of work emerged which was peculiarly American.

The bindings of the colonial period in this country were
never so elaborate as the best of those contemporarily executed in England, for reasons clearly dictated by the primitive conditions of the frontier settlements in which they
were turned out. The general run of decorative work was
typically American and is interesting as showing an adapta-
tion of foreign styles, with an increased emphasis upon
utility, in keeping with its environment. It is also, however,
aesthetically pleasing in its charming simplicity.

All work was by no means on the same level of artistic
value, and certain individuals stand out as superior craftsmen. What we know of the work of Ratcliff and Ranger in
the seventeenth century, William Parks and Robert Aitken
in the eighteenth, and George Champley, Henry I. Megarey, and John Roulstone in the nineteenth, shows a competence and distinction which sets them apart. As further

examples of their craftsmanship emerge from oblivion, it will be possible to evaluate their work more critically and to show more specifically what their contributions have been toward establishing an American tradition of bookbinding.

The final years of the eighteenth century mark the highest development of the simple, sturdy colonial bindings; and it is significant that the work of an immigrant from Scotland, namely Robert Aitken, typifies that development and its peculiarly American character. Trained in Scotland as he was, he must have learned a sound technique and the conventions of decoration there, even though the period of his apprenticeship appears to have been of brief duration. His work was done in Philadelphia, and the examples which we have were produced at the close of the War of Independence. Aitken was not put to flight by the war as his countrymen and fellow craftsmen in Boston had been, but remained in Philadelphia throughout. He worked on in a new atmosphere of freedom, and his work reflects just that, without exhibiting signs of the self-conscious nationalism which came later.

The growth of prosperity after the Revolutionary War made the way clear for added emphasis upon decoration and materials. Greater facilities of communication also led to the more immediate adoption of foreign styles. The spirit of emerging nationalism, with its attendant efforts to promote the use of native materials, and the production of tools at home tended to offset any tendency toward slavish imitation of foreign models. Although the general style of the later bindings in America was closer to that abroad than that of the colonial period had been, it never lost its American characteristics. The concern for more lavish ornamentation which developed led to the neglect of fundamental processes and to a general weakening of structure. Finally, the pressure of increased book production, which resulted in the mechanization of bookbinding, was responsible for the introduction of plate or panel stamps in modern edition binding.

## SUPPLEMENT TO PART I

ALTHOUGH less than a dozen articles on early American bookbinding have been published in the past twenty-five years, work is going on, and additional publications are in prospect. A revised and enlarged edition of Hannah D. French's pioneer study is nearing completion.

To the dealers and librarians formerly contributing in this field, the conservators are now added. A tremendous impetus to the study of early American bookbinding, plain and decorated, has been provided by Willman Spawn, Restorer of Manuscripts of the American Philosophical Society. Anticipating the disappearance of source material through damage and lack of interest in preservation, Mr. Spawn has been collecting rubbings over the last ten years until he has an archive of about eight thousand. Out of this source Willman Spawn and Carol Spawn, his wife, have written the two most recent and most substantial articles. Further contributions by them will follow.

The article by Carol and Willman Spawn entitled "The Aitken Shop, Identification of an Eighteenth-Century Bindery and Its Tools" in: *Bibliographical Society of America Papers,* vol. 57, Fourth Quarter, 1963, pp. 422–437, gives a full account of the binding of Robert Aitken and his daughter, Jane, based on almost six hundred documented bindings. More recently the Spawns have written of a lesser known craftsman, "Francis Skinner, Bookbinder of Newport: An Eighteenth-Century Craftsman Identified by His Tools" in: *Winterthur Portfolio* II, 1965, accounting for more than one hundred bindings by Skinner

(1708/9–1785), product of "the longest career of any known American bookbinder of the eighteenth century."

Additional articles have been published concerning small national groups of binders and their work, individual binders, and single signed bindings. As far back as 1948, Hazel Dreis, a professional bookbinder, reported on her examination of a group of Pennsylvania German bindings from the Ephrata Cloister and from Lancaster, chiefly from the point of view of technique, under the title "Lancaster, Pennsylvania, Bookbindings: An Historical Study" in: *Bibliographical Society of America Papers,* vol. 42, Second Quarter, 1948, pp. 119–128. An article by Hannah D. French on "Scottish-American Bookbindings" in: *The Book Collector,* VI, no. 2, Summer 1957, pp. 150–159, describes six examples from Colonial North America. Miss French followed this article with "The Amazing Career of Andrew Barclay, Scottish Bookbinder, of Boston" in: *Studies in Bibliography,* XIV, 1961, pp. 145–162, giving biographical information, an account of his travels and descriptions of six Barcley bindings done in Boston, five of them bearing labels. William A. Jackson's "Our Ingenious Ancestors" in: *Walpole Society Note Book,* 1963, pp. 3–6, is concerned with binders' labels, most specifically with that of Francis Skinner which Mr. Jackson suggests may be the earliest in use by any American binder.

Two single works signed in gold directly on the spines by two different binders of the late eighteenth century, one working in Philadelphia and the other in Boston, are presented in articles by Edwin Wolf, II, and by Hannah D. French. In "A Signed American Binding on the First American Edition of Shakespeare" in: *Shakespeare Quarterly,* XII, Spring 1961, pp. 152–154, Mr. Wolf describes Thomas McKean's set of the first American Shakespeare, now the property of the Library Company of Philadelphia. To the best of Mr. Wolf's knowledge this was "the only early American binding known with the binder's name impressed on the exterior of the binding, in the manner commonly practised by the Frenchmen, Bozerian and Simier and others." This unusual phenomenon was matched when a Boston binding similarly signed was reported to Hannah D. French by Carolyn Horton, the conservator who worked on it. For her article on this town Bible of Salisbury, Connecticut, Miss French took her title, "Bound in Boston by Henry B. Legg," from the tooling at the foot of the spine. The article appeared in: *Studies in Bibliography*, XVII, 1964, pp. 135–139.

Dealers, collectors, librarians and conservators have made their contributions towards a comprehensive history of American bookbinding. Such a history could be immeasurably speeded by preparation of certain bibliographies: a directory of the Boston booktrade, 1636–1820, comparable to the one for New York, compiled by George McKay, and those for Philadelphia and for Rhode Island compiled by H. Glenn and Maude Brown; compilations of newspaper items on the arts and crafts in New England and in Virginia, similar to those by A. C. Prime for Philadelphia, Maryland and South Carolina, and by Mrs. R. S. Gottesman for New York City.

Hannah D. French

EDITOR'S NOTE: Just as the supplements were going to press, word was received that Dr. Ernst Kyriss, the distinguished German historian of bookbinding, is preparing an article on 19th century New York illustrated books with signed bindings. The article is scheduled for appearance in 1967.

# APPENDIX A

## LIST OF AMERICAN BINDERS
### 1636-1820

THIS list has been collected from a number of sources, chief among them, Isaiah Thomas's *History of Printing in America,* The Grolier Club's *Catalogue of Ornamental Leather Bookbindings Executed in America Prior to 1850,* Eddy's *Account Books Kept by Benjamin Franklin,* Tapley's *Salem Imprints,* and the long files of City Directories for Boston, New York, and Philadelphia available in the American Antiquarian Society and the New York Public Library.

Binders who worked in several different capacities are so designated, e.g.: bookbinder, stationer, and bookseller. Names which carry no descriptive phrases were originally described as bookbinders only.

An asterisk marks the names of those binders, of whose work examples have been identified.

### Albany, New York

Ellison, Abraham. State Street. 1793-1797.
  Bookseller and bookbinder.
*Seymour, William. 1820.
Spencer, Henry. Spencer's Albany Bookstore & bindery in Market Street. 1793-1797.
Spencer, Thomas. At his Bookstore a few doors north of the Low Dutch Church in Market Street. 1793-1794.
Webb, Thomas S. 1797.
Wilson, Stewart. Opposite the main guard. 1759.
  Bookbinder and bookseller.

### Annapolis, Maryland

Green, Jonas. 1765.
*Parks, William. 1728.
  Printer and bookbinder.

### Boston, Massachusetts

Amory, John. Union Street. 1749.
  Bookseller and binder.
Andrews, William. 51 Marlborough Street. 1796-1805.
Andrews & Goodwin. 32 Summer Street. 1803, 1805, 1809, 1813.
Armstrong, John W. 70 State Street. 1807.
Baker, Charles. Butolph Street. 1816.

*Barclay, Andrew. At the Bible in Cornhill. 1764.

Bedlington, Timothy. 47 Cornhill. 1816, 1818, 1820.

Belknap, Nathaniel. Head of Scarlet's Wharf, North End. 1723.

Bell, David W. Congress Street. 1818.

Bradlee, Thomas. Congress Street. 1810, 1813.

Broats, Henry. Warren Street. 1810.

Brots, Henry. Sea Street. 1813.

Brown, John. Devonshire Street. 1813.

Burnton, Thomas H. Essex Street. 1816.

Butler, Alford. Lower End of King-Street, near the Crown Coffee-House, at the head of the Long-Wharf. 1729-1742.
Bookseller and binder.

Butler, Alford, son. Newbury Street. 1796-1807.    74 Middle Street. 1809.

Buttolph, Nicholas. 1690-1728.

Cambridge, Charles. Pleasant Street. 18ᴄ9, 1810.    Eliot Street. 1813.    27 North Street. 1818.    North Russell Street. 1819.

Clark, George. Congress Street. 1816.

Copeland, William M. H. 18½ Cornhill. 1820.

Cushing, John. Spring Lane. 1818.

Dashwood, Samuel, Jr. Water Street. 1809.

Dennis, Michael. 1736-1763.
Bookseller, stationer, and binder.

Douglas, John. 1768.

Edwards, Joseph. Cornhill. 1723.
Bookseller and bookbinder.

Eliot, John. At the Great Elms, South-End. 1728-1771.
Bookseller and bookbinder.

Eliot, Samuel. Cornhill. 1740-1745.
Binder and stationer.

Ellison, A. Newbury Street. 1771.
Bookseller and binder.

Felt, David. 4 Kilby Street. 1813.

Fleet, Thomas. Pudding Lane near the Town House. 1730.
Printer and binder.

Fletcher, James F. 10 State Street. 1805.

Fletcher & Lecain. State Street. 1806.

Gardner, James. Link Alley. 1798.

Gerrish, Samuel. 1708.    At the Sign of the Buck in Marlborough-Street. 1712.    North Side of the Town-House. 1716.
Bookseller and bookbinder.

Goodwin, William. House, S. Federal Court. 1810.    Marlboro Place. 1813.

Gould, John R. 92 Court Street. 1816.

Gray, Benjamin. 1719-1751.
Bookseller and bookbinder.

Gray, Harrison. Spring Lane. 1816.

Hancock, Thomas. Anne Street, near the Draw-Bridge. 1726.
Bookseller and bookbinder.

Harrison, Charles. Over against the Brazen-Head in Cornhill. 1739-1745.
Bookseller and bookbinder.

Henchman, Daniel. Cornhill, Corner of King Street, opposite the Old Brick Meeting House. 1713-1761.

Hodgson, John. Marlborough Street. 1762-1782.
　Bookseller, stationer, and bookbinder.
Hudson, Henry. Congress Street. 1820.
Hurd, Benjamin. Derne Street. 1813, 1816.
Hurd, Benjamin, & Gould, John. 1800-1805.　Court Street. 1809.　9 N.
　Side Court Street. 1810.
Jaquith, Moses. Chambers Street. 1818, 1820.
Kent, James. No. 2 Suffolk Bldg. 1806.
Kent & Proctor. No. 2 Suffolk Bldg. 1805.
Kettell, Thomas. S. Russell Street. 1818.
Kidder, Joseph B. 57 Hanover Street. 1820.
Kidder, Stephen. Devonshire Street. 1813.　8 State Street. 1816.
Kidder, Thomas B. & Stephen. Dorsett Lane. 1810.
Kneeland, Daniel. *ca.* 1759-1789.
　Plain bookbinder.
Lang, William. At the Gilt Bible, Marlboro'-Street. 1760.
　Bookseller and bookbinder.
Langdon, John. Cornhill. 1770.
　Bookseller, stationer, and binder.
*Larkin, Benjamin. 46 Cornhill. 1789-1803.
Lecain, Francis. House, Common Street. 1809.
Legge, Henry B. Eliot-Street. 1798.　Congress Street. 1800.　State Street.
　1803.
Leverett, Thomas. Cornhill. 1753-1778.
　Bookseller, binder, and stationer.
Lincoln, Elijah. 43 Cornhill. 1820.
Long, William. (William Lang?). At the Sign of the Stayes, the South Side
　of the Town-House. 1760.
Loring, Benjamin. 13 Exchange Street. 1805, 1813, 1816, 1818.　7 State
　Street. 1809, 1810.
Loring, Benjamin & Josiah. Water Street. 1798.　State Street. 1800.
Loring, Josiah. Devonshire Street. 1805.　School Street. 1809, 1810.
　Bookbinder and paper ruler.
Love, Bennett. In Anne Street, near the Bridge. 1726.
MacAlpine, Walter. Near the Mill-Bridge, afterward in Union-Street near
　the Town Dock. 1743.
　Bookseller and binder.
MacAlpine, William. Marlborough-Street. 1753-1776.
　Bookseller, printer, and binder.
Marsh, Bela. 88 Newbury-Street. 1820.
　Bookbinder and stationer.
Mein, John. At the London Bookstore, north side of King Street. 1764-1769.
Munroe, Francis & Parker. 4 Cornhill. 1809.
　Printers, bookbinders, and booksellers.
Nowell, William. 1671-1672.
Parker, John D. Pleasant Street. 1813.
Parker, Samuel. Court Street. 1803-1805.
Pemberton, John. School Street. 1731-1759.
Perry, Michael. Under the West-End of the Town House. 1695.
　Publisher, bookseller, and bookbinder.
Phillips, Eleazer. (Charlestown.) 1711.
　Bookseller and binder.

Phillips, John. Stationers-Arms, Corn-Hill. 1725-1763.
    Bookseller and binder.
Pocorney, Joseph. Creel Square. 1810.
Proctor, Nathaniel. At the Bible and Dove in Anne-Street. 1727-1766.
Pulsifer, Joseph. Back Street. 1805-1809.    39 Back Street. 1813.    41 Back
    Street. 1818.    House, 4 Snowhill Street. 1810.    House, 17 Prince
    Street. 1813, 1818.
Rand, Thomas. Cornhill, near the Sign of the Three Nuns, afterward in
    Anne Street. 1745.
    Stationer, bookseller, and binder.
*Ranger, Edmund. 1671-1705.
    Bookbinder and bookseller.
*Ratcliff, John. ca. 1661-1682.
Robinson, Samuel. 1723-1771.
    Bookseller and bookbinder.
*Roulstone, John, jun. Congress Street. 1803.    Half Court Square. 1805-
    1807.    Devonshire Street. 1809. (House — 16 Newbury Street.)    10
    State Street. 1810-1823.    76 State Street. 1825.
Sanders, John. 1636.
Sawyer, Nathan. Congress Street. 1820.
Scott, James. 10 State Street. 1813.
Snelling, Joseph. Fish-Street, corner of Boarded-Alley. 1767-1784?    Gover-
    nor's Alley. 1796.    Whitebread Alley. 1798.    51 Marlboro Street.
    1800.    Spring Street. 1803.    8 Winter Street. 1805.    6 N. Russell
    Street. 1813.
Spence, John. 50 Cornhill. 1818.
Sprint, Bartholomew. 1685.
Steele, Alexander. Back Street. 1789-1800.
Stimpson, Charles. 12 & 13 Exchange Street. 1816, 1818, 1820.
Tucker, Isaac. 56 Cornhill. 1803.
    Blank-book manufacturer and bookbinder.
Webb, John. House, Court Street. 1809.    Butolph Street. 1810.    Friend
    Street. 1813.    N. Russell Street. 1816.
Webb, Samuel. Anne-Street. 1757-1792.
    Binder and bookseller.
Welles, Charles. 1 Water Street. 1820.
Wells & Webb. 32 Ann Street. 1805-1806.
West, David. 36 Marlborough Street. 1789.
    Bookbinder and stationer.
Wharton & Bowes. 1761.
    Booksellers, stationers, and binders.
While, James. Ponars and Willis' Printing Office in Queer Street. 1776.
    Bookbinder and account-book ruler.
White, Timothy. Marshall's Lane. 1755.
    Bookseller and plain binder.
Wilder, Ephraim. 66 Ann Street. 1810.
Wilder, Joseph. Mill Lane. 1805.    Sea Street, Newbury Street. 1810.    Fed-
    eral Street. 1813.    Essex Street. 1816.    Purchase Street. 1818.
Williams, William B. 76 State Street. 1818.
Winter, Joshua. Union Street. 1745-1761.
    Bookseller, stationer, and binder.

## Charleston, South Carolina

*Bailey, David. *ca.* 1796.
Taylor, James. 1771.
Woods, Robert. 1764.

## Elizabeth, New Jersey

Jones, John. Near to Mrs. Cheetwoods mill. 1757.

## Ephrata, Pennsylvania

*Bruederschaft, Ephrata. *ca.* 1738-1794.
    Printers, bookbinders, and publishers.

## Germantown, Pennsylvania

*Liebert, Peter. Upper end of Germantown. 1778.
    Printer and bookbinder.
*Sower (Sauer), Christopher. 1738-1758.
    Printer, paper maker, ink manufacturer, and bookbinder.
Sower, Christopher, Junior. ?-1784.
    Type founder, paper ruler, ink manufacturer, and bookbinder.

## Keene, New Hampshire

Webb, Thomas S. 1790-1796.

## Lansingburgh, New York

Shaw, John. 1798.

## Mendon, Massachusetts

Goodale, Ephraim. 1798.

## New Brunswick, New Jersey

Deare, Lewis. 1813.
    Printer and binder.

## New York, New York

Ackley, James. 62 Stone Street. 1800.
Allen, Luman H. 10 Lumber Street. 1818, 1819.     20 Wall Street. 1820.
*Allen, Thomas. No. 12 Queen Street. 1792.
    Binder and bookseller.
Anderson, Nicholas. 250 Greenwich. 1814-1817.
Anderton, T. The Sign of the Orange Tree in Cannon's Wharf. 1764.
    Bookbinder, letter-case, and pocket-book maker.
Arnold, Philip. Chatham Street. 1797.
Barclay, James. 6 Beaver Lane. 1819.     199 Spring Street. 1820.
Batty, Robert. 19 Ferry Street. 1816, 1817.
Beatty, Robert. 229 Water Street. 1820.

Bell, Nathaniel. 438 Pearl Street. 1796-1797.     94 Chatham Street. 1798-1799.     Bowery. 1800.     222 Broadway. 1801.     220 Bowery. 1802-1804.     82 Bowery. 1805.     69 William Street. 1806.
  Bookbinder and stationer.
      56 Gold Street. 1807-1808.          45 Beaver Street. 1810, 1815-1816?
      12 Ferry. 1820.
  Bookbinder.
Bell & Smith. Chatham Street. 1799-1800.
  Bookbinders and stationers.
Black, John. Cedar Street. 1796.     93 Beekman Street. 1801-1805.
  Bookbinder, bookseller, and stationer.
Bliss, David. 6 Slate Lane. 1804.          56 Maiden Lane. 1805-1806.          291
      Greenwich. 1807.     287 Greenwich. 1808, 1811, 1815.
  Bookbinder and bookseller.
Bowers, Alexander D. 1 Bancker Street. 1812.     18 Bancker Street. 1818.
Bradford, John. 20 Henry Street. 1809.     9 Beaver Street. 1810, 1812, 1815, 1816, 1819.     16 Reed Street. 1811.
*Bradford, William. At the sign of the Bible. 1693-1743.
  Printer and bookbinder.
Brewer, James. 3rd near Rivington. 1804-1806.
Brooks, Philip. Dock Street. 1775.
Brown, Christian. 9 Division Street. 1801.     70 Water Street. 1802-1804.     71 Water Street and 137 Front Street. 1805.     71 Water Street. 1806.     23 Murrage Street. 1807.     71 Water Street. 1808-1810.     52 Beaver Street. 1817-1819.     Water Street. 1820.
Brown, Duncan. 1759.
Brown, Samuel. Maiden-Lane near the Fly-Market. 1761.
  Printer and bookbinder.
Burnton, J. J. 21 Orchard Street. 1808.     1 Division Street. 1809.     28 Cedar Street. 1810.
Burnton, Thomas H. 28 Cedar Street. 1800-1802.     116 Broadway. 1803.     151 Water Street. 1805.     71 John Street. 1806.
Burrell, Joseph. 13 Partition Street. 1804-1806.
Burrell, J. & Co. 80 Water Street. 1803.
  Bookbinders and stationers.
Burrill, John. Hester Street. 1814, 1817-1819.
Burtis & Crane. 80 Cherry Street. 1805.
  Bookstore and Lottery Office, 1806-1810; 19 Peck Slip.
Burtsell, Peter. Beekman Street. 1796-1799.     35 Beekman. 1801.     10 Wall Street. 1803-1810.     22 Barclay Street. 1802.
  Bookseller, stationer, and bookbinder.
Campbell, Samuel. 1795.
  Printer, bookseller, and bookbinder.
*Champley, George. 61 Barclay-Street. 1820.
Childs, Francis, & Co. 1794.
  Printer, publisher, bookseller, stationer, and binder.
Christie, Alexander. 3 Rider Street. 1796-1798.
Cillis, James H. 102 Liberty Street. 1820.
Cills, James H. Hester Street. 1816.
Clark, William S. 20 Norfolk Street. 1818.

Cleland, Charles. 37 Maiden-Lane. 1789-1792.

Cochran, John. 48 Chapel Street. 1815-1819.    54 Cedar Street. 1820.

Codey, William. 68 William Street. 1819.

Collard, Archibald. 312 Broadway. 1809.

Collard, Archer. 91 Beekman Street. 1810-1811.    17 Frankfort Street. 1812-1819.    88 Nassau Street. 1820.

Collard and Vandyke. 23 George Street. 1809.

Crane, Benjamin. 80 Cherry Street. 1804-1805.    19 Peck Slip. 1806-1807. 85 Cherry Street. 1808-1820.
   Bookbinder and stationer. See also Burtis & Crane.

Culberston, Henry. 38 Chapel Street. 1803.    38 Lumber Street. 1804-1806. 6 Elizabeth Street. 1807.

Culley, Eliza. 98 James Street. 1819.    104 Bowery. 1820.

Cunningham, Henry. 91 Broad Street. 1806.    127 Greenwich Street. 1807. 51 Second Street. 1808, 1815-1819.

Curtis, William. 77 Harman Street. 1816.

Darling, William. Chamber Street, near the Almshouse. 1801.

Davis, Charles. 1 Moore Street. 1811.    118 Front Street. 1812.

Dawson, George. 110 Pearl Street. 1816.

Day, John. 7 Division Street. 1818-1819.    347 Pearl Street. 1820.

Day, John & William. 347 Pearl Street. 1820.

Day, William. 17 Harman Street. 1815-1819.

Dearborn, Nathaniel. 171 William Street. 1811.

Debevoise, P. J. 251 Greenwich. 1801.

De Foreest, Henry. At the House of Peter Zenger, or at his House opposite the Sign of the Black-Horse. 1735-1750.
   Bookbinder and blank-book manufacturer.

Delamontagnie or Delamontayne, John. 25 Chamber Street. 1804-1806. 27 First Street. 1809.    91 Murray Street. 1817-1819.    46 Chrystie Street. 1820.

Devilliers, Joseph. 2d Street. 1804-1806.

Dey, John. 17 Oliver Street. 1819.

Drummond, Peter. 194 Front Street. 1796.

Dubois, Peter. 251 Greenwich. 1802.

Dunham, David. 32 Rivington Street. 1818.

Duyckinck, Evert, jun. 102 Pearl Street. 1820.

Elliott, Charles. 382 Water Street. 1820.

Essex, William. 116 Cherry Street. 1797.
   Bookbinder and stationer.

Evans, Samuel. Between the Old-Slip and Coenties Market. 1765.
   Bookbinder and stationer.

Evans, Titus. 60 James Street. 1801.    262 Williams Street. 1802-1806.
   Bookbinder and grocer.

Fenwick, Thomas. Above industry furnace. 1799.    L. Catherine Street. 1800, 1802, 1803.    Anthony Street. 1804-1819.

Ferguson, Francis. 102 Pearl Street. 1803.

Forbes, George. 175 William Street. 1807.    49 Division Street. 1817-1818. 87 Bowery. 1820.
   Bookbinder and bookseller.

Forbes, Samuel B. 87 Bowery. 1820.
   Bookbinder and bookseller.

Foster, John. 3 Chapel Street. 1820.
Foster, Joseph. 288 Broadway. 1820.
Foster & Scott. 73 South Street. 1819.
Fraser, Elias. 137 Bancker Street. 1815-1817.
Fraunces, D. P. 33 Church Street. 1807.
Friend, George. Corner Orchard and Grand. 1801-1802.
Frowde, William. Mott Street. 1804-1806.
Furman, Lydia. 21 Pell Street. 1809-1810.
Gale, Marinus. 66 Ann Street. 1796-1797.     36 Lombard Street. 1798.
      2 Ferry Street. 1800-1801.     63 Ann Street. 1802.
Garson, John. 65 Leonard Street. 1815-1819.
Garson, Thomas. 40 Water Street. 1815.     Vesey Street, c. Church. 1820.
Gilchrist, Eliza, widow. 6 republican alley. 1810.
Gomez, Benjamin. Maiden Lane. 1791-1800.
   Bookbinder and stationer.
Green, William. Maiden Lane. 1775-1776.
   Bookseller and bookbinder.
Greenleaf, Thomas. 196 Water Street. 1787-1798.
   Printer and bookbinder.
Griffith, Hugh M. 238 Greenwich Street. 1798.     36 Lombard Street. 1799.
      358 Pearl Street. 1800.     88 Water Street. 1801-1802.     131 Green-
      wich Street. 1803-1804.     2 Ann Street. 1804-1805.
Guerson, Thomas. 39 Elm Street. 1819.
Haines, Benjamin. 223 Greenwich Street. 1802.
Hall, Christopher. 61 Gold Street. 1812, 1814.     1 Gold Street. 1817.
Hendlen, Thomas. 39 Liberty Street. 1811.
Hendricks, Thomas. 60 Essex Street. 1815-1818.
Hodge, Robert. 38 Maiden Lane. 1785, 1786.
   Publisher, printer, and binder.
Holmes, Latham. 290 Pearl Street. 1819.
Holmes, N. B. 276 Greenwich Street. 1818-1820.
Horsey & Co. 110 Pearl Street. 1817.
Hulsart, Corn. B. 157 Division Street. 1820.
   Bookbinder and stationer.
Hunt, William. 9 Leonard Street. 1809.     13 Leonard Street. 1810.
Hutson, Francis. 2 Republican Alley. 1818.
Hyndshaw, John. At the sign of the Bible, near the Old-Slip Market. 1745.
   Bookbinder and bookseller.
Jansen, George. 248 Pearl Street. 1804.     116 Broadway. 1805-1808.     17
      George Street. 1809-1810.     15 Chatham Street. 1811.
   Bookbinder, bookseller, and stationer.
Jansen, Lewis B. 11 Chatham Street. 1812, 1814-1816.
Jansen, Thomas B. 344 Water Street. 1798.     15 Chatham Street. 1811.
Jansen, Thomas B. & Co. 150 Water Street. 1799.     248 Pearl Street. 1803-
      1805.     116 Broadway. 1805-1806.
   Booksellers and stationers.
Johnson, Joseph. Duke Street. 1731-1734.
Johnson, Samuel. 31 Third Street. 1807-1808.     61 Catherine Street. 1809.
      27 Nassau Street. 1810, 1811.     20 Orange Street. 1816.
Johnston, E. & R. 385 Pearl Street. 1801.     64 Chatham Street. 1802.

Johnstone, Elkhanah. 383 Pearl Street. 1800.    50 Maiden Lane. 1803.    53
    Liberty Street. 1804-1805.    Division Street. 1806.

Judah, Napht. 47 Water Street. 1796-1799.    112 Pearl Street. 1800.
    Bookbinder and stationer.

Keese or Keys, Vincent. 30 Lumber Street. 1818-1819.    William Street.
    1820.

Kent, James G. 29 Bayard Street. 1814-1819.    140 Hester Street. 1820.

Kilbreth, John. 39 Lombardy Street. 1816.

Lake, Daniel. 51 Cliff Street. 1815-1817.

Lealand, B. 71 Pump Street. 1814-1819.

Lee, William, Jr. 9 Division Street. 1814-1815.

Leedell, George. 1773.

Leland, Belarmine. 81 Wall Street. 1820.

Lent, D. & J. Palnier. 68 Mulberry Street. 1806.

Levy, Benjamin. 47 Third Street. 1808.

Lewis, Jansen B. 11 Chatham Street. 1816.    See Jansen, Lewis B.

Lewis, John. Fair Street. 1796-1798.    70 Gold Street. 1799.

Loudon, Samuel. 5 Water Street. 1790.    110 Pearl Street. 1798-1800.    2
    Broad Street. 1801.    102 Pearl Street. 1802.    188 Pearl Street. 1805.
    Printer, binder, and bookseller.

Lyons, Michael. 128 Reed Street. 1815.

*MacAlpine, Robert. Hanover Square and Seaver Street. 1742-1769.
    Bookbinder and bookseller.

M'Donald, Duncan. 81 Chapel Street. 1820.

McEwen, Malcolm. 1748.

M'Kenzie, Hugh. 178 William Street. 1810.    59 Williams Street. 1819.

M'Queen, William. 56 Cedar Street, corner of Lumber Street, rear of the
    City-Hotel. 1820.

Marshall, Gilbert. 27 Stone Street. 1808-1809.    59 William Street. 1810.

Martin or Martine, Henry. Jefferson. 1806.    27 Elizabeth. 1807.    196
    Bowery. 1808.    Corner Pump and Mott Streets. 1810.    Mott Street.
    1811.

Martin, John. 142 Grand Street. 1820.

Masterton, David. 6 Ludlow Street. 1820.    183 Duane Street. 1810.    85
    Fair Street. 1812-1819.

Megarey, Henry I. 138 Broadway. 1819-1821.
    Stationer.

Merrifield, Preston. 69 Pine Street. 1819.

Mertoney, John. Pump Street. 1803.

Mesier, Peter A. 107 Pearl Street. 1796-1810.
    Bookbinder, stationer, and bookseller.

Miller, Alexander. 35 Reed Street. 1798.    61 Harman Street. 1799.    35
    Reed Street. 1800-1803.    49 Church Street. 1806.

Miller, John. 10 Frankfurt Street. 1796.    30 Frankfurt Street. 1797.    6
    Chamber Street. 1798.

Mills, Robert. 14 Cliff Street. 1796.

Mills, Timothy. 14 Ann Street. 1803 (grocer).    14 Ann Street. 1804 (book-
    binder).    104 Pearl Street. 1805.    102 Pearl Street. 1806-1810.    99
    Pearl Street. 1811-1814.    52 & 54 Beaver Street. 1815-1820.

*Mitchell, Edward. 9 Maiden Lane. 1796.    Fisher Street. 1797.

Montayne or Delamontayne?, John. 27 Chamber Street. 1806.   68 Chamber
Street. 1807.   Reed Street. 1808.   269 Greenwich. 1815.
Montgomery, John B.  39 Robinson Street.  1817-1819.     318 Pearl Street.
1820.
Moore, Robert.  Corner of First and Grand.  1801.     108 Water Street.  1802.
38 Pearl Street.  1803-1810.     196 Water Street.  1811.     38 Pearl
Street. 1815-1818.     329 Greenwich Street.  1820.
Bookbinder and stationer.
Moore, Samuel.  196 Water Street.  1812.
Morston, David.  29 First Street.  1814.
Myers, Benjamin.  71 John Street.  1798.
Myers, John D.  70 Frankfurt Street.  1819.
Myers, William.  139 Church Street.  1809.     394 Pearl Street.  1810-1818.
Myers, William & John.  70 Frankfurt Street.  1820.
Nicholas, Ebenezer.  12 Clarke Street.  1820.
Niven & Clussman.  68 William Street.  1815.
Nutter, Valentine.  Opposite the Coffee-House Bridge.  1773-1790.
Bookbinder and bookseller.
Ogilvie, Isaac.  9 Oak Street.  1809.     Broadway.  1814.
Olmstead, James.  156 William.  1806.     71 Stone.  1807.     61 Pearl Street.
1810-1820.
Paine, P.  1765.
Parker, John A.  62 William Street.  1818.
Parsons, Chester.  99 Pearl Street.  1810.
Pemberton, William.  361 Water.  1796.     35 George Street.  1797.     6 Au-
gustus Street.  1799-1800.     16 Reed.  1801.     6 Augustus.  1802.
Perkins, Thomas.  24 Charlotte Street.  1809.     27 Elizabeth Street.  1810-1811.
Perry, Robert.  Gibbs Alley.  1803.     17 Elizabeth.  1807.     Cor. of Mott and
Pump.  1809.     27 Elizabeth.  1810-1815.
Phillips, Andrew.  Grand Street.  1819.     10 Roosevelt Street.  1820.
Pierce, Daniel.  3 Warren Street.  1816.
Ponier, Jacob.  386 Greenwich Street.  1819.
Price, Samuel.  58 Anthony Street.  1808.
Reynolds, Thomas.  30 Lumber Street.  1815, 1818.
Ronoldus or Ronalds, John.  188 Pearl Street.  1803-1805.
Bookbinder and stationer.
Ross, David.  Thames Street.  1817.
Sackett, Joseph.  75 Warren Street.  1797, 1799.     235 Greenwich Street.  1805.
Orange Street.  1806.     1 Chapel Street.  1809.     6 Chapel Street.  1810.
Chapel Street.  1811, 1814, 1815, 1820.
Bookbinder and stationer.
Saffen, Samuel.  31 Partition.  1808.     17 Ann.  1809.     188 Pearl Street.  1810-
1811.
Sands, E.  49 Fulton Street.  1820.
Schenck, James R.  22 Cedar Street.  1811.
Schenck & Turner.  1 Pine Street.  1812-1815.     20 Slote Lane.  1815.
Scott, John.  republican alley.  1811.     1 Bancker Street.  1812-1818.
Seymour, James.  68 William Street.  1820.
Shedden, John.  94 Water Street.  1807-1808.
Sherman, Henry A.  74 John Street.  1815.

Sinclair, George. 196 William Street. 1801.    54 Chatham Street. 1802. 332 Water Street. 1803.    207 Water Street. 1804-1806.    235 Broadway. 1807.    259 Broadway. 1808-1810.    257 Broadway. 1811-1817. 131 Prince Street. 1820.

Bookbinder, stationer, and proprietor of a circulating library.

Sinclair, Hector. Church Street. 1819.

Slay, Edward. 51 Gold Street. 1814.

Smith, Daniel. 94 Chatham Street. 1799-1800.    70 Vesey Street. 1801-1807, ?1812-1816.

Bookbinder, stationer, and lottery office.

Smith, Nathaniel. 15 Cedar Street. 1819-1820.

Smith, Thomas. 96 Gold Street. 1806.    13 Barclay Street. 1807, 1809, 1810, 1811.    80 Nassau Street. 1808.    Pump Street. 1812-1816.

Somerindyke, J. 1765.

Sowarby, James. 42 Elizabeth Street. 1817.

Starr, Charles. 20 State Street. 1820.

Starr, Samuel. 18 Thames Street. 1819.

Stevens, William. Corner of Roosevelt and Bancker Streets. 1810.    Roosevelt Street. 1811-1820.

Stores, ———. 70 William Street. 1810.

Swain, William. 100 Reed Street. 1805.    241 Pearl Street. 1806.    10 Cliff Street. 1807.    241 Pearl Street. 1808-1817.    240 Pearl Street. 1809.

Sylvester, James. 17 Henry Street. 1820.

Taylor, Vermilye. Grand Street. 1818-1819.    13 Spring Street. 1820.

Thomas, James. 173 Water Street. 1819.

Thomas, John F. 6 Catherine Market. 1818.

Thompson, Henry. Church Street. 1812.

Thompson or Thomas, John F. 99 Pearl Street. 1807-1808.    126 Pearl Street. 1809-1819.    163 Water Street. 1820.

Bookseller and bookbinder.

Thompson, Robert R. 17 Cedar Street. 1809.    11 Thomas Street. 1810. 175 Church Street. 1811.    205 Church Street. 1812-1819.    49 Leonard Street. 1820.

Titus, William. Cherry Street. 1817.

Tribe, Lazrus Nixon. 61 Cliff Street. 1811.    89 Fair. 1812-1819.    50 Eldridge Street. 1820.

Turner, Levin. 27 Stone Street. 1810-1811.    146 Washington Street. 1812, 1815, 1817-1819.    59 Stone Street. 1816.    19 Beaver Street. 1820.

Vandyck or Vandyke, Thomas. 44 Warren Street. 1802-1804.    9 George Street. 1805-1807.    1 Peck Slip. 1808.    24 George Street. 1809. 19 Barclay Street. 1810.    127 Chandler Street. 1811.    Chamber Street. 1812.

Van Ranst, Nicholas. 32 Lumber Street. 1804-1809.    5 Cliff Street. 1810-1811.

Van Ranst & Burrell. 6 Lumber Street. 1805.

Vanwater, Dow. 67 William Street. 1811.

Vermilye, William. 9 Anthony Street. 1808.

Walker, John. 29 Fisher Street. 1807.    55 Second Street. 1808.

Walker, William. 7 Fisher Street. 1802-1806.    29 Fisher Street. 1807-1808. 29 Bayard Street. 1809-1819.    32 Eldridge Street. 1820.

Watt, James. 1757-1761.
West, William. Pell Street. 1806.
Whitlock, James. 32 Pike Street. 1816.
Wilbur, Curtis. Broome Street. 1817.
Willis, William. 208 Pearl Street. 1796.     19 Cheapside. 1797-1802.
*Wilson & Nichols. Pine Street, corner of Broadway. 1826.
Wortman, John. 20 Doyer Street. 1808.     5 Thomas Street. 1809.     10 Bay-
     ard Street. 1810-1811.     65 Leonard Street. 1817-1819.     5 Oak
     Street. 1820.
Wright, Thomas. 29 George Street. 1802-1804.     43 Harman Street. 1804.
     12 Bowery. 1805-1806.     4 bancker Street. 1811.     144 Chamber.
     1814-1817.     49 Sullavan Street. 1820.
Young, Robert. 106 Bowery. 1816.

## Newburyport, Massachusetts

Emerson, Bulkeley. 1760.
     Postmaster, bookseller, and binder.

## Norwich, Connecticut

Brooks, Philip. 1778.

## Philadelphia, Pennsylvania

Ackley, James. S. Broad Street. 1810.     7 Watkins Alley. 1811.
*Aitken, Jane. 1802-1810.
     Printer and bookbinder.
*Aitken, Robert. Front Street, nearly opposite the London Coffee-House,
     afterward in Market Street. 1769-1802.
     Printer, engraver, bookseller, and bookbinder.
Aitken, Robert & Son. High & Market Street. 1795.
     Bookbinders and printers.
Alichin or Allchin, George. Black Horse Alley. 1801, 1802.     13 High Street.
     1805, 1809-1811, 1816, 1819.
Allinson, David. 12 Pear Street. 1802.
Anderson, Robert P. Bryan's Court. 1816.
Anderson, William. 39 Locust Street. 1819.
Anderton, John (T.?). London Bookstore in Second-Street. 1768.
Arthur, James. 11th Street below Vine. 1819.
Auner, Peter. 79 Cherry Street. 1820.
Baker, John & Samuel. Sterling Alley, between Cherry Alley & Pace Street.
     1785.
Baker, Samuel. 70 Elm Street. 1793.
Baldwin, John. 28 Sugar Alley. 1820.
Bashford, Norbury. 1 Elbow Lane. 1819.
Bate, Thomas. 164 Cherry St. 1802.
Bennett, John B. 125 Cedar Street. 1816.
Boate, Thomas. 108 W. Cedar Street. 1804.     181 N. Front Street. 1805,
     1806.     133 Vine Street. 1809-1810.     County Line to Germantown.
     1811.     Camden, N. J. 1818, 1820.
Bockus, Daniel. 112 S. Tenth Street. 1816, 1817.
Boddy, John. 124 N. Fifth Street. 1817.

Bolton, Thomas. Arch, corner of Mulberry Street. 1795, 1796.   Oak N. L. 1806.

Bradford, Andrew. Second Street, at the sign of the Bible. 1718.
Printer, binder, and bookseller.

Braeutigam or Brecutigam, Daniel (David?). 100 N. Second Street. 1790, 1791, 1793, 1796, 1797.

Brigham, Hugh. Grezels Alley. 1802.   142 Spruce Street. 1804.

Buglass, Caleb. 1774-1797.   29 Front Street. 1791.   Priest's Alley. 1796.
Bookbinder and bookseller.

Buglass, Mary. 12 Combes Alley. 1801, 1816, 1819.
Bookbinder and bookseller.

Burn, William. Little Seventh Street. 1804.

Burns, Amariah. 12 Cresson's Alley. 1816, 1817, 1819.

Burns, David. Arch Street. 1795.

Bussing, Thomas. Beach Street. 1819-1820.

Butler, Edward. 153 Walnut Street. 1811.

Cameron, John. 67 S. Front Street. 1793-1801.   137 S. Front Street. 1809, 1811.
Bookbinder and stationer.

Carpenter, John. 59 North 3rd Street. 1804, 1806, 1809, 1811.   34 Coats Street. 1816, 1817, 1819, 1820.

Cleland, Charles. 31 Walnut Street. 1804-1806.

Cochlan, James. 44 Cherry Alley. 1798.

Cochran, Hugh B. Relief Alley. 1798.   108 Sassafras Alley. 1804, 1806, 1809, 1811.

Coglan, John. 37 North 6th Street. 1802, 1804.   276 North Second Street. 1805.

Condie, Thomas. 20 Carter's Alley. 1796, 1797.   22 Carter's Alley. 1804-1811.

Widow of T. Condie. 22 Carter's Alley. 1817.

Connor, Michael. Cherry Street. 1795.

Conrad, Peter. 161 High Street. 1816.   18 Pewterplatter Alley. 1817.

Cook, Samuel. 8 Harmony Court. 1819.

Cooper, G. 46 South 5th Street. 1809.

Cooper, William. 1806.

Cooper & Ogden, Carlyles Street. 1809.

Cresson or Crisson, James. 20 Strawberry Alley. 1790, 1791.

Crissey, James. 35 S. Front Street. 1816.   319 N. Second Street. 1817, 1819.

Crofts, ——. 1752.

Culin, George. 2 Goddard Alley. 1816.   9 Goddards Alley. 1817, 1819.

Curtis, John. 43 N. Fourth Street. 1793, 1795, 1797.
Bookbinder and stationer.

Cyphert, Conrad. Corner Fifth & Walnut Streets. 1793.

Datey, Edward. 38 Elder Street. 1817, 1819.

Davies, William. Chestnut Street. 1727.

Davis, Benjamin. 214 S. Fifth Street. 1820.

Davis, John. 50 Appletree Alley. 1811.   12 Stall's Court. 1816.   15 Fromberger Court. 1819-1820.

Davis, William. 309 Walnut Street. 1820.

Deal, Michael. 13 South Sixth Street. 1809.   Near 17 Wagner's Alley. 1810.

Deal, Nicholas. Near Wagner's Alley. 1811.

Dean, John. Laetitia Court. 1775.
Dellap, Samuel. 1771.
Denoon, James Johnston. 34 Carters Alley. 1796.
*De Silver, Robert. Mead Alley. 1801.   13 Grays Alley. 1804.   8 Pear
    Street. 1805-1806.   110 Walnut Street. 1809, 1810, 1811, 1816, 1818,
    1819.   218 High Street. 1820.
    Bookbinder and bookseller.
De Silver or Desilver, Thomas. 12 Cressons Alley. 1804.   12 Grays Alley.
    1805.   152 South Sixth Street. 1806, 1809, 1811, 1816.   2 Decatur
    Street. 1818, 1820.
    Binder, stationer, and bookseller.
Detune, Francis. N. Front Street. 1795, 1796, 1798.
Dickenson, John. North Sixth Street. 1790-1791.
Dickinson, Morris. 38 S. Fourth Street. 1793.
Doyle, Francis. 157 South Sixth Street. 1811.
Duncan, Robinson. N. Sixth Street. 1801.
Dungan, James. 36 Moravian Alley. 1802-1817.
Dunlap, David. 14 Quarry Alley. 1804.
Widow of David Dunlap. Coats Alley. 1819.
Edelmann, Jessie. 32 N. Fourth Street. 1805.
Fletcher, Joshua. Little Pine Street. 1809, 1816-1820.
Frant, Peter. 62 Cherry Street. 1816.
Furdge, Henry. 6 Dock Street. 1819.   3 Farmers Row. 1820.
    Bookbinder and bottler.
Garson, Thomas. 6 Carters Alley. 1819.
Gaskell, Benjamin. 18 Bank Street. 1810-1820.
Gasson, Thomas. 6 Carters Alley. 1820.
Gentle, James. Spruce, between Second and Front Street. 1785-1796.
Geyer, Andrew or Andreas. Second Street. 1767.   Front Street. 1790-1791.
    Bookbinder and bookseller.
Gibbons, John. 144 N. Third Street. 1791.
Goodman, C. 30 Cherry Street. 1811.
Goodwin, Joseph. In Second Street, near Blackhorse Alley. 1742.
    Bookseller, binder, and stationer.
Grant, John. N. Fourth Street. 1795-1796.   1 Watkins Court. 1802.
Grant, Peter. 1805.   124 North Fifth Street. 1806, 1817.
Haas, Samuel. 7 Elfriths Alley. 1805.
Hanfe or Hanse, Samuel. N. Fourth Street. 1795.   170 S. Second Street.
    1810, 1816, 1819, 1820.   12 Cressons Alley. 1804, 1806, 1809, 1811, 1817.
Harry, David "Black." Laetitia Court. 1755.
    Bookbinder and bookseller.
Hellings, John. 37 Pewterplatter Alley. 1810.   83 Callowhill. 1809, 1811.
Henderson, Guy. 99 Cherry Street. 1816, 1819, 1820.
Hermstead, Joseph. 7 Elbow Lane. 1819.
Hickman, Nathaniel. 5 N. Front Street. 1819.   53 High Street. 1820.
Hinchman, Benjamin. 36 Carters Alley. 1816-1817.
Hockinhall, John. 2 Carters Alley. 1793.
Holland, Nathaniel. 1747.
Howorth, George. 368 N. Second Street. 1811.   Darby & High Street. 1819.
Howorth & Marot. Darby & High Street. 1819.

Hyde, George. Carters Alley. 1795.    147 Chestnut Street. 1797, 1801.    149 Chestnut Street. 1802.    71 Chestnut Street. 1816, 1819.

Hyde, George & Co. 77 Chestnut Street. 1806, 1809, 1817.

Hyndshaw, John. At the Sign of the Two Bibles, in Market Street, over against the Presbyterian Meeting-House. 1730.
    Bookseller and bookbinder.

James, Samuel. 3 Marshall Court. 1819.

*January, Benjamin. Front, between Market & Chestnut Streets. 1785, 1793, 1795, 1796.

Jenkins, John J. 123 Race Street. 1820.

Jones, William. N. Fourth Street. 1801.
    Bookbinder and whalebone cutter.

Katz, John J.    Over Phoenix Hose House. 1819.

Kausselt, George. 130 Callowhill. 1810.    180 Callowhill. 1811.

Kennedy, William. Buttonwood Lane. 1819-1820.

Kurtz, Charles. 125 N. Second Street. 1811, 1816.

Lampley, Richard. 479 N. Second Street. 1810.    Francis Lane. 1819.

Laycock, John. 24 Elizabeth Street. 1810.

Le Bretran, A. 175 North 3rd Street. 1806.

Limbeck, David. 1753.
    Bookbinder and bookseller.

Limeburner, George. Flower Alley. 1819.    Noble Street. 1816, 1817, 1819, 1820.

Limeburner or Limeburger, Philip. 185 N. Second Street. 1793, 1795, 1798. 45 Vine Street. 1804-1811.
    Bookbinder and stationer.

Locker, James. Emlen's Alley. 1816-1819.

McCalpin, Walter. 80 N. 3rd Street. 1790-1793.

M'Cassey, John & A. 3 Knight Court. 1809.

M'Causland, Alexander. 204 South 4th Street. 1819.

M'Dougall, John Douglass. Chestnut Street. 1774-1775.
    Printer, binder, and stationer.

MacGill, Robert. Corner of Laetitia Court, afterward in Second Street. 1771-1778.
    Binder and bookseller.

McNeal, Isaac. 54 N. Fourth Street. 1820.

Magnet, Daniel. 147 Cherry Street. 1806.

Marshall, Gilbert. 39 Prune Street. 1819.

Martin, James. 88 N. Fifth Street. 1809, 1811, 1820.

Mason, Isaac N. 3 Chestnut Street. 1816, 1820.    Watkins Alley. 1809, 1811, 1819.

Maxwell, Hugh. Chestnut Street. 1798.

Mentz, George W. 71 or 79 Sassafras Alley. 1804-1820.

Metz, William. Corner Race & Fourth Streets. 1785.

Meyer, Jacob. 179 N. Second Street. 1810, 1816.

Miller, Joseph & Walker, Chester. Sassafras Street. 1795.

Mintz, Elizabeth. 68 Race Street. 1796.

Mitchel, William. Farmers Row. 1795-1797.

Moreau de St. Méry, Médéric Louis Élie. S. Front Street, No. 84, corner of Walnut Street. 1794.
    Printer, binder, stationer, and bookseller.

Morgan, William V. Wood Street. 1819.    Middle Alley. 1820.

Morris, Daniel. 184 St. Johns Street. 1802.

Morris, George. Relief Alley. 1805, 1806, 1811, 1819.    2 Dock Street. 1819, 1820.

Morris, Thomas. 26 Spruce Street. 1809-1810.

Morton, Thomas. Blackhouse Alley. 1811.    10 Goforth Court. 1820.

Muir, James. Pewterplatter Alley. 1785-1796.

Muir, W. Near Market Wharf. 1753.

Muir & Hyde. 33 Pewterplatter Alley. 1793.

Murdock, Thomas. 2 Fromberger's Court. 1816, 1820.    14 Sassafras Alley. 1809, 1819.

Murphy, William G. 368 N. Third Street. 1816.    Francis Lane. 1819.

Murray, James. 1819.

Murray, John. 43 Sassafras Alley. 1804.    171 N. Second Street. 1805-1811.

Myers, Jacob. 189 North 2d. Street. 1809.

Myers, William. 204 N. Second Street. 1797-1798.    18 North 4th Street. 1802, 1804.    Cherry Street. 1805.

Nagle, Samuel. 3 Little Pine Street. 1817.

Oat, James. 5 Clawges Court. 1816.

Oat, Joseph. 80 North 3d Street. 1802, 1819.

Ogden, Abraham. 7 Elfreiths Alley. 1810, 1816.    6 Blackhouse Alley. 1817.

Otto, Henry. 216 N. Second Street. 1798.

Parker, John A. 190 Cherry Street. 1820.

Patton, David. N. Second Street. 1795-1801.    Ridge Road. 1805, 1810. Greenleaf Alley. 1802-1809.

Patton, Robert. N. Second Street. 1790-1791.

Payn, John. Ann Street. 1801.

Peters, Thomas. Strawberry Alley. 1785-1801.    3 Cherry Street. 1802-1811.

Peters, William. 140 Walnut Street. 1804.

Poters, Thomas J. 3 Cherry St. 1796.

Potter, William W. 36 Carters Court.    1816, 1819. 1820.    113 South 2d Street. 1809, 1811, 1819.

Potts, Stephen. Market-Street, opposite the Shambles.    Third Street, opposite the Church-alley; at the Bible and Crown, in Front-Street. *ca.* 1730-1749.

Poulson, Zachariah. Sign of the Bible in Second Street. 1763-1804. Bookbinder, bookseller, and stationer.

Price, Samuel C. Malt Alley. 1811.

Reed, William. 75 Green Street. 1819.    Davis Court. 1820.

Reinhold, G. Christoph. Second Street, afterward in Market Street. 1763-1773. Bookbinder and bookseller.

Riddle or Riddal, James. Chestnut Street. 1801-1802, 1804-1806, 1811-1817. 44 S. Eighth Street. 1816, 1820.

Roach, John. 10 N. Front Street. 1820.

Robertson, Duncan. Hoffmans Alley. 1797-1798.

Saits, ——. 1742.

Schreiner, Jacob. 110 N. Eighth Street. 1820.

Schreiner, William. 3 Patons Court. 1816, 1820.

Schriner, ——. 7 Hasting Alley. 1817.

Schuppy or Schippius, or Schuppey, or Schuppley, W. Strawberry Alley. 1743-1753.
  Bookbinder and bookseller.
Seyfert, Charles. 120 S. Fourth Street. 1819.
Seyfert, Conrad. 10 Pear Street. 1816.    18 Pear Street. 1817, 1819.
Sharpless, Joseph. 30 Arch Street. 1817.    21 N. Fourth Street. 1820.
Shields, James. 14 Carters Alley. 1804, 1809, 1811.
Shoemaker, David. 76 North 4th Street. 1804.
Skeriatt, George A. 152 S. Ninth Street. 1816, 1820.
Skeriatt, George S. 15 Watson Alley. 1819.
Smallwood, ——. 26 Spruce Street. 1805.
Snyder, Henry. 12 Knights Court. 1804-1806.    Buttonwood Lane. 1819.
Sower or Sauer, David. 66 N. Third Street. 1796-1797.
  Bookbinder and stationer.
Sower & William Jones. 66 N. Third Street. 1796.
Taylor, Joseph & Shadrach. 384 N. Second Street. 1816.
Taylor, Samuel. At the Book-in-hand, corner of Market and Water Streets. 1765-*ca.* 1781.
  Bookbinder and bookseller.
Thompson & Dailey. 74 Dock Street. 1809, 1811.
Thomson, Peter. 107 Vine Street. 1816-1817.
Trickett, William. 5's. Front Street. 1773.
  Bookseller and bookbinder.
Tucknis, John. Rutters Alley. 1795-1798.    Pattons Court. 1804-1811.
Tucknis, Luke. Greenleaf Alley. 1801.    Pattons Court. 1802-1805.
Wakeling, Samuel. Arch or Mulberry Street. 1795, 1798.
Wallace, John. 13 Waggoners Alley. 1802.    147 N. Sixth Street. 1805, 1810. 127 N. Sixth Street. 1802-1811.
Wallace, Thomas. 378 S. Second Street. 1810, 1816.    5 Garrigues Court. 1809, 1817.
Wardell, Phillip. Rose Alley. 1820.
Warden, Phillip. 81 Callowhill. 1809.
Wiatt, John. 408 N. Third Street. 1816.
Wiatt, Solomon. 368 N. Second Street. 1805-1810.    31 High Street. 1819-1820.
Wieatt, Solomon. 23 North Street. 1804-1819.
Wight, Thomas. 13 Sterling Alley. 1820.
Wightinburg, Michael. 124 Coates Road. 1809-1810.
Wiley, James. Sassafras Alley. 1809-1811.
Mrs. Wiley, widow. 47 Strawberry Lane. 1819.
Willis, Henry. 142 N. Third Street. 1793.
Wilson, George. Frankford Road. 1810.    19 Church Alley. 1806, 1811.
Wittenburg, Michael. 23 South 4th Street. 1804.
Woodhouse, William. Front Street, near Chestnut Street. 1765-1795.
  Printer, bookbinder, and bookseller.
Worn, Philip. Pemberton Alley. 1816.    110 Vine Street. 1819.
Young, William. 1790.
Zeller, Jacob. 119 & 121 N. Third Street. 1797-1819.
  Bookbinder and corder.

## Portsmouth, New Hampshire

Furber, Thomas. 1764.
   Printer and plain binder.

## Salem, Massachusetts

Cushing, Isaac. 1802.
Dabney, John. 1791.
   Bookbinder, bookseller, postmaster, and proprietor of circulating library.
Macanulty, Bernard Brian. 1795.
Prince, Thomas. 1806.
   Printer, blank-book manufacturer, and binder.
Snelling, Joseph. 1784-1788.
Steele, Charles. 1804.
   Bookseller, stationer, and bookbinder.
West, Samuel. 1807-1835.
Williams, Mascol. 1755-1770.
   Bookseller, binder, postmaster, and stationer.

## Williamsburg, Virginia

Parks, William. 1742.
   Printer and bookbinder.

## Wilmington, Delaware

*Craig & Lea. 1791.
Ferris, Benjamin. 1769-1770.
   Stationer and binder.
Williamson, James. 1774.

## Worcester, Massachusetts

Merriam, George. 1794.
Miller, Joseph. 1794.
Salter, John. 1794.
Whittemore, Clarke. 1794-1806.

# APPENDIX B

## *LIST OF AMERICAN BINDINGS*

This list of existing American bookbindings supplements The Grolier Club's *Catalogue of Ornamental Leather Bookbindings Executed in America Prior to 1850*. It is limited to bindings done in the 1820's or earlier, and, with two or three exceptions, to those examined personally by the author.

The main body of the list, arranged alphabetically by author, gives author, title, imprint, location, and the name of the binder when it is known. A finding list, arranged alphabetically by owners, follows the main list.

ALLEINE, RICHARD. Heaven Opened, Or, a Brief and Plain Discovery of the Riches of God's Covenant of Grace. Being the Third Part of Vindiciae Pietatis. Boston: Printed by B. Green & J. Allen for Elkanah Pembroke, 1699.
    In the Boston Public Library.

AMERICAN PHILOSOPHICAL SOCIETY. Transactions . . . 2d ed. corr. Philadelphia: Printed by R. Aitken & Son, at Pope's Head in Market-Street, 1789.
    In the John Carter Brown Library.

BARLOW, JOEL. The Columbiad, a Poem. Philadelphia: Printed by Fry & Kammerer for C. and A. Conrad and Co. . . . 1807.
    In the Chapin Library. Binder's ticket: 'Bound by R. De Silver, No. 110 Walnut Street, Philada.'

BIBLE. ENGLISH. The Holy Bible Containing the Old and New Testaments; Newly translated out of the Original Tongues. . . . Philadelphia: Printed and Sold by R. Aitken . . . 1782.
    Copies in the John Carter Brown Library, the Library of Congress, the New York Public Library.

BIBLE. ENGLISH. The Holy Bible. Trenton, N. J.: Printed and sold by Isaac Collins, 1791.
    Copies in the American Type Founders' Library, and in the Library of Congress. Binder's ticket: 'Craig & Lea, Stationers & Bookbinders, Wilmington, Delaware.'

BIBLE. ENGLISH. The Holy Bible. . . . with the Apocrypha. . . . Worcester: Isaiah Thomas, 1791. 2 vols.
    In the American Antiquarian Society.

BIBLE. ENGLISH. The Self-Interpreting Bible . . . to which are annexed Marginal References . . . by the late Reverend John Brown. . . . New York: Printed for T. Allen, and sold at his Book and Stationary Store, 1792.
    In the Henry E. Huntington Library. Binder's ticket: 'Bound and Sold by Thomas Allen, No. 12, Queen Street, New-York.'

BIBLE. GERMAN. Biblia. Das ist: Die Heilige Schrift Altes und Neues Testaments. . . . Germantown: Gedruckt bey Christoph Sauer, 1743. 1st ed. 1763. 2d ed.
> Biblia. Das ist: Die ganze Göttliche Heilige Schrift. 1776. 3d ed.
> In The Grolier Club Library.

BIBLE, INDIAN. The Holy Bible: Containing the Old Testament and the New. Translated into the Indian Language. . . [by John Eliot]. Cambridge: Printed by Samuel Green and Marmaduke Johnson, 1663.
> Copies owned by J. K. Lilly, Jr. and the Harvard College Library.

BIBLE. O. T. PSALMS. A New Version of the Psalms of David. Fitted to the Tunes Used in Churches. By N. Brady, D.D. Chaplain in Ordinary, & N. Tate, Esq; Poet-Laureat, to her Majesty. Boston, N. E.: Printed by J. Kneeland, and S. Adams, in Milk-Street for Thomas Leverett, in Cornhill, 1765.
> Two bindings in the New York Public Library.

BIBLE. O. T. PSALMS. A New Version of the Psalms of David. Boston: Printed by D. Kneeland, for J. Eliot, at the Tree of Liberty, 1766.
> In the New York Public Library. Binder's ticket: 'Books Bound and sold Gilt or plain by Andrew Barclay, next door but one North of the three Kings in Cornhill Boston.'

BIBLE. O. T. PSALMS. A New Version of the Psalms. . . . Boston: Printed for Nicholas Bower, 1774.
> In the American Antiquarian Society.

BIBLE. O. T. PSALMS. The Psalms. Boston: Printed for J. Phillips at the Stationer's Arms, next door to Mr. Polbiers near the Dock, 1729.
> In the Library of Congress.

BIBLE. O. T. PSALMS. Psalms carefully suited to the Christian Worship in the United States of America. . . . Hudson: Printed for William E. Norman, by Harry Croswell, 1805.
> In the Henry E. Huntington Library. Binder's ticket: 'Bound at Parson's Bindery.'

BIBLE. O. T. PSALMS. A Version of the Book of Psalms. . . . Charleston: Printed by J. MacIver, 1796.
> In the Library of Congress. Binder's ticket: 'David Bailey, Book-binder, from London.'

BIBLE. O. T. PSALMS. Bay Psalm Book. The Psalms, Hymns and Spiritual Songs of the Old and New Testament. . . . Printed by Samuel Green at Cambridg in New-England, 1651.
> In the New York Public Library. Bound by John Ratcliff.

BIELBY, LORD BISHOP OF LONDON. A Summary of the Principal Evidences for the Truth and Divine Origins of the Christian Revelation. 3d ed. Charlestown: Pr. by Samuel Etheridge in Charlestown, for E. and S. Larkin, No. 47 Cornhill, Boston, 1800.
> In the American Antiquarian Society.

BLACKWELL, THOMAS. Forma Sacra; or a Sacred Platform of Natural and Revealed Religion. . . . Boston: Pr. & sold by William M'Alpine at his Printing-Office in Marlborough-Street. 1774.

In the New York Public Library. Advertisement at back: 'At the Shop of William M'Alpine, May be had by the Quantity or single, Tate and Brady's Psalms, Watt's Psalms and Hymns, Spelling-Books, Psalters Primers, &c. — Account Books of different Sizes, with a Number of other Books in Divinity, History, &c. N. B. As the above Books are mostly printed and bound by said M'Alpine, he is determined to sell at the lowest Prices, and will warrant all such to be neatly bound, &c.'

BLAIR, HUGH. Lectures on Rhetoric and Belles Lettres. Philadelphia: Printed and Sold by Robert Aitken at Pope's Head in Market Street, 1784.

Owned by Dr. Samuel Woodhouse.

BOSTON. SYNOD, 1680. A Confession of Faith owned and consented unto by the Elders and Messengers of the Churches assembled at Boston in New England. May 12, 1680. Being the Second Session of that Synod [by Increase Mather]. Boston: Printed by John Foster, 1680.

Copies in the libraries of the Connecticut Historical Society, and of its Librarian, Albert C. Bates. Bound by John Ratcliff. A third copy in the Boston Public Library.

BUCKMINSTER, JOSEPH STEVENS. Sermons. . . . Boston: Printed by John Eliot, No. 5, Court Street, 1814.

In the Henry E. Huntington Library.

The Christian's Duty. . . . Germantown: Printed by Peter Liebert and Son, 1791.

In the Library of Congress.

CICERO, MARCUS TULLIUS. M. T. Cicero's Cato Major, or his Discourse of Old-Age: With Explanatory Notes. Philadelphia: Printed & Sold by B. Franklin, 1744.

In the American Antiquarian Society.

COLDEN, CADWALLADER DAVID. Memoirs, prepared at the Request of a Committee of the Common Council of the City of New York, and presented to the Mayor of the City, at the Celebration of the Completion of the New York Canals. . . . Printed by Order of the Corporation of New York, by W. A. Davis. 1825.

Copies owned by Philip Hofer and the New York Public Library. Signed on the spine: Wilson & Nichols.

CONNECTICUT. LAWS. The Book of the General Laws for the People within the Jurisdiction of Connecticut. . . . 1672. Cambridge: Printed by Samuel Green, 1673.

In the Connecticut Historical Society. Bound by John Ratcliff.

Federalist: A Collection of Essays, written in Favour of the New Constitution, as agreed upon by the Federal Convention. September 17, 1787. New York: J. & A. M'Lean. 1788. 2 vols.

In the New York Public Library. Ticket: 'Printed and bound at Franklin's Head, no. 41 Hanover Square.'

GOLDSMITH, OLIVER. The Vicar of Wakefield, n. t. p.
In The Grolier Club Library. Binder's ticket: 'G. Champley, Fancy Binder, 61 Barclay-St., New York.'

HARRIS, THADDEUS MASON. Hymns for the Lord's Supper. . . . Boston: Printed by Sewell Phelps, No. 5 Court Street, 1820.
In the Henry E. Huntington Library.

HOLLINGWORTH, LEVI. Ship Freight Book. n. t. p.
In the Historical Society of Pennsylvania. Binder's ticket: 'Benjⁿ. January, Stationer & bookbinder in Water street, a few Doors below the Drawbridge . . . Philadelph; Where all Sorts of Account Books are Made Ruled to any Pattern. He likewise sells all Sorts of Stationary Wares at the Lowest Rates.'

HORSMANDEN, DAVID. A Journal of the Proceedings in the Detection of the Conspiracy formed by Some White People, in Conjunction with Negro and other Slaves, for Burning the City of New-York in America, and Murdering the Inhabitants. . . . New York: Printed by James Parker at the New Printing-Office, 1774.
In the Library of Congress.

HUBBARD, WILLIAM. A Narrative of the Troubles with the Indians in New-England. . . . Boston: Printed by John Foster, in the year 1677.
Copies owned by Carroll A. Wilson, A. S. W. Rosenbach, the American Antiquarian Society and the John Carter Brown Library. Bound by John Ratcliff.

HUMPHREYS, DAVID. The Miscellaneous Works of Colonel Humphreys. New-York: Printed by Hodge, Allen and Campbell, 1790.
In the Boston Athenaeum.

Institutio Graecae Grammatices Compendaria in Usum Regiae Scholae Westmonasteriensis. London, Roger Norton. 1656.
In the Boston Public Library.

LANGHORNE, JOHN. The Correspondence of Theodosius and Constantia. . . . London: Printed for Walker and Edwards . . . 1817.
In The Grolier Club Library. Binder's ticket: 'G. Champley, Fancy Binder, 61 Barclay-street, New York.'

MASSACHUSETTS BAY COLONY. The Book of the General Lawes and Libertyes Concerning the Inhabitants of the Massachusetts. . . . May, 1649. Cambridge. Printed [by Samuel Green]. According to Order of the General Court . . . 1660.
In the American Antiquarian Society. Bound by John Ratcliff.

MASSACHUSETTS BAY COLONY. The General Laws and Liberties of the Massachusetts Colony: Revised & reprinted. By Order of the General Court Holden at Boston, May 15th, 1672. Cambridge: Printed by Samuel Green, for John Usher of Boston. 1672.
In the American Antiquarian Society. Bound by John Ratcliff.

MATHER, INCREASE. A Call from Heaven. To the Present and Succeeding Generations. Boston: Printed by John Foster, 1679.
In the Mather Collection of the Alderman Library, University of Virginia. Bound by John Ratcliff.

MATHER, INCREASE. A Collection of Tracts, 1670-1680.
 In the Mather Collection of the Alderman Library, University of Virginia. Bound by John Ratcliff.

MATHER, INCREASE. Practical Truths Tending to Promote the Power of Godliness. Boston in New England: Printed by Samuel Green upon assignment of Samuel Sewall, 1682.
 Copies in the New York Public Library and the Mather Collection of the Alderman Library, University of Virginia. Bound by Edmund Ranger. Another copy in the Connecticut Historical Society. Bound by John Ratcliff.

MELLEN, JOHN. Fifteen Discourses upon Doctrinal Connected Subjects, with Practical Improvements. . . . Boston: N. E. Printed and sold by Edes and Gill, in Queen Street, 1765.
 In the Massachusetts Historical Society. Binder's ticket: Andrew Barclay.

NEW YORK. PROVINCE. Votes and Proceedings of the General Assembly of the Colony of New-York. [New York] William Weyman, printer [1764].
 Copies in the Collections of L. C. Karpinski, The Grolier Club, the New York Historical Society, and the John Carter Brown Library. Inscribed: Bound by Robert McAlpine.

NEW YORK. STATE. Transactions of the Society Instituted in the State of New York, for the Promotion of Agriculture, Arts, and Manufactures. New York: Printed by Childs & Swaine, 1792.
 In the Boston Athenaeum.

The Order for Morning and Evening Prayer . . . [in Mohawk]. The Third Edition. . . . For the Six Nation Indians in the Province of Quebec. Printed in the year 1780.
 In the John Carter Brown Library.

PETYT, GEORGE. Lex Parliamentaria; or, A Treatise of the Law and Custom of the Parliaments of England. By C. P. Esq. London: Printed and Reprinted in New-York and sold by William and Andrew Bradford in New-York and Philadelphia, 1716.
 Owned by the Rosenbach Company of Philadelphia.

PHILADELPHIA SOCIETY FOR PROMOTING AGRICULTURE. Memoirs. . . . Philadelphia, Jane Aitken, 1808. Vol. 1.
 In the Ridgway Branch of the Library Company of Philadelphia.

PROTESTANT EPISCOPAL CHURCH IN THE UNITED STATES OF AMERICA. The Book of Common Prayer. . . . As revised and proposed to the Use of the Protestant Episcopal Church. Philadelphia: Printed by Hall and Sellers, and sold for the benefit of sundry Corporations and Societies, instituted for the support of the widows and children of deceased clergymen, 1786.
 Copies in the John Carter Brown Library, and in the Library of Congress.

PROTESTANT EPISCOPAL CHURCH IN THE UNITED STATES OF AMERICA. The Book of Common Prayer. . . . New York: Printed by Hugh Gaine, by direction of the General Convention at the Bible, Hanover-Square, 1793.
 In the Henry E. Huntington Library.

PROTESTANT EPISCOPAL CHURCH IN THE UNITED STATES OF AMERICA. The Book of Common Prayer. . . . Boston: Printed by Manning and Loring, for I. Thomas and E. T. Andrews, Faust's Statue, No. 45 Newbury-Street, 1794. In the American Antiquarian Society.

PROTESTANT EPISCOPAL CHURCH IN THE UNITED STATES OF AMERICA. The Book of Common Prayer. New York: Hugh Gaine, 1795.
Copies in the Pierpont Morgan Library, and in the William L. Clements Library. Signed binding: 'Roulstone, J. Binder, Boston.'

PROTESTANT EPISCOPAL CHURCH IN THE UNITED STATES OF AMERICA. Book of Common Prayer. New York: Printed and sold by T. & J. Swords, No. 160 Pearl St., 1810.
In The Grolier Club Library. Binder's ticket: 'William Seymour, Fancy Blank Book Binder, Albany.'

PROTESTANT EPISCOPAL CHURCH IN THE UNITED STATES OF AMERICA. The Book of Common Prayer. New York: Henry I. Megarey, 1820.
In the American Antiquarian Society.

[PUGLIA, JAMES PH.]. The Complete Disappointment, or a Touch at Modern Times: a Comedy in Three Acts, written by Me, Author of the Embargo, &c. Philadelphia: Printed for the Amateurs By . . . 1789.
In Harvard College Library.

[PUGLIA, JAMES PH.]. The Embargo, a Comedy in Three Acts written by Me, Author of &c., &c., &c., &c., &c., &c.
Philadelphia: Printed for the Amateurs By . . . 1788.
In Harvard College Library.

REFORMED CHURCH IN THE UNITED STATES. Neu-vermehrt-und vollständiges Gesang-Buch. Worinnen sowohl die Psalmen Davids. . . . Philadelphia: zu finden bey Ernst Ludwig Baisch, in der Szey-Strasse, nahe bey der Rees-Strasse, 1774.
Copies owned by Dr. A. S. W. Rosenbach, Cornelius Weygandt, the Historical Society of Pennsylvania, and the Library of Congress.

ROWE, ELIZABETH. Devout Exercises of the Heart. . . . New York: Tiebout & O'Brien for E. Mitchell at 9 Maiden-Lane, [n.d.]
In the William L. Clements Library.

SCOTT, SIR WALTER. Lord of the Isles. New York: Published by J. Eastburn & Co. Literary Rooms, Broadway, 1818.
Owned by the Rosenbach Company of Philadelphia.

SEWALL, SAMUEL. Commonplace Book.
In the Massachusetts Historical Society. Inscribed: 'Samuel Sewall, his Booke, Decemb. 29, 1677. Bound by Jno. Ratcliff.'

SEWALL, SAMUEL. Notebook.
In the Boston Public Library. Inscribed: 'Decemb. 22, 1677. Bound by John Ratcliff. This together with my clasped Book in quarto cost 18d fr Binding.'

———— Volume 5.
In the Boston Bublic Library. Inscribed: 'Bound by Samuel Sewall, Septr 30, 1697.'

SEWALL, SAMUEL. [Sermon Notebook.]
In the Boston Public Library. Bound by Edmund Ranger.

SEWARD, ANNA. Memoirs of the Life of Dr. Darwin. Philadelphia: At the Classic Press, for the Proprietors. Wm. Poyntell, & Co. 1804.
In The Grolier Club Library.

TILLOTSON, JOHN. Sermons Preached upon Several Occasions. 5th ed. corr. London: Printed for Ed. Gellibrand, at the Golden Ball in St. Paul's Churchyard, 1681.
In the American Antiquarian Society. Binder's ticket: 'Books Bound and sold Gilt or plain by Andrew Barclay, next door but one North of the three Kings in Cornhill Boston.'

TYLER, ROYALL. The Contrast, a Comedy; in five Acts: written by a Citizen of the United States: Performed with Applause at the Theatres in New-York, Philadelphia, and Maryland; and published under an Assignment of the Copy-Right by Thomas Wignell. . . . Philadelphia: From the Press of Prichard & Hall in Market Street, between Second and Front Streets, 1790.
Owned by Mr. Hall P. McCullough.

[A Volume of Pamphlets from the Mather Collection. No. 703.]
In the American Antiquarian Society. Bound by John Ratcliff.

[A Volume of Pamphlets from the Mather Collection. No. 787. Another Volume, No. 838.]
In the American Antiquarian Society. Bound by Edmund Ranger.

[A Volume of Tracts, 1657-1681. Church Catalogue No. 551.]
In the Henry E. Huntington Library.

WASHINGTON, GEORGE. A Collection of the Speeches of the President of the United States to both Houses of Congress, at the opening of every Session, with their Answers. . . . Printed at Boston, by Manning and Loring for Solomon Cotton, jun. Bookseller and Stationer, Sold by him, at his Bookstore, No. 51, Marlborough-Street, July, 1796.
In the Boston Athenaeum.

WASHINGTON, GEORGE. Washington's Political Legacies. To which is annexed, an Appendix, containing an account of his illness, death, and the national tributes of respect paid to his memory, with a Biographical Outline of his Life and Character. Boston: Printed for John Russell and John West, 1800.
In the Boston Public Library.

WATTS, ISAAC. Hymns and Spiritual Songs. Edinburgh, 1778.
Owned by Mrs. Harry MacNeill Bland.

WILLARD, SAMUEL. A Compleat Body of Divinity. . . . Boston in New England: Printed by B. Green and S. Kneeland for B. Eliot and D. Henchman and sold at their shops, 1726.
Copies in the Boston Public Library and Columbia University Library.

WILLARD, SAMUEL. Covenant Keeping. The Way to Blessedness. . . . Boston in New England: Printed by James Glen, for Samuel Sewall, 1682.
Copies in the Connecticut Historical Society and the Massachusetts Historical Society. Bound by Edmund Ranger.

WILLARD, SAMUEL. The Just Man's Prerogative, a Sermon Preached Privately, Sept. 27, 1706. On a Solemn Occasion: For the Consolation of a Sorrowful Family, Mourning Over the Immature DEATH of a Pious SON, viz. Mr. Simeon Stoddard, who was Found Barberously Murdered in Chelsea-Fields near London May 14, 1706 . . . Boston, N. E.: Printed by B. Green, and Sold by Nicholas Boone at his Shop, 1706.
In the Massachusetts Historical Society.

WILLIAM AND MARY COLLEGE, WILLIAMSBURG, VIRGINIA. The Charter and Statutes of the College of William and Mary in Virginia. In Latin and English. Wiliamsburg: Printed by William Parks, 1736.
Copies in the Library of the College of William and Mary, and in the John Carter Brown Library.

## Ownership and Location of Extant Bindings

### *Owned by Individuals*

ALBERT C. BATES, Hartford, Connecticut.
Boston. Synod, 1680. A Confession of Faith. . . .

MRS. HARRY MACNEILL BLAND, New York, New York.
Watts. Hymns and Spiritual Songs.

PHILIP HOFER, Cambridge, Massachusetts.
Colden. Memoirs.

LOUIS C. KARPINSKI, Ann Arbor, Michigan.
New York. Province. Votes and Proceedings. . . .

J. K. LILLY, JR. Indianapolis, Indiana.
Bible. Indian. The Holy Bible.

HALL P. McCULLOUGH, North Bennington, Vermont.
Tyler. The Contrast.

A. S. W. ROSENBACH, Philadelphia, Pennsylvania.
Hubbard. A Narrative of the Troubles with the Indians in New-England. . . .
Reformed Church in the United States. Neu-vermehrt-und vollständiges Gesang-Buch.

THE ROSENBACH COMPANY OF PHILADELPHIA.
Petyt. Lex Parliamentaria.
Scott. Lord of the Isles.

CORNELIUS WEYGANDT, Philadelphia, Pennsylvania.
Reformed Church in the United States. Neu-vermehrt-und vollständiges Gesang-Buch.

CARROLL A. WILSON, New York, New York.
Hubbard. A Narrative of the Troubles with the Indians in New-England. . . .

SAMUEL WOODHOUSE, Philadelphia, Pennsylvania.
Blair. Lectures on Rhetoric and Belles Lettres.

## Owned by Libraries

ALDERMAN LIBRARY, UNIVERSITY OF VIRGINIA. Charlottesville, Virginia.
  Mather. A Call from Heaven.
  Mather. A Collection of Tracts.
  Mather. Practical Truths.

AMERICAN ANTIQUARIAN SOCIETY. Worcester, Massachusetts.
  Bible. English. The Holy Bible . . . . 1791.
  Bible. O. T. Psalms. A New Version of the Psalms. . . . 1774.
  Bielby. A Summary of the Principal Evidences. . . .
  Cicero. Cato Major.
  Hubbard. A Narrative of the Troubles with the Indians in New-England. . . .
  Massachusetts Bay Colony. The Book of the General Lawes. . . . 1649.
  Massachusetts Bay Colony. The General Laws. . . . 1672.
  Protestant Episcopal Church in the United States. The Book of Common Prayer. 1794.
  Protestant Episcopal Church in the United States. The Book of Common Prayer. 1820.
  Tillotson. Sermons Preached upon Several Occasions.
  Volume of Pamphlets from the Mather Collection. No. 703.
  Volume of Pamphlets from the Mather Collection. No. 787.
  Volume of Pamphlets from the Mather Collection. No. 838.

AMERICAN TYPE FOUNDERS' LIBRARY. Columbia University. New York, New York.
  Bible. English. The Holy Bible. 1791.

BOSTON ATHENAEUM. Boston, Massachusetts.
  Humphreys. Miscellaneous Works.
  New York. State. Transactions of the Society . . . for the Promotion of Agriculture, Arts, and Manufactures.
  Washington. Collection of Speeches.

BOSTON PUBLIC LIBRARY. Boston, Massachusetts.
  Alleine. Heaven Opened.
  Boston. Synod, 1680. Confession of Faith.
  Institutio Graecae Grammatices Compendaria.
  Sewall. Notebook.
  Sewall. Sermon Notebook.
  Washington. Political Legacies.
  Willard. Compleat Body of Divinity.

CHAPIN LIBRARY. Williams College. Williamstown, Massachusetts.
  Barlow. The Columbiad.

COLUMBIA UNIVERSITY LIBRARY. New York, New York.
  Willard. Compleat Body of Divinity.

CONNECTICUT HISTORICAL SOCIETY.
  Boston. Synod, 1680. Confession of Faith.
  Connecticut. Laws. Book of the General Laws. . . . 1672.
  Mather. Practical Truths.
  Willard. Covenant Keeping.

GROLIER CLUB LIBRARY. New York, New York.
  Bible. German. Biblia. . . . 1743.
  Bible. German. Biblia. . . . 1763.
  Bible. German. Biblia. . . . 1776.
  Goldsmith. Vicar of Wakefield.
  Langhorne. Correspondence of Theodosius and Constantia.
  New York. Province. Votes and Proceedings.
  Protestant Episcopal Church in the United States. Book of Common
    Prayer. 1810.
  Seward. Memoirs of the Life of Dr. Darwin.

HARVARD COLLEGE LIBRARY. Cambridge, Massachusetts.
  Bible. Indian. The Holy Bible.
  [Puglia.] The Complete Disappointment.
  [Puglia.] The Embargo.

HENRY E. HUNTINGTON LIBRARY. San Marino, California.
  Bible. English. Self-Interpreting Bible. 1792.
  Bible. O. T. Psalms. Psalms. 1805.
  Buckminster. Sermons.
  Harris. Hymns for the Lord's Supper.
  Protestant Episcopal Church in the United States. Book of Common
    Prayer. 1793.
  A Volume of Tracts, 1657-1681.

HISTORICAL SOCIETY OF PENNSYLVANIA. Philadelphia, Pennsylvania.
  Hollingworth. Ship Freight Book.
  Reformed Church in the United States. Neu-vermehrt-und vollstän-
    diges Gesang-Buch.

JOHN CARTER BROWN LIBRARY. Providence, Rhode Island.
  American Philosophical Society. Transactions.
  Bible. English. The Holy Bible. 1782.
  Hubbard. A Narrative of the Troubles with the Indians in New-Eng-
    land. . . .
  New York. Province. Votes and Proceedings.
  Order for Morning and Evening Prayer. 1780.
  Protestant Episcopal Church in the United States. Book of Common
    Prayer. 1786.
  William and Mary College. Charter and Statutes.

LIBRARY COMPANY OF PHILADELPHIA, RIDGEWAY BRANCH. Philadelphia, Penn-
    sylvania.
  Philadelphia Society for Promoting Agriculture. Memoirs. Volume I.

LIBRARY OF CONGRESS. Washington, D. C.
  Bible. English. Holy Bible. 1782.
  Bible. English. Holy Bible. 1791.
  Bible. O. T. Psalms. Psalms. 1729.
  Bible. O. T. Psalms. Psalms. 1796.
  Christian's Duty.
  Horsmanden. Journal of the Proceedings. . . .
  Protestant Episcopal Church in the United States. Book of Common
    Prayer. 1786.

Reformed Church in the United States. Neu-vermehrt-und vollständiges Gesang-Buch.

MASSACHUSETTS HISTORICAL SOCIETY. Boston, Massachusetts.
Mellen. Fifteen Discourses.
Sewall. Commonplace Book.
Willard. Covenant Keeping.
Willard. The Just Man's Prerogative.

NEW YORK HISTORICAL SOCIETY. New York, New York.
New York. Province. Votes and Proceedings.

NEW YORK PUBLIC LIBRARY. New York, New York.
Bible. English. Holy Bible. 1782.
Bible. O. T. Psalms. Bay Psalm Book. 1651.
Bible. O. T. Psalms. New Version of the Psalms. 1765.
Bible. O. T. Psalms. New Version of the Psalms. 1766.
Blackwell. Forma Sacra.
Colden. Memoirs.
Federalist.
Mather. Practical Truths.

PIERPONT MORGAN LIBRARY. New York, New York.
Protestant Episcopal Church in the United States. Book of Common
Prayer. 1795.

WILLIAM L. CLEMENTS LIBRARY. Ann Arbor, Michigan.
Protestant Episcopal Church in the United States. Book of Common
Prayer. 1795.
Rowe. Devout Exercises of the Heart.

WILLIAM AND MARY COLLEGE LIBRARY. Williamsburg, Virginia.
William and Mary College. Charter and Statutes.

*PART II*

# The Rise of American Edition Binding

*By JOSEPH W. ROGERS*

# The Rise of American Edition Binding

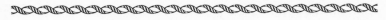

## CHAPTER I

## *INTRODUCTION*

THE literature of bookbinding has never disclosed the well-ordered steps by which modern edition bookbinding, particularly as it is found in America, emerged and became distinct from its parent craft — hand bookbinding. On the one hand, authors dealing with the art of bookbinding have seldom deigned even to notice its mechanical offspring. The literature of machine bookbinding, on the other hand, is virtually non-existent; that which does exist is preoccupied with mechanical and technical details. When I first undertook the task of studying the origin and development of publishers' bookbinding in this country, there had been no attempt whatsoever to trace this evolution here or elsewhere. It was after I had completed the bulk of my research that Douglas Leighton's lecture on modern bookbinding was published. This book, I found, duplicated much of the material on the English origin of publishers' bookbinding that I had already collected. However, since Mr. Leighton was primarily concerned with the English phase of the problem, my material on the American aspects remains valid and is still, I feel, a distinct contribution to the subject. In this study, therefore, I not only chronicle the replacement during the nineteenth century of hand-bookbinding processes by machines, particularly those of American origin, but also offer an explanation of the movements responsible for the first development of edition bookbinding as an industry distinct from the craft of hand bookbinding.

Needless to say, the inventors of the nineteenth century required the solid, fundamental methods of the seventeenth-

and eighteenth-century craftsmen on which to build. The productions described by Miss French in the preceding section of this volume, the product of men employing age-old methods revised from time to time as external conditions demanded, formed a necessary point of departure for the innovations to come.

The progression of modern machine binding from hand binding followed a course which may be divided into four reasonably distinct phases. In the first phase we find bookbinders performing all their processes with hand-manipulated tools. Next we find bookbinders, under the pressure exerted by the increased speed of printing machines, seeking methods of simplifying and speeding up their processes while still being forced to work largely with tools. Our third stage is that in which machines are progressively introduced to handle certain of the manipulations while the balance of the processes are still done by hand. The last phase is that in which the great majority of the bookbinding processes are performed by machine, a phase which marks the complete breaking away of the great modern industry from the parent craft of hand bookbinding.

It is impossible to consider bookbinding as an independent industry. Its very existence, and the nature of its existence, is dependent upon the printing industries. Coming logically, as it does, at the end of the series of processes through which a book must go to reach publication, it is an essential feature of book production. This is particularly true in England and America, where the continental style of the paper-bound book has never found lasting favor. The modern edition binding is essentially a more or less permanent yet inexpensive substitute for the permanent but expensive hand binding. It is characterized by the mechanical nature of its production and by the fact that its cost is merely one of a number of costs assumed by the publisher, rather than a cost to be assumed and determined by the individual book buyer.

To realize fully the impetus that gave rise to edition bookbinding, it may be well to review briefly some of the significant developments that preceded it. After centuries of use, the old wooden hand printing press had been to a large extent replaced by the iron hand press, the first of which was introduced by the third Earl Stanhope in 1798. There followed improved models, notably those of the Americans George Clymer (1816) and Samuel Rust (1827). Dr. William Church of Vermont also produced an iron hand press, patented in England about 1821, which, with the addition of ink rollers, brought the hand press, in theory at least, to its highest degree of perfection. Other evolutionary processes, assisted by the discovery of the glue and molasses ink roller by Benjamin Foster in 1813, led to the successful completion of the cylinder press in the following year by Friedrich König of Saxony. The Fourdrinier paper-making machine was perfected by Louis Robert and Leger St. Didot in France in 1799, was brought to England in 1804, and to the United States in 1827. Stereotype plates made with plaster matrices, a process invented by William Ged of Edinburgh, were early introduced to the printing world by the third Earl Stanhope after 1802 and in the United States between 1811 and 1813. They were followed by the curved plates made with papier-mâché matrices developed by M. Genoud in France in 1829, which made possible the modern rotary press. The first important invention of a composing machine—that of Dr. William Church—was patented in England in 1822. These far-reaching inventions in printing and paper-making equipment, occurring primarily in the few years between 1798 and 1830, were inventions that greatly increased the speed of production in the printing industry.

A new day was dawning, too, in the field of publishing. The first four decades of the nineteenth century saw the founding of many great publishing houses that have lasted to the present day, among them Lippincott in Philadelphia,

Putnam, Appleton, and Harper in New York, and Little, Brown and Houghton Mifflin in Boston. The rapid growth of population and the zealous work of the proponents of popular education were creating a reading public which hundreds of small publishers were ill-equipped to supply. Native American authors at last had a potential American audience which held promise of sufficient remuneration to make authorship a self-sustaining if not lucrative profession. Publishers far-sighted enough to take advantage of the new mechanical improvements found ready markets for their vastly increased production and thereby set their firms on solid financial foundations that have endured to this day. The situation in the printing and publishing fields was one of flux and change, the future course of which was to be largely determined by the nature and variety of the inventions of the nineteenth century. It was imperative that so essential a part of the bookmaking process as bookbinding be speeded up to keep pace with the revolutionary developments taking place in related trades.

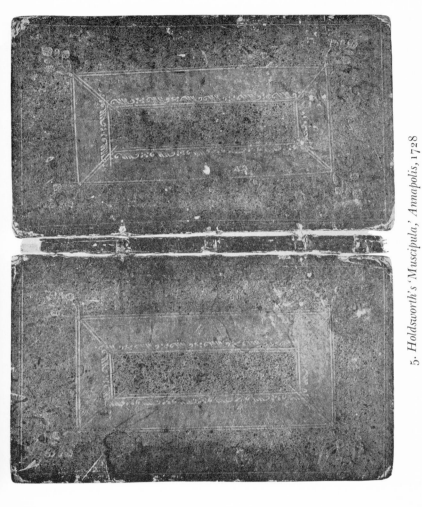

5. Holdsworth's 'Muscipula,' Annapolis, 1728

6. *Cicero's 'Cato Major,' Philadelphia,* 1744

7. 'Lex Parliamentaria,' New York and Philadelphia, 1716

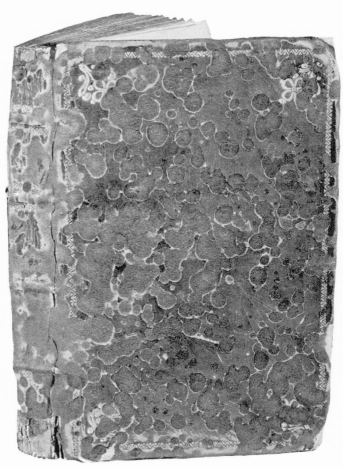

8. *Mather's 'Practical Truths,' Boston,* 1682

9. Mather's 'Call from Heaven,' Boston, 1679

10. *Horsmanden's 'Journal,' New York,* 1744

11. *Gesang-Buch, Philadelphia,* 1774

Books Bound and Sold, Gilt or plain, by Andrew Barclay, Next Door but one to the sign of the Three KINGS in Cornhill, BOSTON

Books Bound and Sold, Gilt or Plain by Andrew Barclay, next Door but one to the three KINGS, in Cornhill Boston

Samuel Taylor
BOOK-BINDER & STATIONER,
the Corner of Market & Water Street
PHILADELPHIA.
Binds all sorts of Books, in the Neatest
Manner, Gilt or plain, as new Practised
in England &c. where Merchants
and others may have all sorts of
Account Books made and Ruled
to any Pattern at the Lowest Prices.
He likewise Sells Bibles Common
Prayer Books, Spelling Books, Shop
Books, Pocket Books, Writing Paper,
Sealing Wax Wafers, Pens, Pencils,
and most other sorts of Stationary
Wares, also all sorts of Ink &c.

14. *'The Psalms,' Boston,* 1729

15. 'The Christian's Duty', Germantown, 1791

16. '*The Book of Common Prayer,*' *Philadelphia,* 1786

17. *'The Order for Morning and Evening Prayer'*
*(In Mohawk), (Quebec)* 1780

18. *Aitken's 'Bible', Philadelphia,* 1782

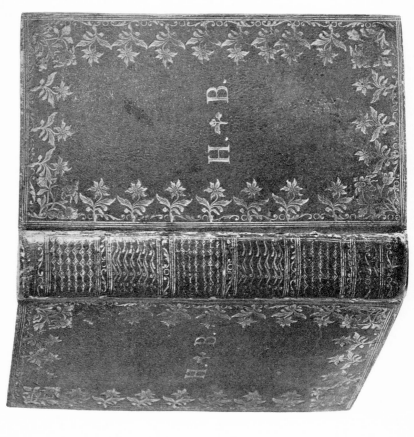

19. *Watts's 'Hymns and Spiritual Songs,' Edinburgh, 1778*

20. *Humphreys' 'Miscellaneous Works, New York,* 1790

21. 'A Collection of the Speeches of the President
of the United States,' Boston, 1796

22. 'Transactions of the Society Instituted in the State of New York, for the
Promotion of Agriculture, Arts, and Manufactures,' New York, 1792

23. Langhorne's 'Correspondence of Theodosius and Constantia,' London, 1817

24. 'Washington's Political Legacies,' Boston, 1800

## Bookbinder's Tools & Stock

| | | |
|---|---|---|
| 2 Standing Presses | 50.00. | |
| 1 New Cutting Press | 4.00 | |
| 2 good — do | 8.00 | |
| 2 old do | 3.00 | |
| 1 pr Screws for Sewing bench | 0.50 | |
| × 4 bundles Narrow Slabb? | 1.00. | |
| 23 do. Maple do for Childs. books | 7.66⅔ | |
| 1 Binder's Plough, new | 1.00 | |
| 1 sett Lettering tools 4to | 6.00 | |
| 1 do do do 8vo | 5.00 | |
| 1 do. do. do 12mo | 5.00 | 91. 16⅔ |
| × 1 pr Bookbinders Shears | 2.00 | |
| × parcel broken Pasteboard | 0.50. | |
| 1 sett New Lettering tools 8vo | 5.00. | |
| 6 stamps Large Apartment of Stamps, flowers &c | 25.00 | |
| 6 Rollers for Lettering tools | 4.50 | |
| × 2 bundles Slabboard | 0.10 | |
| × 200 pos Large Clasps | 4.00 | |
| 2 Large Ivory polishers | 1.00. | |
| Sponge | 0.20. | |
| × 1 Hand press Small | 0.75 | 43. 5 |
| 6 Boles | 4.00. | |
| 2 Polishers | 0.75. | |
| 3 Sewing benches | 2.25 | |
| 4 Gold Cushion &c | 1.00 | |
| 1 Beating hammer | 1.00 | |
| 1 Backing do. | 0.20. | |
| 6 Pallats | 2.00 | |
| 34 Gilding Tools | 30.00 | |
| 2 Press Pins | 0.75. | |
| 2 Iron bars | Dr 2.00 | 43.95 |
| 14 Folio boards | 2.00 | |
| 22 4to do | 2.50. | |
| 16 8vo do | 1.00 | |
| 4 Seats | 1.00 | |
| 1 Paring knife | 0.12½ | |
| 2 pr Dividers | 0.33⅓ | |
| × one pr Shears Large | 5.00. | |
| 2 pr Small do | 0.33⅓ | |
| 1 Saw | 0.50. | 11. 90 |
| 2 Letter Cases | 2.50 | |
| 1½ doz. 12mo Horns | 0.75 | |
| 1 pr Iron backing boards | 1.00 | |
| 1 sett Lettering tools 12mo old | 1.25 | |
| 1 do Do. do. 4to old | 1.50. | |
| 1 Iron Stand frame, Iron pan for gilding | 2.00. | |
| 1 sett Lettering Tools Old 8vo | 1.00 | |
| 6 Pallats | 1.50. | |
| 1 sett Folio Letter & 2 sts figures | 2.00 | 14. 33 |
| | | $ 204.4 |

25. *Isaiah Thomas's Account of Stock, April, 1796*

26. 'The Book of Common Prayer,' New York, 1795

28. *Brady & Tate's 'New Version of the Psalms,'*
*Boston,* 1774

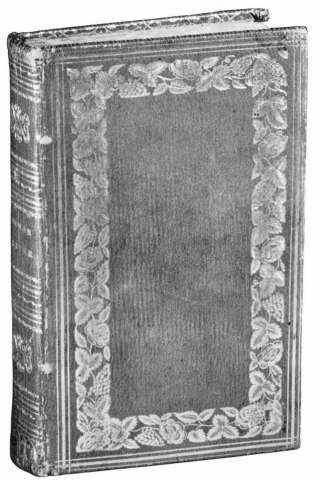

29. 'The Book of Common Prayer,' New York, 1820

(Plate Nos. 30-40)

*The following Plates illustrate typical book Cloth Finishes found on American Edition Bindings in the approximate order of their appearance. The bindings shown are reproduced through the courtesy of the New York Public Library and with their permission.*

30. *Morocco or imitation leather pattern.*
*Taylor's 'District School,'* 1834

31. *Watered pattern. Shepard's 'Autobiography,'* 1832

32. *Diaper pattern. Reed's 'Six Months in a Convent,'* 1835

*33. Ribbon-embossed pattern.*
'*The Christian's Defensive Dictionary,*' 1837

34. *Bold ribbed pattern. 'Life of Columbus,'* 1839

35. *Fine ribbed pattern. Carlyle's 'French Revolution,'* 1841
*Note name of binder on broad blind-stamped band at top*

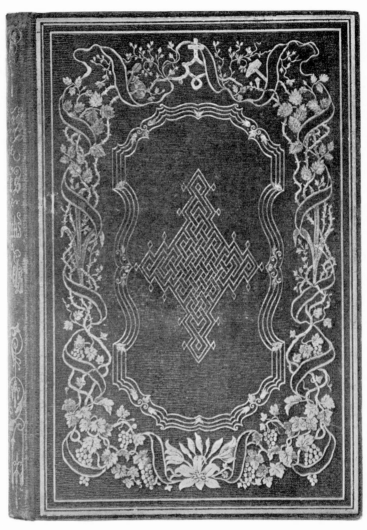

36. *Ripple grain pattern. 'Scenes in the
Lives of the Patriarchs and the Prophets,'* 1846

37. *Close bead grain pattern. 'The New Priest,'* 1858

38. *Wave grain pattern. 'Mother Goose for Grown Folks,'* 1860

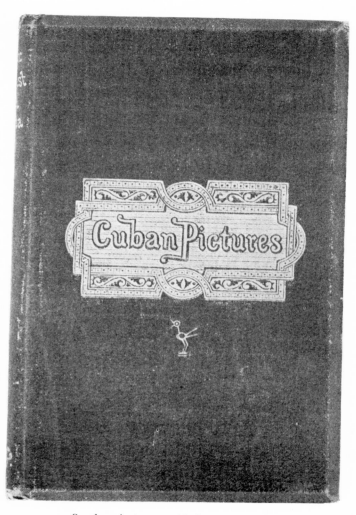

39. *Sand grain pattern. 'Cuban Pictures,'* 1865

40. *Dot and line pattern. 'Lyra Anglicana,'* 1865

*41. Plan of the rolling press,
the first bookbinding machine*

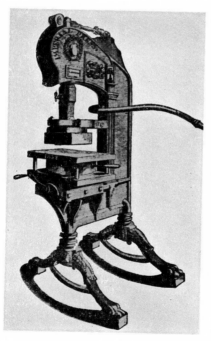

*42. The Imperial arming press,
the first embossing press*

43. *An early cloth-embossing machine of English manufacture*

44. *An American embossing press of the 1850's*

45. *A hand backing machine of* 1870

46. *A stabbing machine of* 1860

47. *An early folding machine, the first bookbinding
machine operated by steam power*

48. *The Smyth four-feed arm type sewing machine*

49. *A hand-operated sawing machine of the late fifties*

50. *Hydraulic dry-pressing or smashing machine,*
*designed to compress folded sheets*

51. *Case-making machine of* 1895

52. *Casing-in machine of* 1903

*53. Rolls for the graining of sized cloth*

54. *Cover of the* 1885 *Gorenflo Specimen Book*

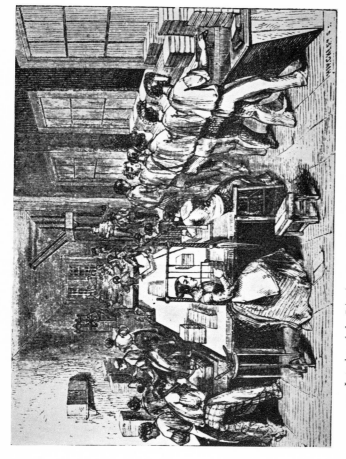

55. *Interior of the Lippincott and Grambo bindery in Philadelphia, 1852*

56. *Shelves of mediaeval and Renaissance volumes in contemporary bindings in the rare book room of the Newberry Library, Chicago*

57. *Eighteenth-century books in paper bindings*

58. *Nineteenth-century books in leather and cloth bindings*

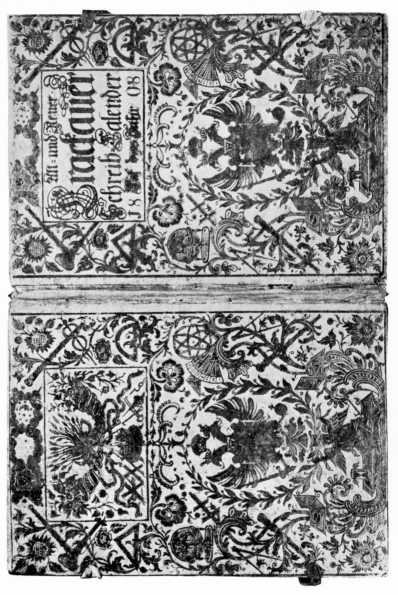

59. *'Alt-und Neuer Crackauer Schreib-Calender auf das Jahr 1808'*

60. *How to attach new cords to broken old ones*
*and how to fasten them to the old covers*

61. *Douglas Cockerell's trial binding on blank paper for the*
*Codex Sinaiticus at the British Museum.*
*White pigskin back, Spanish mahogany boards, silver clasps*

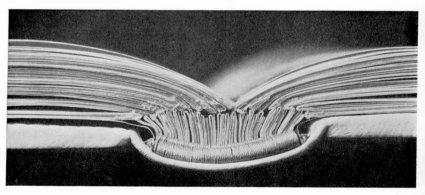

62. *Douglas Cockerell's trial binding for Codex Sinaiticus at the British*
*Museum, showing how the sections are thrown out from the back on guards*

63. *Three early printed books, bound by Douglas Cockerell in* 1902 *and* 1904 *in morocco over binders board, decorated with blind and gold tooling. In the Newberry Library, Chicago. The volume on the left is the* 1483 *edition of Cavalca's 'Specchio di Croce'; the large volume on the right the 'Epistolae' of St. Jerome, printed in* 1469 *in Naples(?); the book in the foreground Jehan Petit's sixteenth-century edition of Mantuani's 'Parthenice Mariana'*

64. *A group of early nineteenth-century volumes in original half-leather bindings with marble paper sides. In the collection of Isadore G. Mudge*

65. *A group of early nineteenth-century volumes recently rebound in old marble papers with leather backs and corners. In the collection of Isadore G. Mudge*

66. *Half-leather bindings with Douglas Cockerell's marble papers used on the sides. In the Newberry Library, Chicago. The tall volume on the left is a copy of Paolo Giovio's 'Elogia,' Basel, Pedrus Perna,* 1575; *in the middle background is Brocman's 'Ingwars Säga,' in a Stockholm,* 1762 *edition; on the right Fortunio's 'Regole grammaticali,' printed at Venice in* 1550; *and, in front, Buonanni's 'Discorso sopra la prima cantica,' Florence,* 1572

67. *On the left, pamphlets bound in unattractive materials and by over-sewing. On the right, attractive materials and sewing through the fold*

68. *A group of pamphlets hand-sewn through the fold and bound in paper-covered boards by Charles M. Adams*

69. *Attractive, legible lettering on standard library bindings (right group) does not cost more than ugly lettering (left group)*

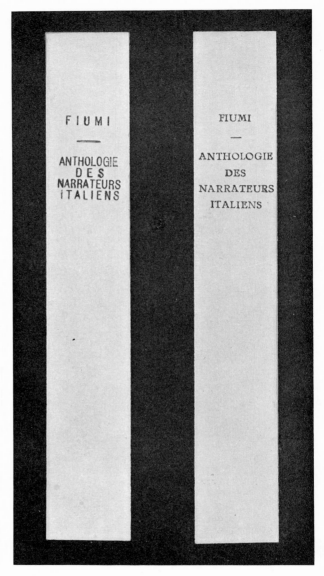

70. *The use of tall, condensed gilding type (left) is not always the best solution of the problem of the long title on a narrow back. On the right, a normal type, well spaced, is much more legible and attractive*

72. After nearly five hundred years of sewing through the fold.
Two leaves from a book printed in the fifteenth century

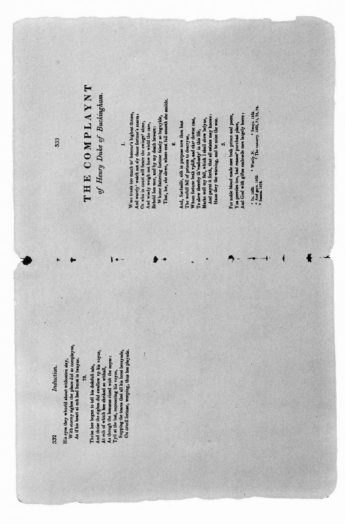

73. After one hundred and twenty-five years of sewing through the fold, and fourteen years of oversewing. Pages from the 'Mirror for Magistrates,' London, 1815. Rebound July, 1926

# THE RISE OF EDITION BINDING

## The Introduction of Cloth

EARLY in the nineteenth century forces were in action which were to produce fundamental changes in the time-honored binding processes that would largely determine the future course of publishers' bookbinding. While these forces were also to be responsible for the production of the first bookbinding machine, as will be shown in the next chapter, they produced two developments of even greater basic importance. These innovations, which came in response to the need for greater speed, simplicity, and economy in book production, consisted of the invention of the casing process and the introduction of cloth as a binding material.

The use of cloth as a binding material in England has been the subject of intensive study by John Carter, whose admirable publications on this subject present the most authoritative evidence available.[1] His studies were preceded by those of Geoffrey Keynes[2] and Michael Sadleir,[3] whose primary interests, however, were directed elsewhere; Mr. Carter has gone considerably deeper into the matter. On the basis of his work it may be assumed without question that calico or muslin cloth was first used practically and regularly for a binding material sometime between 1820 and 1825. Although his sources do not reveal the actual date, Mr. Carter is of the opinion that it can be placed at least as early as 1822 or 1823. Whatever further investigation may reveal, it is unlikely that this fundamental tenet,

[1] John Carter, *Binding Variants in English Publishing, 1820-1900* (London: Constable, 1932). *Publisher's Cloth; An Outline History of Publisher's Binding in England, 1820-1900* (New York: Bowker [1935]).

[2] Geoffrey Keynes, *William Pickering, Publisher* (London: The Fleuron, 1924).

[3] Michael Sadleir, *The Evolution of Publishers' Binding Styles, 1770-1900* (London: Constable, 1930).

accepted by such an authority as Douglas Leighton,[4] will be disproved: that the use of unfinished muslin for publishers' bindings was extensively practised in London by 1825 at the latest.

Some evidence has come to light recently which would indicate that cloth was used before 1800 in the United States. Miss French has reviewed these interesting facts on page 91 of this volume. While this definitely establishes the use of cloth at this earlier date I am unable to consider these practices as anything other than evidence of isolated attempts to find a substitute for leather that was at once usable by the bookbinder, attractive to the book buyer, and cheap. It is true that velvets and silks were being used concurrently with the first muslins for the bindings of annuals and other gift books to an extent that places the style well beyond the experimental stage, yet their influence upon the introduction of a serviceable cloth binding is extremely questionable. It seems to me that the final acceptance of the cloth binding of the 1820's depended upon these factors: practicability at the bindery, serviceability and attractiveness for the book buyer, and the formulation of new binding techniques to which the material was particularly adaptable. Canvas could not have been very attractive to the adult book buyer, nor velvet and silk very serviceable. Muslin was the successful compromise, but it had to wait until binders could use it successfully and until they had developed a simple and economical technique of using it—namely, casing.

Moreover, the simple matter of the scarcity of cloth-bound books dated before the 1820's, and their prevalence in the twenties and thirties, indicates, if nothing else, that *general* adoption of the cloth style did not come about until the 1820's. An examination of the earliest cloth-bound books of American origin which have come to my atten-

4 Douglas Leighton, *Modern Bookbinding; A Survey and a Prospect* (New York: Oxford [1935]).

tion has revealed that they were bound in the same types and colors of cloth as were used by English binders of the same period.

The earliest example of an American book bound in cloth which has come to my attention was printed in New York by J. and J. Harper in 1827. This book, *Rome in the Nineteenth Century,* was bound in half purple cloth with paper-covered boards. The most logical inference, apparently, is that the idea of using cloth as a cover material was, like so many patents of the period, 'communicated from abroad,' in this case from England. A contemporary statement (February, 1822) by Thomas Prince, a bookbinder of Salem, Massachusetts, indicates how closely American bookbinders followed English bookbinding fashions, when he said, with obvious pride, that he bound his books 'in the good old English style.'[5] The prevalence of American books published between 1827 and 1830 bound in red or purple unfinished muslin, the same colors and material used in England since 1825, unquestionably points to England as the immediate source of the custom. This belief is further strengthened by the fact that in 1820 only thirty per cent of all the books sold in America were of American manufacture, the balance being importations from England. American bookbinders thus had every opportunity to observe and copy innovations originating in England. Their subservience to English leadership in the production of book cloth through nearly the whole of the nineteenth century constitutes a story of such unusual interest that extended treatment in a later chapter is required.

Whatever further research into the problem may tell us about the origins of cloth as a cover material, it is nevertheless true that its general and rapid adoption by English and American bookbinders for publishers' binding satisfied to some degree the demand for economy in binding without

[5] Harriet Sylvester Tapley, *Salem Imprints, 1768-1825* (Salem, Mass.: The Essex Institute, 1927), p. 205.

a comparable loss in permanency. As a matter of fact, it was the development of the casing process to replace the slower and more complex process known as boarding that gave the greatest impetus to the growth of publishers' or edition bookbinding as a separate branch of the craft.

## *The Beginnings of Casing*

Place an edition binding and a hand binding side by side and one significant feature will be noticed; while the hand binding may be quite obviously the more expensively produced, there will be little difference in the apparent strength of the two bindings. While the one may be covered with leather and the other with cloth, both books will be enclosed in boards, will open with equal ease, and may at first be equally firm and compact. The differences in the two types of binding are not so much a difference in external appearance as in internal construction. It is characteristic of American and other edition binders throughout the nineteenth century that they have attempted always to give edition bindings the appearance of hand bindings.

Thus, in order to discover the point of divergence of extra and edition bindings from their common stock, any examination of exteriors will result in doubtful findings. It is the internal construction of the book which matters. Of all the processes employed in the building of a book none are more important than sewing the signatures together and fastening them inside the covers. An examination of these processes, it is believed, will show with fair accuracy the emergence of actual edition bookbinding.

In European bindings during the Middle Ages the pages of a book were tied or sewn to thongs of leather or parchment. The thongs were then attached to heavy wooden boards and a strip of leather was pasted around the back over the edges of the boards. Because of their tendency to crack and split, the parchment and leather thongs were replaced by stout hemp cords which were found to give greater strength to the binding.[6] When the back was covered with leather these cords caused parallel ridges to appear on the spine of the book. Since the cords were usually placed evenly apart, these ridges divided the back into panels which, eventually, were used to carry decoration and author-and-title information.

In the Near East, however, the evolution of sewing proceeded along a somewhat different course. The first primitive step of holding the book within its wooden covers by strings of gut without the use of a leather back was followed by an advanced stage in which the signatures were sewn together by a chain-stitch. In the latter method the back of the book was pasted to the leather strip or to a leather strip reinforced on the inside by a piece of linen. This method produced a smooth back, a characteristic of Islamic bindings since the ninth century.[7]

Influenced by the smooth back of Islamic books the European bookbinders towards the end of the Middle Ages attempted to produce a smooth back without giving up the use of the cords or bands characteristic of Western binding technique for several centuries. This tendency reached a climax around the middle of the eighteenth century when the sawn-in back became a widely accepted, if doubtful, practice. The sawn-in back was produced by cutting grooves across the fold of the signatures with a small saw. These grooves were just deep enough to contain the cords or bands so that a perfectly smooth back resulted.

At the beginning of the nineteenth century the cords were still fastened securely to the boards, usually by making two holes in the boards for each cord end, through which they were drawn and fastened. However, the increasing demand for books in inexpensive bindings made

[6] Hans Loubier, *Der Bucheinband von seinen Anfängen bis zum Ende des 18. Jahrhunderts* (2nd ed., Leipzig: Klinkhardt & Biermann, 1926), pp. 2-7.
[7] Sir Thomas W. Arnold and Adolf Grohmann, *The Islamic Book* (n.p., The Pegasus Press, 1929), pp. 37, 44, 57.

it necessary not only to find a serviceable and inexpensive substitute for leather but also to simplify the methods by which the cover was attached to the books. This was achieved through the gradual modification of traditional methods.

For example, the normal permanent binding of the period was of full leather over boards that had been laced on. The trimming of the edges was done with the plough *after* the boards had been laced on; hence, the books were trimmed individually, one at a time. To effect a slight saving in time this process was modified by trimming the edges *before* the boards were laced on, which permitted the binder to trim several copies at a time unencumbered by the boards. The boards could then be laced on and the full leather cover added as usual. Although the net result was practically the same in each case, books bound by the earlier procedure—called 'in-boards,' since the pages were trimmed after the boards had been added—were more expensive at the binders' than those trimmed 'out-of-boards,' the newer method.

It was also customary, at the time, to employ for many books a temporary binding called 'boards,' consisting of 'a simple covering of paper and board which, in its original intention, was only a means of keeping pages in readable form while the purchaser decided whether the book was worthy of a library binding.'[8] Catering to the growing number of book buyers who could afford neither to buy a book permanently bound nor to have a leather binding added after purchase, binders improved upon this type of binding by using extra quality marbled or colored papers over the board and obviated the use of gold stamping on the spine by the use of printed paper labels. This style, called 'extra boards,' was more expensive than 'boards,' yet much less expensive than the 'out-of-boards' binding. Thus the ideal represented by the edition binding was gradually

[8] Leighton, op. cit., p. 9.

being approached: good bindings were being made at lower cost, and low-cost bindings better.[9]

While 'out-of-board' binding could not be called 'casing,' since the cases were not being made as units, nevertheless the method of trimming books in batches before boarding is definitely a step in that direction. Another important step was accomplished by fraying the cord ends and pasting them to the inside of the boards, rather than lacing them through holes in the boards. When the endpapers were subsequently pasted down, they covered the ends of the cords and thus assisted in holding the boards— now the case—to the book. So by foregoing the undoubted superiority of lacing as to strength, this method of handling the cords made it *possible* for cases to be made separately and as units. Completed books so made retained sufficient strength to satisfy the vast majority of book buyers.

This process has since come to be known as casing, and now constitutes the chief structural difference between edition and hand bookbinding. The date of its first introduction marks the beginnings of edition bookbinding. While it is impossible to fix that date definitely, it is possible to approach it fairly closely. On the basis of the examination of more than fifty American books issued between 1800 and 1850, it may be said with reasonable certainty that it occurred at some time between 1825 and 1835. I have in my possession a cased book which is dated 1831. It is a publication of J. and J. Harper and is bound in the full red cloth typical of the time. The particular title of this volume is the publisher's Stereotype Edition of *The Young Duke,* a two-volume novel 'by the author of "Vivian Grey." '

The cases were, of course, made by hand, the processes of cutting the boards and cloth to proper size, gluing the boards to the cloth and turning in the edges over the boards remaining hand work for many years. They were made by hand, in fact, until the last decade of the century

9 Leighton, op. cit., pp. 12-14.

when the case-making machine was introduced. The modern terms 'hand-casing' and 'machine-casing' have come into use to distinguish the periods prior to and following the invention of casing machines. They serve also to re-emphasize that casing contributed to the industrialization of the craft through modification of traditional methods rather than by means of mechanical invention.

It is important to note in this connection that the establishment of binderies catering particularly to publishers' work began in America at least as early as 1832 with the founding of Benjamin Bradley's bindery in Boston (see p. 179). That the introduction of cloth, the casing process, and the machines treated fully in the next chapter should be followed so closely by the founding of edition binderies, points clearly to the fact that it was because of these innovations that edition binderies could be established. All of these influences, and the great strides being taken at the time in the printing industry, made the growth of edition bookbinding as an industry a matter of certainty. It is my opinion, based upon the evidence available, that the strongest of these influences must have been the origin of the casing process, replacing as it did the venerable hand process of boarding. A simplification of an involved process that had required much time and skill on the part of the bookbinder, it became a rapid and economical procedure, well adapted to keeping the bookbinder in step with the growing economy and speed of the book printer. With the introduction of subsequent inventions, each contributing additional cheapness and speed to binding processes, the edition bookbinding industry in the United States grew with ever greater rapidity as the years went by.

Following 1835, casing was rapidly adopted in America as the accepted practice in binding publishers' books. The types of paper used for the backing strip varied greatly, some binders zealously using the heaviest and toughest papers they could find, while others employed almost any type of scrap paper found lying around the office. Such slipshod methods soon became noticeable in the weakness of the hinge, the spot at which bindings first began to disintegrate. In order to provide more strength at this vulnerable spot, edition bookbinders adopted the use of a light, loosely woven linen crash to replace the customary paper backing strip. The crash backing strip had the advantage of being uniformly strong of itself, and, in attaching it to the back of the book and to the boards, the glue easily penetrated the interstices between the threads and, hardening, held the crash tightly. Crash was probably first used in backing strips between 1845 and 1855.

As casing became an accepted practice, the cords to which the signatures were sewn gradually came to lose almost entirely their original function of forming the bond which held the pages of a book within its cover. I have seen volumes issued around mid-century in which there was absolutely no attempt to affix the cord ends to the boards. Their lack of utility as bonds had by that time come to be fully recognized. It was impossible to dispense with them entirely, however, for they were still needed as something to which the signatures could be sewn. It was not until the Smyth sewing machine was invented that the cords became no longer useful, for it was possible with the sewing machine to sew the signatures to each other, eliminating entirely the need for cords. Thus, after 1882 cords were doomed, although many bookbinders gave them up slowly and reluctantly.

In such a manner was the trade of edition bookbinding born. Partly as a result of the need for speed and economy in all printing trades, partly as a result of the mechanical aids beginning to be produced, but chiefly as the result of the hand-casing method of attaching the covers to books, a distinct branch of the bookbinding trade was evolved.

This branch of the trade has so enlarged and expanded since that time that today it is difficult to find books, produced and marketed commercially, which are bound in any other way, regardless of price, class, or quality of printing.

# CHAPTER III

## THE MECHANIZATION OF BOOKBINDING PROCESSES

### The Invention of Machines Operated by Hand

AT the same time that the industry of edition book-binding was being born through the evolution of the casing process and the use of cloth to facilitate that process, mechanical genius was becoming interested in the problem of devising machines to replace hand-book-binding processes. The first product of that interest was the English invention in 1823 of the rolling press,[1] a machine designed to supplant the hand process known as beating (Fig. 41). The process involved consisted of pounding the pages with a heavy hammer to drive out air from between the pages after sewing. The machine consisted of two heavy iron rollers, one on top of the other, actuated by means of a hand crank and fly-wheel which turned the rollers through a series of cog wheels. The books were compressed by passing them between the rollers, much as water is removed from clothes in a wringer. That this was an innovation conceived independently of the introduction of cloth is evident from the simple fact that the processes of beating the pages and of covering the volume have no immediate dependence upon each other. An examination of the successive inventions in any one field of mechanics clearly shows that a great majority of them are really only improvements upon earlier ones, the earlier containing innovations making those following it possible. In this instance there is nothing about the rolling machine that would in any way affect the use of cloth as a binding material, nor is there any way in which cloth bindings might influence the invention of the rolling machine. Thus, while it is true that the introduction of cloth does mark in

[1] Charles Henry Timperley, *A Dictionary of Printers and Printing* (London: Johnson, 1839), p. 887.

time the beginnings of invention in bookbinding, it is also true that inventors were concerning themselves with the bookbinding processes and would have done so whether the cloth binding was introduced or not. The coincidence in time of these two factors points with gratifying clarity to the period between 1820 and 1825 as the beginning of the trend towards mechanization of the bookbinding processes.

Timperley estimated that the rolling press would compress in one day as many books as could be beaten by two bookbinders in a week's time with the beating hammer. Apparently it was sufficiently successful in England to throw many bookbinders out of work. It is said, for example, that a paper dated December 16, 1830, and issued by nearly five hundred journeyman bookbinders of London and Westminster requested their employers to give up the use of this machine.[2] This might indicate that bookbinders were unused to the experience of having one of their time-honored hand processes eliminated by a machine. By inference, this occurrence makes it apparent that this was the first major invention in the field of bookbinding, and perhaps substantiates the conclusion drawn in the preceding paragraph.

It is to be remembered, of course, that this was an English invention. That machines similar in principle should soon be made in the United States was an inevitable consequence, for American mechanics were still closely bound to English customs and practices. While it is known that rolling presses were being made by 1840 in the machine shop of James Maxwell at 259 Bowery, New York,[3] it is probable that they were being made in the early thirties at the latest. Both the date and the manner of their transmittal

[2] *The Working-man's Companion. The Results of Machinery, Namely, Cheap Production and Increased Employment, Exhibited* (3rd ed., London: Knight, 1831), p. 157.

[3] *American Repertory of Arts*, Vol. I, no. 1 (February, 1840). (Advertisement on back cover.)

to America are unknown. It was the common practice of English workmen, upon migrating to America, to bring technical knowledge which would enable them to reproduce the plans of machinery from memory. This leads me to suspect that such a procedure was followed in this case. After putting such plans on paper upon his arrival, an immigrant workman could have his press made by a machinist.

There were, of course, no manufacturers who made bookbinding machines exclusively in these early years. Almost any machinist would turn out the iron parts of a standing press on order, and there were plenty of wood-workers to make sewing presses, ploughs, and other simple tools of the bookbinder. The age of specialization in manufacture was, however, beginning, and certain machinists began specializing in bookbinders' equipment. The customary terse description of many of these in the early directories merely as 'machinist' makes it difficult to single out those catering to the bookbinding trade, yet among them must be included Bernard Sheridan, who founded in 1835 the manufacturing concern now known as the T. W. and C. B. Sheridan Company,[4] and James Maxwell, referred to above, who opened his shop sometime before 1840.

England saw also in 1832 the invention of the embossing press, probably the Imperial arming press (Fig. 42), manufactured by Cope and Sherwin, which was designed for the purpose of stamping decorative designs and grains on cloth covers. That such a machine should have engaged the attention of inventors so early in the history of edition bookbinding is undoubtedly the result of a tendency to conceal the texture of the cloth as much as possible. It is apparent that the book-buying public found it difficult to accustom themselves to simple, unadorned cloth bindings. Bookbinders were doubtless aware of this aversion and were, in addition, annoyed at their inability to prevent glue from penetrating the unfinished muslin when making

---

[4] *Bookbinding Magazine,* Vol. XV, no. 3 (March, 1932), p. 26.

cases. It was also impossible to do any sort of blind or gold stamping — the cloth would not take and hold the impression, nor would gold adhere to it.

These problems were solved through the efforts, apparently, of Archibald Leighton, of Leighton & Eels, London binders, when at his instigation a method of preparing sized cloth was perfected about the same time that the Imperial arming press was introduced. Together, these innovations eased the work of the bookbinder and made it possible to disguise the offending muslin in numberless ways. The methods used to achieve this none too admirable deception will be discussed more fully in the next chapter. Douglas Leighton[5] attaches great importance to this machine, which was described by John Hannett in 1835,[6] and was known variously as arming, embossing, or stamping press. It is undoubtedly one of the chief developments in the mechanization of bookbinding, insofar as it made possible the decoration of book covers in styles and designs limited only by the abilities of the brass die engravers (see p. 169 ff.).

Embossing presses were being manufactured in the United States by 1838.[7] Bernard Sheridan manufactured and marketed letter-copying and embossing presses almost from the beginning. Embossing presses have since been made in a wide variety of forms by many manufacturers, and have been employed by bookbinders for embossing in blind, gold, or color on paper, cloth, leather, and other surfaces. A standard type in use during the last half of the century is illustrated in Figure 44. The particular machine shown was manufactured by the Isaac Adams Company of Boston. Many were used also as smashing machines, the purpose of

[5] Leighton, op. cit., pp. 20-21.
[6] John Hannett [John Andrews Arnett, pseud.], *Bibliopegia; Or, The Art of Bookbinding, In All Its Branches* (London: Groombridge, 1835), pp. 170-171.
[7] Fred S. Tipson, Treasurer, T. W. & C. B. Sheridan Company. Letter to author, June 5, 1934.

which was to drive out air from between the pages before casing so that the book would be firm and compact.

While English inventors produced a special cloth-embossing machine (Fig. 43) soon after the introduction of sized cloth to the binding world,[8] the versatile embossing machines made in the United States were often adapted to the work of imparting all-over grains to sized cloth through the employment of flat plates rather than rollers as were used on the English machine (see also p. 169). The very versatility of the embossing machine made it an essential item of equipment in all edition binderies.

## The Application of Power

Power for the rolling and the embossing presses was supplied entirely by hand, the chief feature in their design being the fact that they increased mechanically the compression possible by the strength of one man. The application of power other than hand power to machines of all kinds was a problem that had been engaging the attention of men from the day of James Watt. It has been recorded that König's cylinder press was run successfully by steam in 1811. Steam was slow to secure a foothold in America, however; the presses of the Harper brothers, for instance, were turned by horse power for many years.[9]

The use of steam power to run bookbinding machines was also slow to become an accepted practice. It was first applied to the stamping or embossing presses, mentioned in the preceding section, which were manufactured by Bernard Sheridan. According to Mr. Fred S. Tipson, treasurer of the T. W. and C. B. Sheridan Company, power stamping presses were introduced in the United States about 1845.[10] Steam was, of course, not immediately ap-

---

[8] George Dodd, *Days at the Factories.* Ser. I. — London. 'A Day at a Bookbinder's' (London: Knight, 1843), pp. 363-384.

[9] Joseph Henry Harper, *The House of Harper* (New York: Harper, 1912), p. 25.

[10] Tipson, op. cit.

plied to all machines then in use, nor even to those being
introduced at this time. For example, the first of a long
series of patents on hand backing machines was granted in
1845, and while it was the forerunner of the later and more
elaborate power rounder and backer, it could hardly be
considered of itself an important step forward. These backing machines, designed to facilitate the forming of grooves
along the back edges into which the boards were to be fitted, probably reached the point of production soon after
the first patent was granted, although the first concrete evidence appears in Hickok's catalogue for 1870.[11] The machine illustrated (Fig. 45) consists of two clamps, one fixed
immovably to an iron frame support, the other to a screw
actuated by a hand wheel which permitted the clamps to
be brought together on either side of the book with some
power. The operator then proceeded to back and round
the book with his backing hammer, the clamps being so
made that the groove to hold the boards naturally resulted.
By this time job backers, as they were usually called, were
standard edition bindery equipment, and continued to be
such for more than thirty years. They are, in fact, often
found in binderies to this day, especially those doing hand
binding and library rebinding.

In the first portion of this book Miss French refers (page
17) to a method of holding signatures together by 'stabbing'
holes from side to side or in the center of the fold through
which thread was inserted and tied. Since it was a relatively
simple process it is not surprising to find stabbing machines
(Fig. 46) in production at a fairly early date. The machine
marketed by W. O. Hickok as early as 1860[12] consisted of a
movable head, to which needles could be affixed in varying
numbers and positions, mounted on a table a little below
waist-high. Signatures placed against guides on the table
were perforated neatly and uniformly when the workman

---

[11] W. O. Hickok Company. *Illustrated Catalogue* . . . (Harrisburg, Pennsylvania: Hickok, 1870), p. 19.

[12] W. O. Hickok Company. *Illustrated Catalogue* . . . (1860), p. 8.

brought the needles down upon the signatures by means of a foot-treadle attachment. As a method of sewing this was, of course, not ideal. The Smyth sewing machine, soon to be described, largely superseded it for edition work, yet this same type of machine is often used in library binderies today for pamphlet work.

The first bookbinding machine owing its invention directly to the availability of steam power was the folding machine, first successfully produced by Cyrus Chambers, Jr., of Philadelphia. In 1856 he took out his first patent, and followed it immediately with many others covering various improvements. His essential idea has been used in almost all other folding machines marketed, and no great variance from that principle can be noticed in modern machines. In early machines the paper was placed in its first position by hand (Fig. 47). At that point a long, light wooden bar with a narrow edge descended upon the center of the sheet, forcing it between a series of small, flat-surfaced wheels which carried the sheet between two cylinders resting lightly together, thus making the fold. By adding, in successive stages, other bars, wheels, and cylinders, as many folds as could be desired could be made in a single sheet of paper.

The problem of folding was not, however, settled once and for all by the Chambers machines. A great many patents on folding machines were secured throughout the rest of the century. Sufficiently different types of folders were later invented to make possible the formation of a rival company which competed with the Chambers folders. This was the Dexter Folder Company formed in 1880 in Des Moines, Iowa.[13]

## The Final Process of Industrialization

During the last half of the nineteenth century inventors became more and more ingenious in their attempts to

[13] Earl D. Rader, Dexter Folding Company. Letter to author, dated September 17, 1934.

conquer by mechanical means the remaining hand processes in bookbinding. The period was, in fact, the golden
age of American invention and machine manufacture, an
era during which American firms first competed to any extensive degree with foreign companies for world-wide
trade. So rapid was the progress made that in the last quarter of the century American companies were the undis-
puted leaders in many fields. This was particularly true in
the printing field, where such men as Mergenthaler and
Lanston with their type-composing machines, Hoe, Miehle,
Gordon, Gally, Colt, and Harris with their printing presses,
and Horgan and Ives with their contributions to photo-
engraving, produced machines and methods of international significance. As will be seen, this was also true in the
production of new bookbinding machines, for American
manufacturers were now prepared to take the initiative
and leadership in this field as well as in others.

The first thread sewing machine for use in bookbinding
was the invention of David McConnell Smyth of Hartford,
Connecticut, in 1856. These machines were manufactured
for and sold to D. Appleton & Company, New York publishers, for their exclusive use.[14] No detailed description of
this machine has come to light, although I assume it to have
been a bona fide sewing machine and not merely a stabbing
machine such as has already been described. While no
American patent for this first book-sewing machine is listed
in the records of the Patent Office, Smyth made further
improvements upon it which he patented in 1868, 1872,
and 1873.

In 1879 Smyth invented and patented his curved-needle
book-sewing machine. In 1880 the Smyth Manufacturing
Company was formed to manufacture and market the machines, the first of which were delivered in 1882. After a
few years of experimentation, two general styles of the ma-

14 George A. Stephen, *Machine Book-sewing, with Remarks on Publishers'
Binding* ([Aberdeen], Aberdeen U. Press, 1908), pp. 4, 5.

chine were evolved, the four-feed arm type and the single-feed arm type. The former was especially adapted to routine edition work, whereas the single-feed arm type was built for such heavier work as the sewing of ledgers and account books. Other variations of the four-feed arm type of machine sewed 'on the "all-along" principle, doing plain . . . sewing, i.e., without tapes or other material at the back, through or over tapes or through the edge of same, or over sunken cords.'[15] Among the firms receiving book-sewing machines in the early years of this company were the following: William B. Burford, Indianapolis; E. Fleming & Company, Boston; H. O. Houghton, Cambridge; and the American Bible Society, George McKibbin Company, and J. J. Little Company, all of New York.[16]

The Smyth four-feed arm type sewing machines found an immediate and world-wide market, because of the speed and efficiency with which sewing could be accomplished. An average operator of the four-arm type machine could sew fifty to fifty-five signatures a minute; an expert operator could do as many as seventy a minute. Too, the stitches were taken through the fold as in sewing by hand and at many times the speed of hand sewing. Within the next thirty years several thousand machines had been sold to the leading binderies of Europe and America, and of Australia, South Africa, India, and Japan as well.[17] A more modern version of this machine is shown in Figure 48.

In order to eliminate the 'band' on the back of a book caused by the cords to which the signatures were sewn, it was customary, as stated earlier, to make with a small hand-saw shallow cuts across the back about one-sixteenth of an inch deep into which the cords could be sunk. By 1856 a sawing machine was in common use which greatly facili-

[15] Stephen, op. cit., pp. 5, 6.

[16] Ian D. Mackenzie, Vice President, Smyth Manufacturing Company. Letter to author, dated June 4, 1934.

[17] *Smyth Bookbinding Machines* (New York: E. C. Fuller Company [n.d.]), pp. 7, 8.

tated this simple process both in time and accuracy.[18] A
series of small circular saws were arranged on a shaft placed
under a table so that the saws would fit into slots cut at
intervals in the table top. The saws, protruding slightly
above the top of the table, cut grooves to the desired depth
when books were passed over them. W. O. Hickok produced
sawing machines of this type motivated by hand power until
the seventies (Fig. 49). In his catalogue of 1874 he illustrates
an improved machine which could be operated by steam as
well as hand power. While the Smyth sewing machine
eventually doomed saw cuts, customary practices were not
easily given up, and saw cuts and cords persisted for many
years after the sewing machine was in general use.[19]

American leadership in the production of bookbinding
machines continued with the finally successful invention
of a rounding and backing machine. Inventions of machines to aid or replace the hand operations of rounding
and backing had appeared, as previously mentioned, from
time to time during the century, though none of these went
much beyond the 'tool' stage. The problems involved in
these processes were never successfully solved until the
Crawley rounder and backer was introduced to the trade
by the E. C. Fuller Company, probably in 1892.[20]

The first patent taken out by Crawley for a rounder and
backer was in 1876. A second patent was secured in 1877
and the last in 1892, showing a period of sixteen years of
experimentation. This machine, like the Smyth sewing
machine, was popular both at home and abroad. It solved,
mechanically, two of the hand-bookbinding processes requiring much skill on the part of the hand binder.

The need for an effective and simple 'smashing machine'
was supplied in the eighties with the so-called hydraulic

18 James Bartram Nicholson, *A Manual of the Art of Bookbinding* (Philadelphia: Baird, 1856), p. 171.
19 W. O. Hickok Company. *Illustrated Catalogue* . . . (1860), p. 13; (1870),
p. 15; (1874), p. 19; (1880), p. 33; (1883), p. 36.
20 Tipson, op. cit.

dry-pressing machine marketed by Hickok (Fig. 50).[21] This machine, still in common use, compresses and ties in a bundle twenty or more uncased books at a time. Books so compressed may be cased at once or conveniently stored for casing at a future date.

Although the practice of making cases as separate units had been characteristic of edition bookbinding since the 1830's, the cutting of the boards and backstrips, gluing them to the cloth, and folding the edges over had been done by hand since the beginning. It was not until the last decade of the nineteenth century, that attention began to be given to the speeding up of that process. One of the first machines produced to facilitate this process was the case-smoothing machine introduced by the George H. Sanborn & Sons Company of New York prior to 1891. This machine consisted of two soft rubber rollers working like a clothes wringer moving continuously from power derived by a pulley from an overhead shaft, and relieved the case maker of a number of hand motions with a bone folder formerly needed to affix the book cloth to the boards and glue the edges down tight.[22]

The first machine to inaugurate the modern era of 'machine-casing' was the Sheridan covering machine, introduced in 1893. These machines, the first of which were added to the binderies of R. R. Donnelley & Sons Company, Frank A. Munsey Company, and the Government Printing Office,[23] performed mechanically all the hand operations in case-making except the cutting of the cloth and boards. The most active inventor who had been working on the problem of case-making machines was A. Bredenberg, who secured four patents for such a machine between May 31, 1892, and October 24, 1893, although it is not known

[21] W. O. Hickok Company. *Illustrated Catalogue . . .* (1883), p. 48.
[22] *Sanborn's Paper Cutting Machines and Bookbinders' Machinery* (New York: Geo. H. Sanborn & Sons [1891]), p. 52.
[23] Tipson, op. cit.

whether it was his invention that the Sheridan Company marketed.

Two years later the Smyth Manufacturing Company issued a case-making machine to do the same type of work. It was made in two sizes and was entirely automatic in operation except that the cloth had to be fed by hand (Fig. 51).[24] Both the Sheridan and Smyth machines found substantial markets at home and abroad and have since been improved a number of times.

In 1901 the Smyth Company introduced a cloth-cutting machine 'designed to carry a roll of bookbinder's cloth of standard length and diameter and at one operation to cut it up into rectangular sheets of any desired proportion within the range of the machine.'[25]

The gathering of signatures into books had been a hand process from time immemorial until the first automatic power driven gathering machines were introduced by the T. W. and C. B. Sheridan Company between 1900 and 1903.[26] As book production increased during the nineteenth century, gathering became increasingly a problem. Factory girls walked miles every day around the sides of a long table picking up one signature after another from the piles of signatures ranged along its edges until a complete book had been assembled, only to repeat the process *ad infinitum*. One genius, sometime during the last two or three decades of the century, at least saved the poor girls' feet by devising a rotating table on which the signatures were arranged, the girls picking up a signature from each pile as it went by. The gathering machine utilized the earlier method, and replaced human fingers with mechanical ones, requiring the attendance of only one or two boys to see that no single pile of signatures ran low.

By this time all the forwarding processes from folding to

24 Mackenzie, op. cit.
25 *Smyth Bookbinding Machines*, op. cit., p. 42.
26 Tipson, op. cit.

sewing, on the one hand, and the making of the titled and decorated case, on the other, were completely mechanized. There yet remained the problem of affixing the case to the block of pages to form the completed book. This process was first successfully conquered mechanically with the introduction in 1903 of the Smyth casing-in machine (Fig. 52).[27] Only a single operator was required to feed uncased books to the machine and remove the cased books from it, all other operations being automatically handled by the machine.

Although I have made the nineteenth century my particular field of study, the productions of the present century are richly deserving of thorough study and separate treatment as soon as it may be possible. Incidental to my study I have been impressed by the fact that recent developments have consisted primarily in the improving and perfecting of existing machines, although certain new machines designed to perform some of the smaller steps in edition bookbinding have been placed on the market. For example, machines were invented that affixed the end-papers to the first and last signatures, glued on the crash and paper back-linings after rounding, and still others that combined in a single operation two or three processes formerly handled on individual machines. The modern forms of the machines mentioned specifically in these pages have become so complex within recent years that a detailed treatment of them on these pages becomes impossible.

Let it suffice to say that edition bookbinding today is almost completely a mechanized industry. As such, it no longer requires the skilled craftsmen so characteristic of the industry in its early stages. Bookbinders these days are mechanics rather than craftsmen, for they must know intimately the technical make-up of their incredible machines. Even the highly specialized work of finishing has been sim-

[27] Mackenzie, op. cit.

plified by the use of genuine and imitation gold and other metals on paper rolls in the stamping machine. Where genuine gold leaf is required in gold stamping and gilding of the edges, however, hand work must still be employed. In all other respects, edition bookbinding today is a completely mechanized industry.

# CHAPTER IV

# THE MANUFACTURE AND DECORATION OF BOOK CLOTH

MY apparent preoccupation with the origins of edition bookbinding on the one hand and the gradual replacement of hand processes by machines on the other, has deferred to this point a presentation of the extraordinary story of book cloth manufacture and decoration in America. The importance of this story to the whole subject of edition bookbinding is conditioned not only by the fact that it is unusual but also because it is an integral part of the subject about which little information has so far been available. It is made interesting by the fact that it admits failure on the part of American manufacturers to achieve leadership in a field in which it might have been expected. It shows, too, how mechanical ingenuity has aided and abetted, in the past and at present, the deliberate and conscious misrepresentation of materials sold to the book-buying public.

## Manufacture of Book Cloth

The part played by the introduction of cloth as a binding material in the rise of edition binding has already been described. It was pointed out, also, that the first cloths used in America were of the same types and styles as those being used in England at the same time. This fact, coupled with the knowledge that the importation of both ideas and materials from England was at that time the rule rather than the exception, makes it logical to accept the premise that the cloths used in the United States in the early years of the industry were of English manufacture and that they were imported into this country ready for use. Would it not also be logical to assume, knowing of the rapidity with which American machinery manufacturers produced bookbinding machines for American buyers, that American

cloth manufacturers would hasten to monopolize the domestic book cloth market? The parallel, however, does not
hold good.

Possibly the most dramatic evidence available is contained in the table on this page and in the accompanying
illustrations (Figs. 30-40). John Carter provides the basis for
this comparison in the classification he prepared to desig-
nate the chief styles employed by English book cloth manufacturers in the decoration of their product.[1] These styles,
appearing at various times and having more or less distinct periods of popularity, he has dated as closely as possible through examination of many examples of English
edition bindings. In comparing American edition bindings
with his classification we get the following amazing result:[2]

| Cloth Classification | Found on English books | Found on American books |
|---|---|---|
| Morocco (imitation leather) | Early thirties | 1834 |
| Watered | Early thirties | 1832 |
| Diaper | 1833 (?) | 1835 |
| Ribbon-embosser's cloth | 1834 | 1837 |
| Bold ribbed | 1840's | 1839 |
| Fine ribbed | —— | 1841 |
| Ripple-grain | 1840's | 1846 |
| Close bead-grain | 1858 | 1858 |
| Wave-grain | 1859 | 1860 |
| Sand-grain | Early 1860's | 1865 |
| Dot and line | 1860's | 1865 |

Thus we see that as the several styles were produced in England they appeared almost simultaneously on American
books. This indicates one of two things: either American
book cloth manufacturers slavishly copied English designs
as they saw them, or the cloth was the actual English product imported ready to use. That the latter explanation is
the correct one is easily explained.

[1] Carter, *Binding Variants*, p. xviii.
[2] For this comparison the collection of early cloth-bound books in the
New York Public Library was consulted.

Book cloth manufacture in England naturally had a head start through the activities of such influential men as Archibald Leighton, William Pickering, and others, and through the active co-operation of such experts as James Leonard Wilson. Douglas Leighton seems fairly cautious when he says, referring to England, that 'book cloth manufacturing came to be recognized as a distinct trade around 1840.'[3] The foregoing table, for example, lists several distinct book cloth styles prevalent before 1840, which would indicate that production was going forward on a sufficiently large scale to permit the exportation of sizable quantities to America. Although James Leonard Wilson did not have himself listed in the London directories as a book cloth manufacturer until 1843, nevertheless, as Mr. Leighton remarks, he was 'almost certainly in business earlier.'[4] It is thus apparent that England was the chief source of the book cloth used in America during these early years. It is more startling to realize that English cloth was used in America to the practical exclusion of domestic cloth throughout nearly the whole of the nineteenth century.

One of the earliest results of the growing industry of edition bookbinding was the establishment of bookbinders' supply houses, more commonly called 'bookbinders' warehouses.' Among the first of these was that established by Hermon Griffin in 1833 at 114 Nassau Street, New York. In the words of his grandson, Edward C. Griffin, chairman of the present firm of Griffin, Campbell, Hayes, Walsh, Inc., he 'conceived the idea that there was a very great demand for bookbinders' supplies and machinery, as at that time there was great difficulty in purchasing the various articles which were necessary in the manufacture of books.' Among the articles handled from the beginning was book cloth imported from England from the firm of Wilson and Bentley. The Griffin firm continued to import

[3] Leighton, op. cit., p. 27.
[4] Ibid.

English cloths throughout the century, adding the Winterbottom line in the 1870's.[5]

In 1827 Matthias Baldwin, later to found the famous
Baldwin Locomotive Works, established a machine shop
at 15 South Sixth Street, Philadelphia, where he made,
among other things, 'book rolls from brass.' One of his employees was a boy named John C. Copper who took over the
business in 1840 and re-formed it as a bookbinders' supply
house. This firm, unlike that just mentioned, is reported to
have handled domestic rather than imported book cloth according to Owen Shoemaker, who, with Joshua L. and
Charles J. Shoemaker, bought out the business in 1880, and
re-formed it under the name of J. L. Shoemaker & Company.[6]

In 1864 or 1865, the firm of Louis Dejonge & Company,
originally established on Staten Island in 1846 as paper
converters, added a line of bookbinders' supplies, beginning with imported leathers and soon adding book cloth
to their line. They first handled cloth made in England
by the Garfine Company, and later became the chief distributor in America for Winterbottom book cloths, still
an important feature of their line.[7]

It was in 1868 that Archibald Winterbottom began manufacturing book cloth in Manchester, England. The Winterbottom product gradually came to be of world-wide importance, although the Griffin price-lists of October 15,
1875, and the 1880's merely list their cloths as 'English
Book Cloth' in 1875, with the added statement in the later
issue 'Wilson's and others.'[8]

Following Archibald Winterbottom's death in 1882 the
firm was carried on under the title 'Executors of Archibald
Winterbottom,' and later as 'Archibald Winterbottom &

[5] Letter to author, dated December 4, 1939.
[6] Owen Shoemaker, J. L. Shoemaker & Company. Letter to author, dated
November 24, 1939.
[7] Hans Clasen, head, Bookbinders' Supplies Dept., Louis Dejonge & Company. Interview, November 14, 1939.
[8] H. Griffin & Sons, *Price-list of Bookbinders' Stock and Machinery* (New
York: Griffin, 1875), p. 5. H. Griffin & Sons, *Condensed Price-list* (New York:
Griffin [n.d.]), p. 5.

Sons.' In November, 1891, 'The Winterbottom Book Cloth Co. Ltd., was formed ... by eight firms who were then manufacturing Bookbinders Cloth, including "Archibald Winterbottom & Sons of Manchester, England" and the "Interlaken Mills, Providence, Rhode Island" Mr. G. H. Winterbottom (one of Mr. Archibald Winterbottom's sons) acting as Chairman of the Company from its inception until his death in November 1934.'[9]

The significant point I wish to make clear is that English book cloth was the standard article in use in America throughout the century. Further support for this statement is available in the results of an investigation prompted by a letter addressed to the Department of State, Washington, D. C., from the manager of a leading cotton mill in Rhode Island, in which he says, in part:

For years, the manufacture of book cloth was controlled in this country by an English syndicate who manufacture in England, and because of this the export of book cloths from the United States has been prevented, the parent company reserving for itself the markets of the world. Manufacture of book cloth has, however, been started in the United States by others, as well as by the corporation which I represent, and we have a profitable demand for our products at home.

In response to this letter, Thomas W. Cridler, Third Assistant Secretary of State, gave instructions to consular officers in all parts of the world, under date of January 24, 1899, to investigate the book cloth markets of their respective posts, and report their findings. The report is nothing short of amazing. The world-trade seems to have been divided pretty largely between Winterbottom and two or three German firms. German cloth was preferred in France, Greece, Mexico, and Guatemala, and of course, was the principal article consumed at home. In Belgium, Denmark, Italy, Sweden, Norway, Argentina, and Uruguay little preference was indicated between the German and

[9] W. G. Davison, The Winterbottom Book Cloth Co., Ltd. Letter to author, dated March 28, 1935.

English articles. Winterbottom, however, was the chief source of supply in Austria-Hungary, the Netherlands, Ireland, Scotland, Canada, West Indies, Japan, Korea, Persia, Syria, and Australia. Even Germany is said to have secured its best grades from Manchester.[10]

It was not until the establishment of Interlaken Mills in 1883 that any serious threat to English supremacy in this field was made by American firms. It is a matter of tradition among the present officers of the firm that Interlaken was the fourteenth American concern to 'dabble' in the making of book cloth.[11] Only two of the thirteen earlier companies have I been able to isolate so far, the earlier of which was the firm of Abbot & Wilcomb who were located at 32 Liberty Street, New York City in 1844.[12] The other firm, and apparently the only one that had any measure of success prior to 1883, was the New York Dyeing and Printing Establishment on Staten Island, more commonly known as the 'Staten Island Dye Works.'

This firm was organized in 1819 as a cloth dyeing and finishing establishment under the firm name of Barrett, Tileston and Company, soon after changed to the New York Dyeing and Printing Establishment. The leading spirit in the early years of the company was Colonel Nathan Barrett, who withdrew from the firm in 1851 following a disagreement with his partners over his purchase of some land in the name of the company. In the following year Colonel Barrett, his nephews, Nathan M., Joseph H., and Edwin B. Heal, and Abraham C. Wood, opened a rival plant nearby under the name Staten Island Fancy Dyeing Establishment, Barrett, Nephews & Co. Both companies flourished well into the twentieth century amid what must have been

10 United States Bureau of Foreign Commerce, 'Book Cloth in Foreign Countries,' *Special Consular Reports*, XX, Part 1 (Washington: Government Printing Office, 1900), 15-44.

11 J. Frank Morrissey, Treasurer, Interlaken Mills. Letters to author, dated November 6 and 13, 1939.

12 *The New York Business Directory, for 1844 & 1845* (New York: Doggett, 1844), p. 18.

a goodly amount of confusion on the part of their respective patrons, to say nothing of the puzzle it presents at first to the historian.[13]

A book cloth division was established in the New York Dyeing and Printing Establishment sometime prior to 1877 which was undoubtedly the most ambitious—as well as the last—of the sporadic and indecisive attempts of American manufacturers to enter the book cloth field. In the year mentioned fifty men were employed in this division of the firm and machinery valued at more than $75,000 was in constant operation.[14] The enterprise, however, found English competition much too strong and discontinued its book cloth division in 1883, the same year in which Interlaken Mills was established.

This firm was founded in the office of Governor Howard of Rhode Island by a group of New England cotton men including the Governor, Edward C. Bucklin, and W. F. Sayles. They erected a plant for the finishing of book cloth at Arkwright, Rhode Island, taking on a number of the men from the book cloth division of the defunct New York Dyeing and Printing Establishment. The oldest American firm manufacturing book cloth now in existence, Interlaken has had an extensive line of substantial cloths in a wide variety of colors and finishes since its early years.[15]

A year or so after the founding of Interlaken Mills, the cotton manufacturing firm of Joseph Bancroft & Sons of Wilmington, Delaware, began the manufacture of book cloth. In 1883 Samuel Bancroft, Jr., went to England to study English methods of manufacture of cloth for window shades, one of the firm's specialties to this day. It is not unlikely that that visit was also responsible for the

[13] Ira K. Morris, *Morris's Memorial History of Staten Island, New York* (West New Brighton [N. Y.]: Author [c. 1900]), 2 vols., II, 468-469.
[14] J. J. Clute, *Annals of Staten Island* (New York: Vogt, 1877), p. 323.
[15] Joseph D. Hall, *Biographical History of the Manufacturers and Business Men of Rhode Island* (1901), p. 314; *Publishers' Weekly* (May 6, 1933), p. 1490; Morrissey, op. cit.

entry of the company into the book cloth field. Among the important Bancroft developments was the introduction of 'Legal Buckram' (known as Number 666) which on June 1, 1908, was selected as standard at a meeting of representatives of the American Library Association, Librarian of Congress, Bureau of Standards, Public Printer, and the Printing Investigation of the Sixtieth Congress.[16]

Holliston Mills was started in 1893 by Herbert M. Plimpton to avoid the then high cost of book cloth necessary for the manufacture of books in his plant, the Plimpton Press, at Norwood, Massachusetts.[17] In company with his brother, Howard E. Plimpton, he founded the Security Manufacturing Company for the manufacture of book cloth, soon changing the name to Holliston Mills. The company has since been greatly enlarged, absorbing the Clinchfield Mills of Kingsport, Tennessee, and establishing a finishing plant and bleachery there, the Federal Book Cloth Company of Long Island City, New York, and the Siegbert Book Cloth Corporation of New York.[18]

Book cloth up to this time was essentially a starch-filled muslin cloth giving a fair amount of satisfactory wear and being adaptable to a wide variety of decorative styles. The booklover who got caught in the rain with a book under his arm, however, arrived home with unnatural color on his fingers or clothes and a spotted, ugly book. The year 1895 saw the results of the first efforts toward a waterproof cloth when the 'Fabrikoid' Company of Newburgh, New York, began producing book fabrics with a special type of coating. Under the management of E. I. du Pont de Nemours & Company, Inc., since 1910, the company has developed an extensive line of pyroxylin coated fabrics which is

16 Samuel B. Bird, Joseph Bancroft & Sons Co. Letters to author, dated November 1 and November 20, 1939. 'Joseph Bancroft & Sons Co.' *Textile Age*, III, no. 9 (September 1939), 26-33.
17 Clasen, op. cit.
18 Harold E. Shaw, Holliston Mills. Letter to author, November 6, 1939.

described, with good reason, as waterproof, washable, grease-proof, scuff-proof, and 'resistant to wear and weather.' [19]

Soon after the Newburgh firm got under way, a rival company was organized in Newark, New Jersey, making a waterproof cloth marketed under the name 'Keratol.' It was successfully used in library rebindings as early as 1903 by the Public Library of Newark.[20] The product of the Keratol Company has, in common with Fabrikoid, been extremely popular for use on school-books, reference books of many kinds and even trade books, and has been extensively used in library rebindings. Similar cloths have been added to the lines of other companies and are available under various trade names. The types of cloth now used in edition bindings are so many and varied that it is impossible to discuss them here.

The bibliographic implications of the foregoing data regarding the firms engaged in book cloth manufacture may now be briefly stated. In general, it can be said that English cloth was used in an overwhelming majority of cases on American edition-bound books during the nineteenth century. Specifically, English cloth was used as a rule from the beginning in the 1820's until the founding of Interlaken in 1883; use of American-made book cloth was the quite rare exception. Apparently the largest exporter of cloth to America was Wilson and Bentley until Winterbottom appeared on the scene; between 1868 and 1883 the Winterbottom product easily predominated. From 1883 to 1900 came the gradual infiltration of domestic book cloth, which will make it difficult to determine the origins of cloth found on American edition bindings of this period until detailed information on the patterns, colors, and weaves of American cloth is available. By 1900 American

[19] Frank R. Price, E. I. du Pont de Nemours & Co., Inc. Letter to author, November 13, 1939.

[20] 'Fifty Years, 1889-1939,' *The Library*, fiftieth anniversary issue, Public Library of Newark, New Jersey, p. 17.

cloth predominated in this country and export possibilities were being exploited. Since that time the domestic market has been controlled unquestionably by domestic manufacturers.

Edition binders have had at their disposal not only an ever increasing variety of cloths, but, since the introduction of sized cloth, a material that was capable of receiving innumerable forms of decoration. The types of decoration employed have always, of course, followed the changing dictates of the taste, good or bad, prevailing during the nineteenth century. While I am not attempting here to treat, except incidentally, the edition binding styles of the past century, I do wish to call attention to the principal methods by which the effects desired were achieved.

## *Graining*

Since 1832 and until the revival of unfinished cloths in the 1920's, book cloth was made in a more or less standardized manner, consisting in the application of a coating, at first of starch and much later of pyroxylin, to a light cloth base. The primary purpose of such coatings from the beginning was to make possible the decoration of book covers. The first step in that direction was to provide the cloth with an all-over pattern which would present an attractive appearance even if the book it covered went untitled and undecorated at the embossing press, as, in fact, often happened in the early 1830's when a paper label still frequently sufficed to carry title information.

While there is an abundance of external evidence regarding the grains imparted to book cloth during the nineteenth century, we have relatively little specific knowledge regarding the processes by which such all-over grains were achieved. In the light of modern methods of graining book cloth, together with one or two earlier references, the general process may be reconstructed fairly accurately.

The requirements for graining the prepared cloth included a plate that was soft enough to be engraved with the desired pattern yet hard enough — or capable of being hardened — to retain its design indefinitely under thousands of severe impressions while heated, and a machine capable of exerting the necessary pressure. Such machines — the embossing or arming presses — were available in England following 1832 and in America not later than 1838. Little information, however, has been recorded regarding the plates used or the makers of them.

It is obvious enough, I think, that the business of making such plates was at first so slight in volume as to comprise merely a side-line for an artisan making similar products for other uses. The nature of the work involved makes it logical to assume that most plates were made by brass engravers — many such are listed in the directories of the 1830's and 1840's — on order from the large bookbinders at first, then by the book cloth manufacturers following the beginnings of that industry in the 1840's. The imperishable nature of the steel engraving made steel also an ideal metal of which to make cloth graining plates. Judging from the frequency with which new cloth grains appeared in England beginning with the 1850's, it is likely that one or more English engravers had developed such work into a profitable specialty.

It is probable that both flat plates and rollers were used from the beginning. George Dodd has described a cloth-embossing machine accommodating engraved rollers which made it possible to grain a roll of cloth in one continuous operation (see Fig. 43).[21] It is also not unlikely that flat plates were used at the same time and possibly to a greater extent, since they were easier to engrave, and could be accommodated on an ordinary embossing or hydraulic press of ample dimension, eliminating the necessity of purchasing a special cloth-embossing machine. The use of the flat plate

[21] Dodd, op. cit., p. 381.

also permitted the graining of cloth in rolls: as one impression was struck and the pressure removed, the cloth was merely moved forward the width of the plate and another impression made. Both rollers and plates are in use today, plates being used the more widely.[22] (Figure 53 illustrates typical graining rolls.)

English control of the book cloth trade in America and the ineffectiveness of American competition until the 1880's kept the American demand for cloth graining plates at a minimum. As we have seen, the American book cloth industry made great strides in the 1880's and 1890's until a profitable demand arose for graining plates. About 1898 or 1899 the F. A. Ringler Company in New York first undertook the manufacture of cloth graining plates in addition to their regular business of electrotyping and general engraving.[23] The founder of the firm, F. A. Ringler, was born in Hesse-Cassel in 1852[24] and came to America shortly thereafter. Although he established his engraving business in 1871, it was not until sometime in the nineties that his interest was turned to graining and embossing plates. About that time he became interested in a galvanoplastik process for the making of imitation leather plates which was first explained in 1886 by Dr. Georg Langbein of Leipzig.[25] Responding to the growing demand in America, the Ringler Company began making embossing plates in imitation leather designs.

This company is now the larger of the two American firms manufacturing cloth graining plates. From its small beginning in the last century it now supplies plates made in about five days from any of the more than two thousand master plates kept in stock. In addition to their use in the

22 Justin F. Schiess, F. A. Ringler Company. Interview, November 28, 1939. Letter to author, dated September 24, 1940.
23 Ibid.
24 Albert Bernhardt Faust, *The German Element in the United States*, 2 volumes in 1 (New York: Steuben Society, 1927), II, 110.
25 Georg Langbein, *Vollständiges Handbuch der galvanischen Metall-Niederschläge (Galvanostegie und Galvanoplastik)* Leipzig: Klinkhardt, 1886), p. 269.

preparation of book cloth, they are used to make imitation leather papers and to produce imitation grains on such leathers as calf and sheep. The company supplies a world-wide market, its exports even exceeding its domestic business.[26]

Briefly, Dr. Langbein's process faithfully reproduced the texture of any animal skin by working from a section of the skin itself. A thin facing of copper was deposited by electrolysis on the skin. This copper facing, when lifted from the skin, was naturally a perfect reproduction except for the fact that it was in reverse. Another coating deposited on this reverse plate, when lifted off, exactly duplicated the texture of the original skin. This plate became the master pattern from which all embossing plates for actual use in graining were taken. Reverse plates made from the master pattern were mounted on a steel back and were used in embossing presses under heat and pressure to impart to paper, starch-filled or pyroxylin-coated cloth, or to such leathers as sheep and calf the appearance of morocco, pigskin, alligator, and scores of other skins with a faithfulness that virtually defied detection. The master plates were retained in stock and used for the production of duplicate embossing plates as they were ordered.

To satisfy the demands for current styles of mechanical grains engravers were set to work at a process that demanded the old-style craftsmanship. Mechanical designs were first cut by hand on a small soft steel roller called a 'mill' or 'knurl,' which was then hardened. The design was then impressed by the mill over the entire surface of a soft steel plate, which was carefully finished by hand. Since the area copied on a mill was necessarily small, plates made by this method were inclined to show a set repeat or pattern, a peculiarity often noticeable in imitation leather products. In the making of embossing rollers the same procedure was

[26] Schiess, op. cit.

followed, the plate being replaced by the roller.[27] This interesting generalization results: prior to the introduction of Dr. Langbein's process, all cloth grains — including the so-called imitation leather and morocco grains of the 1830's — were 'mechanical' grains, produced in the manner just described. Only grains made by Dr. Langbein's process can be strictly called 'imitation leather' grains as that term is now employed by the trade.

It cannot be considered other than a sad commentary upon the integrity of the industry that such elaborate methods have had to be employed to convert a simple, honest material like muslin into something that looked like morocco. One can readily understand the prejudice against cloth held by book buyers in the 1820's, who were accustomed, by and large, to leather-bound books. The publisher's desire to hide the true nature of the material was undoubtedly born of the need to sell his books. When sized cloth became available in 1832 with its capacity for seeming to be what it was not, any ethical scruples publishers and book cloth manufacturers may have had were easily overcome by the increased purchases of books by the multitude who failed to detect the deception. Unfortunately, as cloth binding came to be accepted, methods of achieving more perfect imitations — as, for example, Dr. Langbein's process — were developed to the point where even experts could be confounded. Undoubtedly the modern excuse would substitute 'decoration' for 'deception,' yet the intent to deceive is usually fundamental. In justice to the bookbinding trade it should be said that similar instances of deliberate misrepresentation may be found in other branches of the publishing industries. Yet who is there that will not acknowledge that an honest but uninspired piece of craftsmanship — hand or machine work — is more to be admired than a beautiful fake?

The imparting of all-over patterns or grains to sized cloth

27 Schiess, op. cit.

in quantities for a wholesale market was only a first step in the decoration of books, however, for grained cloths were capable of receiving further impressions of lettering and decoration at the embossing press. These impressions, progressing from simple titles embossed on the spine to elaborate combinations of designs embossed in blind, gilt, or color, were adapted to the individual title at hand, and became the function of the edition binder rather than the book cloth manufacturer. The mechanics of this process constitute another interesting phase of the industrialization of bookbinding, although again I am able to make only casual reference to the decorative styles employed and remain within the limits of this essay.

## Embossing

It will have been observed no doubt that I have approached the several phases of edition bookbinding with these questions in mind: what were the problems? where, when and by what means were they solved? and what were the resultant effects of these solutions upon the industry? I am treating the processes and machines involved in the embossing of designs onto cloth covers in the same way, naturally, although I must necessarily avoid the most inviting by-path uncovered by this study in so doing; namely, the esthetics of design in American edition bindings during the nineteenth century. Though the subject eminently deserves attention, and soon, I believe the more basic problems of technique deserve prior consideration.

We know that cloth bindings could not be decorated except by printed labels until 1832, when sized cloth was first used. With sized cloth available bookbinders soon discovered that not only could grains be imparted to the surface, but also that titling could be done in gold with the finisher's pallet. The earliest example of such work in America that has come to my attention is found on a book dated 1835 bound in a green imitation leather cloth, with this brief form of the title stamped on the spine: *Public Instruction in Prussia.*[28] Its manner of production is obviously the same as that still commonly practised by the extra binder and library rebinder; namely, glairing the back, laying on the gold, assembling brass type in the finisher's pallet, heating the type at the finisher's stove, impressing the letters onto the gold by the force of the finisher's arm, and wiping off the surplus gold with a rag. It is apparent that brass type for bookbinders was readily available, and undoubtedly was a stock item in the Binny & Ronaldson and other type foundries.

The hand binder's tools for the application of gold continued to be used for titles and small decorative ornaments — with some competition, it is true, from the printed paper label — until the embossing press came on the scene. With its introduction in America at least as early as 1838 it became possible to use more elaborate titles and to decorate larger areas. These decorative designs consisted of conventional flower arrangements and other decorative motifs, and were of such a size as to preclude the possibility of their having been produced except under the substantial pressure of the embossing machine. Although they were undoubtedly of brass, they resembled in technique the wood engravings of the period, and apparently were little more than copies of wood-engraved printers' decorations.

While it is probable that many such designs did service for more than one book — and also that as many different designs as there were finishers were used in the binding of one issue of a single book — it quickly became customary, as edition binding equipment grew in size, for ornamentation to be designed especially for the book and to be used for that book only. This meant a decided increase in the demand for brass cover dies, which during this time had

[28] M. Victor Cousin, *Report on the State of Public Instruction in Prussia* (New York: Wiley & Long, 1835).

been made by any number of general engravers, brass name-plate makers, harness decorators, etc. The story of what is probably the oldest firm still in existence specializing in brass cover dies will typify the development of this special branch of the trade.

This was the business founded in 1870 by Edward Gorenflo, who called himself 'Manufacturer of book binders' rolls, hand tools, press stamps, lines, palletts and dies for embossing.' After attending the mechanics' institute of Pforzheim, 1852-1854, he came to America about 1855 and secured employment with the firm of John R. Hoole, at that time advertised as a 'Book-Binders' Furnishing Warehouse,' 124 Nassau Street, New York. Hoole's original business was that of engraver and die maker and was so advertised in 1844. John R. Hoole was succeeded by his son, W. Edmund Hoole, whom we find listed in the 1857 directory three times: E. Hoole, Book-Binders' Warehouse, 114 Nassau Street; Edmund Hoole, Die Sinker, 175 William Street; and E. Hoole, Engraver, 160 William Street. Edward Gorenflo continued with the Hoole firm, becoming a partner in the 1860's, until he formed his own business in 1870.

Gorenflo issued in 1885 an interesting *Specimen Book* and price list of the bookbinders' rolls and hand stamps he manufactured and regularly carried in stock. The cover of this pamphlet (Fig. 54) is particularly notable in that it was printed in three colors and 'is intended as a specimen of my work, the plates are brass, as for stamping a regular cloth cover.'[29] While brass cover dies and hand stamps were his specialty, even so late as 1885, the *Specimen Book* informs us that he was prepared to make, in addition, scarf and glove stamps, hat dies, shirt stamps, seal presses and steel punches.[30] After the death of Edward Gorenflo, the business was carried on by his sons Edward and Stephan.

[29] Edward Gorenflo, *Specimen Book* (New York: Gorenflo, 1885), p. [2].
[30] Ibid., cover.

Stephan is now one of three partners operating the firm.[31]

Another important firm engaged primarily in the production of brass cover dies is the Becker Brothers Engraving Company, 103 Lafayette Street, New York. This firm was organized about 1885 by the brothers Philip and George Becker. Prior to that time Philip Becker had been employed in the die-sinking establishment of James Skelton, at whose death the brothers formed their company, buying out his business and equipment.[32]

The equipment of the die sinker has always been relatively simple, for it was almost completely a hand craft until the introduction of photo-engraving methods early in the twentieth century, in spite of which hand work still is used to a considerable extent. The elaborate and usually delicate designs of the hand stamps of the nineteenth century were engraved entirely by hand on brass plates approximately one-quarter inch in thickness, and were subsequently mounted on iron shafts stuck into wooden handles. The same was true, of course, of blank and gilding rolls. The early introduction of the routing machine made possible the production of considerably more elaborate plates for the stamping press and in much less time. Following preliminary stages of propulsion—probably by foot-treadle and steam—routing machines during the closing years of the century commonly received their power from gas engines (not gasoline). After that they were run by shafting from a large electric motor, and still later changed to individual motors as at present.[33]

Prior to the application of photography to die making, the die engraver worked from layouts and drawings prepared by the publisher. These were submitted in varying degrees of detail and were frequently merely rough

[31] Albert Ammon, Gorenflo Engraving Company. Interview, November 9, 1939.

[32] Philip Becker, Becker Brothers Engraving Company. Letter to author, dated November 27, 1939.

[33] Ibid.

sketches. Much dependence was therefore placed upon the engraver's skill and knowledge of lettering. From the rough designs submitted the engraver prepared a pencil drawing in exact detail for each plate to be made if, as often happened, the binding was to be stamped both in blind and in gilt, or in two or more colors. This drawing was transferred to a brass plate about one-quarter inch in thickness which was turned over to the workman at the routing machine.

By placing various sized cutters in the machine, and working from large areas down to fine lines, the workman cut away the brass to a depth of about one-sixteenth inch, leaving the design standing in relief. The head of the router being stationary except for the vertical movement regulated by the workman's foot, it was necessary for him to move the brass plate about by hand, carefully watching the cutting tool as it cut away the waste brass and left the design remaining. After leaving the routing machine the plate was carefully 'finished' by hand, giving to it small perfections the machine was incapable of producing even in the hands of the most expert operator.

When photography began to be applied to brass die engraving about 1900 it became necessary for the publisher to supply finished drawings or proofs of cover designs and lettering. The transfer of such work to a sensitized brass plate and the initial etched bite into the plate was usually farmed out to a free lance etcher, for the volume of such work did not justify the addition of photographic and etching equipment by the die engraver. The plate was then routed out to the proper depth by the routing machine and finished by hand. Photographically produced dies did not become generally popular, however, until the 1920's, although today approximately three-fourths of the book cover dies are so produced.

The hand stamps, rolls and fillets that formed a substantial part of the die sinker's business in the nineteenth century lost their utility in America around 1900, and have been virtually unavailable here since that time. A growing, though still unprofitable, demand for them now exists as a result of the institution of courses in bookbinding in a number of schools and its growing popularity as a hobby. The best hand tools in use in America today are of German manufacture.[34]

[34] Ammon, op. cit.

# CHAPTER V

## THE GROWTH OF THE INDUSTRY OF EDITION BINDING

THE advent of the cloth binding and the casing process in the late 1820's at first affected, primarily, those publishers who had printing and binding establishments of their own. Such a firm as Harper's in New York, for example, could adapt its plant to produce edition bindings with a minimum of difficulty, since their business was substantial enough to absorb whatever initial outlay was necessary for the purchase of machines and materials, and was growing rapidly enough to permit savings in time and costs to become evident. Those publishers whose binding was handled by individual binders, however, must have found it difficult to persuade their binders to adopt the new style. Eventually their demands were satisfied by the creation of binderies specializing in cloth work.

The first bindery to specialize in cloth work, and hence the first edition bindery of which we have any definite knowledge, was that established by Benjamin Bradley in Boston in 1832. Bradley had secured his training and experience in the shop of Simri Whitney and was Whitney's partner at least from 1828 to 1831 in their shop at 164 Washington Street. In 1832 we find Bradley in sole possession of the bindery at No. 164, and Whitney in partnership with H. G. Terry at 127 Washington Street.[1] From this fact it seems apparent that Bradley was able to buy out Whitney's interest in the firm, and it may very well be that disagreement between the partners on the question of specializing in cloth work had hastened the split. In any event, Bradley's establishment began a prosperous existence of nearly seventy years, whereas both Whitney and Terry went out of business in a few years.

[1] *Stimpson's Boston Directory* (Boston: Stimpson), 1828, p. 291; 1829, p. 284; 1831, p. 332; 1832, pp. 87, 335.

As one of the pioneers in edition binding, Bradley bound all of the publications of Ticknor & Fields; Philips, Sampson & Company; and Crosby & Nichols, and did some of the binding for D. Appleton & Company of New York prior to the establishment of their bindery in 1854. Thomas Y. Crowell, later to found his own publishing company, entered the business with Bradley in 1856 as a youth of twenty. For three years following the death of Benjamin Bradley in 1862 Crowell managed the shop, entering into a five-year partnership with Mrs. Martha M. Bradley, the widow, in 1865.[2] At the end of the five years Crowell obtained complete ownership of the firm, retaining it as property of his publishing firm after it was begun in New York in 1876. The bindery was moved to New York in 1900, and was only abandoned in 1919 after its destruction by fire.[3]

Among the early edition binders of New York perhaps the first that should be mentioned was the firm of Colton & Jenkins. This firm is notable for its practice of embossing the firm name on its bindings, placing the name usually in the wide blind rules forming the frame of the cover design. Whether the idea originated with them is questionable, since some English cloth binders were doing the same thing about the same time. However that may be, I have seen a number of books so marked, the earliest of which was issued in 1843.

This practice was followed by a number of other binders, notably E. Walker & Sons, and E. McWhood, both in New York, and Du Comb & Collins of Philadelphia. E. Walker & Sons operated an establishment of considerable size in the 1840's and 1850's, as attested by an advertising booklet issued in 1850.[4] The only binding bearing the name

[2] *Bookbinding Magazine,* Vol. X, No. 4 (October, 1929), p. 29.

[3] Hellmut Lehmann-Haupt, *The Book in America* (New York: Bowker, 1939), p. 180.

[4] E. Walker & Sons, *The Art of Book-Binding* (New York: Walker, 1850).

of the Walker firm which I have seen was on a book dated 1848, and those bearing the firm names of Du Comb & Collins and McWhood appeared in 1851.

There can be no question but that other binders, especially in Boston, New York, and Philadelphia, became specialists in edition binding in the 1830's and 1840's, although their names have not yet come to light. A great many publishers, also, established binderies as well as printing departments as their business grew. Some of these binderies have been described in histories of publishing; as a rule, however, publishers' memoirs have concentrated upon their lists of authors or upon bookselling or publishing coups memorable in the annals of their firms, rather than upon the mechanical and technical features of their plants. If some omissions seem glaring among the firms catalogued in these pages, blame it upon the preoccupation of the chroniclers of publishing history upon other matters.

Two Philadelphia publishers whose binding plants were notable were J. B. Lippincott & Company and Altemus & Company. The former business was founded in 1836, and sometime prior to 1852 a bindery was established in connection with the printing plant. In 1852 the plant was thoroughly described and illustrated (Fig. 55) in an issue of Godey's *Lady's Book*,[5] and was considered one of the largest plants in existence. Altemus & Company, established by S. T. and Henry Altemus in 1842, soon developed a large edition bindery for the production of their cheap and inexpensive editions.[6]

One of the earliest edition binderies still in existence is that established by Jesse Fellowes Tapley in Springfield, Massachusetts, in 1850. The J. F. Tapley Company moved to New York in 1881 and to its present location at 27-08

[5] C. T. Hinckley, 'Everyday Actualities, No. 6,' Godey's *Lady's Book* [No. 11] (November, 1852), pp. 403-412.

[6] Edwin Troxell Freedley, *Philadelphia and Its Manufactures . . . in* 1857 (Philadelphia: Young, 1858), p. 459.

Thomson Avenue, Long Island City, New York, in 1930.[7]

D. Appleton & Company of New York established its first bindery in 1854, having started in business as booksellers in 1825, and turning to publishing in 1831. In 1855 a printing department was established in Franklin Street. Nine years later they opened a composition and electrotyping plant in Greene Street. With the continued growth of the business they found it necessary to erect a plant in 1867 at 201-219 Kent Avenue, Brooklyn, to house the printing, binding, and composition departments. In 1884, when the plant was described, the bindery occupied five floors 250 feet long and employed about 425 workmen under the supervision of William Matthews, who had been in charge of the bindery since its establishment thirty years before.[8]

The growing publishing business of Chicago produced the great printing firm of R. R. Donnelley & Sons Company, The Lakeside Press, originally founded as Church, Goodman and Donnelley by Richard R. Donnelley in 1864. The history of the firm has been marked by numerous changes in name and address although its place among the leading printing and binding firms of the mid-west has always remained unquestioned.[9]

St. Louis had an edition bindery by 1872, for it was in that year that the Becktold Company was formed by Andrew Wunsch and William B. Becktold. The firm is still located at its original address, 200-212 Pine Street.[10]

An edition bindery was added to the type-setting and stereotype-plate making firm of Little, Rennie & Company of New York in 1876. In this year Mr. Rennie died, the firm of Lange, Little & Company succeeding to the business and

7 J. F. Tapley Company. Letter to author, n.d.

8 Henry Reed Stiles, *The Civil, Political, Professional and Ecclesiastical History . . . of the County of Kings*, 2 vols. (Brooklyn and New York: Munsell [1884]), II, 740-743.

9 E. E. Sheldon, R. R. Donnelley & Sons Company. Letter to author, dated March 13, 1935.

10 A. L. Wunsch, Becktold Company. Letter to author, dated March 14, 1935.

moving to a new eight-story building at 2-20 Astor Place. This firm was dissolved in 1878 and the firm of J. J. Little & Company was formed, the partners being Joseph J. Little and W. Jennings Demorest, publisher of *Demorest's Magazine*. In 1908 Mr. Little built a twelve-story building on East 24th Street, purchasing the Edwin Ives & Sons Bookbindery. Following the death of Joseph J. Little in 1913 the business was administered by the Little Estate Corporation until 1929, when Arthur J. Little, eldest son of Joseph J. Little, purchased the entire interests of the other heirs.[11]

By this time edition binderies appeared on the scene with considerable rapidity. Many were complete book manufacturing plants combining both book printing and binding under the same roof, such as the J. B. Lyon Company of Albany[12] and the W. B. Conkey Company of Chicago[13] established in 1876 and 1877, respectively. In 1880, A. S. Barnes & Company erected a large manufacturing plant in Brooklyn to house their printing, binding, and packing activities.[14] The Plimpton Press was founded in 1882 by Herbert M. Plimpton in Boston, moving to Norwood, Massachusetts, in 1897.[15] The Quinn & Boden Company, Inc., did its first binding in 1882, although the firm dates back to 1874.[16] The firm of L. H. Jenkins, Inc., was established in Richmond, Virginia, in 1884.[17] In 1890 the bindery of George McKibbin & Son was founded in New York, moving to Bush Terminal, Brooklyn, in 1914.[18] Firms estab-

[11] L. H. Porter, J. J. Little & Ives Company. Letter to author, dated March 4, 1935.

[12] Ernest A. Barvoets, J. B. Lyon Company. Letter to author, dated March 18, 1935.

[13] W. S. Conkey Company, *What a Business Man Should Know About Printing and Bookmaking* (Hammond, Indiana: Conkey [*c.* 1929]), pp. 11-13.

[14] Stiles, op. cit., II, 738, 741.

[15] J. L. Ladd, The Plimpton Press. Letter to author, dated March 12, 1935.

[16] M. C. McCarthy, Quinn & Boden Company, Inc. Letter to author, dated March 15, 1935.

[17] Alfred P. Jenkins, L. H. Jenkins, Inc. Letter to author, dated March 18, 1935.

[18] George McKibbin, George McKibbin & Son. Letter to author, dated March 13, 1935.

lished in the 1890's include Brock & Rankin, Inc., Chicago (1892),[19] Braunworth & Company, Inc., New York and Brooklyn (1893),[20] H. Wolff Book Manufacturing Company, New York (1893),[21] American Book Bindery, Inc., New York (1899),[22] and the Engdahl Bindery, Inc., Chicago (1899).[23]

It will be observed that the rapid succession of binderies established in the late seventies, eighties, and nineties coincides with the time of America's pre-emption of leadership in the production of bookbinding inventions and machines, and also with the period of struggle of American book cloth manufacturers to break the English hold on the market. Abroad, American machines sold because they were better than those of foreign make; at home they sold because publishers and manufacturers were faced with a steadily increasing demand for books. The quality of popular education, the degree of literacy, the standard of living were being raised so rapidly that readers of books were increasing both in numbers and in ability to read. They had, moreover, more time for reading and, to a substantial degree, more money with which to buy books. Even those with little money were given access to books in the hundreds of public libraries, large and small, springing up all over the country during those years.

For the general purpose of the publishing trade and the requirements of the average book buyer, the usual edition binding is an eminently satisfactory article, sturdily though mechanically manufactured and pleasantly, often beautifully designed. However, the use given books in public libraries presented new problems to the bookbinding trade, for

19 J. G. Doran, Brock & Rankin, Inc. Letter to author, dated March 16, 1935.
20 C. A. Braunworth, Braunworth & Company, Inc. Letter to author, dated March 11, 1935.
21 *Bookbinding Magazine*, Vol. XVIII, No. 1 (January, 1935).
22 Mary E. Burke, American Book Bindery, Inc. Letter to author, dated March 11, 1935.
23 *Bookbinding Magazine*, Vol. XVIII, No. 1 (January, 1935).

until this time bindings had seldom been called upon to withstand anything other than the ravages of time and the few handlings given them by the owner, his family and, perhaps, a few borrowing friends. Edition bindings had never been intended for any other sort of treatment than this and consequently they were unable to withstand the multiplied use — and abuse — they suffered at the hands of library patrons. The methods evolved to provide the type of binding required for this special type of service is a story in itself, and one that has yet to be told. The final part of this volume, by Dr. Hellmut Lehmann-Haupt, while not primarily concerned with standard library bindings, discusses certain important aspects of the movement for lasting and adequate protection of books.

## SUPPLEMENT TO PART II

ON the whole, very little new information regarding nineteenth century American edition binding has appeared in published form since the data presented in the preceding essay were gathered in the late thirties. The single work most directly related was produced through the efforts of Newton C. Brainard in 1940. This was *The Andrus Bindery, a History of the Shop, 1831–1838,* issued by the Case, Lockwood and Brainard Company of Hartford, Connecticut. The work is interesting for the picture it gives of working conditions and labor-management relationships in the bindery of Silas Andrus in Hartford. It consists of a narrative written by the employees themselves during those years, consisting largely of chatty notes about persons and events. It contributes little, however, to our knowledge of binding techniques or machines.

Edith Diehl's comprehensive work, *Bookbinding; Its Background and Technique* (New York, Rinehart, 1946), while devoted predominantly to the craft or art of hand binding, refers to the development of machine binding and describes it briefly in a few pages. Miss Diehl mentions some of the factors which encouraged the rapid growth of edition binding, particularly in the United States, but does not attempt to detail its development.

Because American edition binding practices in the early nineteenth century had their roots in the techniques used in English binderies, a substantial portion of a recent survey of James Burn and Company is pertinent to the history of American developments in commercial binding. This study by Lionel S. Darley, *Bookbinding, Then and Now* (London, Faber and Faber, 1959), surveys the entire 178-year history of the firm. James Burn was inventor of some of the earliest bookbinding machines, and his firm was one which influenced the adoption of new techniques in the early days.

Two other works of British origin deserve mention. In *Bookbinding for Librarians* (London, Association of Assistant Librarians, 1957), Eric A. Clough refers briefly to the introduction of casing and of binding machines in the nineteenth century, and devotes a chapter to a description of edition binding. He also reviews such recent developments as perfect binding and lamination. References to casing and to several of the machines used for both custom and publishers' bindings are contained also in *A History of English Craft Bookbinding Technique* by Bernard C. Middleton (New York and London, Hafner, 1963). These works are primarily concerned, however, with the techniques of hand binding and preserving library materials.

While peripheral mention of developments in commercial binding may be found in other works concerned with larger aspects of book-trade history, no major study of the changes in method and equipment occurring in the United States since 1900 has yet been made. The first forty years of this century richly deserve early attention, since they encompass the refinement to a high level of the processes and machines traditionally used in edition book-binding, and the first successful development of the "perfect" binding so instrumental in making the paper-back book acceptable to many millions of book users. Documentation of the changes and innovations occurring in this period is available most fully in the binding industry's trade journal, *Book Production Industry,* together with its predecessors *Book Production, Bookbinding and Book Production,* and *Bookbinding Magazine.*

Future students in this field would be particularly well served if members of the industry take steps, individually or collectively, to see that company records and other historical data are preserved and made accessible.

Joseph W. Rogers

*PART III*

# On the Rebinding of Old Books

*By HELLMUT LEHMANN-HAUPT*

# On the Rebinding of Old Books

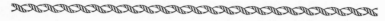

## CHAPTER I

### *INTRODUCTION*

TO put a new binding on an old book is always an unpleasant responsibility. Those who love their books hesitate a long time before they part with what remains of the nice old covers and even the less sentimental feel some doubts when faced with the necessity of rebinding. There seem to be so many perplexing questions about the proper procedure and so little choice as to what to do. Apparently, these problems puzzle owners of a private library as much as professional librarians.

Although I have burned my fingers in trying, unsuccessfully, to put gold letters on a leather back and have occasionally managed to bind a little pamphlet, I am not a bookbinder. But I have always been very much interested in bookbinding of all kinds and have had a good opportunity to study rebinding problems over a number of years and in a variety of places.

It seems to me that there are quite a number of important things that have not been put into print. The literature of bookbinding, like that of any other conceivable topic, has grown in our time to mammoth proportions. There would be no point in repeating the information and advice contained in the practical manuals of bookbinding, some of which are excellent. It would harm no one who feels concerned with the proper care and treatment of volumes entrusted to him to read, or reread, Douglas Cockerell's splendid *Bookbinding and the Care of Books*, first published in London in 1901. A more recent volume, and one that takes into consideration problems peculiar to this country, is Harry M. Lydenberg and John Archer's *The Care and*

*Repair of Books,* published in New York by R. R. Bowker in
1931. There is not much information about how to repair
an old volume and the materials with which to do it which
this book does not contain. While there are one or two
points which I am going to add to that information, it
should be understood clearly that this essay does not attempt
to cover the same ground.

The following pages do not contain instructions on how
to rebind or repair an old volume, but advice as to the best
way to get this done. We might call it the ethics and aesthetics of rebinding that are to be discussed. The reader will
find here some quite general and some quite special considerations, a little history, and a little something about
materials and methods — all presented to help in solving the
many difficult problems encountered in the proper rebinding of old books.

Something worth doing at all is worth doing well. There
are some excellent reasons why this applies to the rebinding of old volumes. In a book there is a relationship of body
and soul that matters. Beauty is not a superfluous luxury
but something that very few of us can live without, whether
we know it or not. The vast majority of old books partake
of beauty, some of them deliberately and obviously, others
incidentally and not so obviously. Replacing the old covers
is a major operation and one that is successful only if the
patient survives. Many precious remnants of the past have
been murdered, to all intents and purposes, by careless or
brutal rebinding. There are very few public collections
that do not contain an uncomfortable number of such
casualties.

It is a very curious thing but nevertheless true that the
least attractive, most 'strictly utilitarian' of new bindings
on old volumes are usually technically unsound and highly
impractical. They are awkward to use, as it is difficult to
open them and to keep them open. They are hard to read
because there is so little inner margin that the right edges

of the left pages and the left edges of the right pages disappear in the depths of the sewing. Fine old engravings are pierced in many places by the 'economical' method of overcasting. It is no exaggeration to say that in choosing such methods for the sake of economizing a few cents per volume, a great many dollars have been lost by the permanent and irreparable damage inflicted at the same time. I am quite willing to prove this to anyone who does not believe it.

Unfortunately, the kind of care recommended on the following pages cannot very well be applied to all old books. It would be nice if they could all be treated with equal respect and consideration, and the day will perhaps come when this is possible. At the present this cannot be done; time and money make it necessary to discriminate.

There is I suppose no uniform way of determining which of the old books in a given collection qualify for preferred treatment and which do not. The individual owner of books, be he a collector or merely someone who prefers to own the books he reads, will know how well he likes each individual volume and how much care he can afford to give the patients on his shelves—even if he may be uncertain about the best way of going about it.

In libraries this will be more difficult to determine. There are not a few libraries (or shall we say collections of books available to the public?) that by their very purpose and definition should attempt nothing but the very best of care, protection, and preservation of every single volume they own. But with most libraries that will not be the case. Most libraries will have to differentiate in the physical treatment of their volumes, and single out those that deserve special care. It would be impossible for a library with large holdings of rare, valuable, and semi-precious books to make a complete segregation in a short time. But it is not impossible to accomplish this necessary task systematically over a period of time.

For instance, most libraries of some size do have collections of special material given them as a unit or crystallizing around some definite starting point. Also, libraries throughout the country have shown themselves increasingly interested in segregating their holdings of old and valuable material into collections set apart, physically and in treatment, from the general run of books on the open shelves. All books contained in these reserve rooms, rare book collections and treasure vaults naturally enter into consideration here. The librarians in charge of these collections will naturally want to do their best. They will certainly welcome a discussion of how to deal with their most serious patients, even if not all will agree with all of the suggestions made on the following pages.

Segregating the rare and valuable material from open shelves is in most libraries a perennial task. Many fine old volumes that should be locked up are still on open shelves in libraries throughout the country. There are theories of dates in circulation by which to determine, once and for all, what books should be segregated. I have heard such suggestions as: all European books before 1700; all American books before 1800 belong in the treasure room. Unfortunately, it is not so simple as that and many worthwhile and valuable volumes will continue to live on the open shelves for a good while yet. It will not be possible at this time to take care of them properly. May I emphasize at this point how important it is that they should at least not be taken care of improperly? This is something that should be possible in every library. It should be possible to make sure that each book, when it does get treated, receives the kind of treatment it deserves. Also, there is no reason why new books, at the time of their acquisition, or at some other definite point in the process of their preparation for the shelves, could not be classified in regard to physical treatment.

The standard library binding while it solves a good many problems admirably and certain problems adequately enough, can rarely be applied successfully to a fine old volume. The fact that it has quite often been used for that purpose is no proof to the contrary. It was never meant for that type of binding at all. There is the possibility of a misunderstanding here. Members of the library binding profession who may be looking at these statements and others further along in this discussion might gather the impression that we are perhaps disregarding their particular problems. That is not the case. It is quite true that this essay approaches rebinding from the point of view of the owner rather than that of the professional binder. But an explanation of the problems and the needs of his client, even if they do not seem to coincide exactly with what he has at present to offer, ought to prove helpful and stimulating to the professional binder. It might very well point the way to a kind of service which, while not readily available at the present time, would greatly increase the usefulness of a bookbinder to the library he wishes to serve. Very much the same thing is true in regard to the bookbinder who caters to private collectors. Many of the suggestions contained in the following pages are unorthodox in so far as they do not correspond readily to existing practices and customs. For that reason they will undoubtedly meet with objections from those who prefer to leave things as they are. Again there is the chance of a misunderstanding here. The following pages do not aim to criticize the current methods of bookbinding for collectors and libraries. They aim to point out why, in the case of fine old volumes, these methods are not always advisable, and they discuss the adjustments and changes recommended to a binder in order to improve his usefulness and, perhaps, to open for him new opportunities for service.

It is also hoped that this discussion may convince the owners of fine old volumes which need attention that, contrary to their belief, they can afford after all to have their books taken care of without undue expense, and in a pleasant and appropriate manner.

## CHAPTER II

### *WHAT IS WRONG WITH THE CURRENT METHODS?*

TWO types of bindings are in general use today for the rebinding of old books. One of them is the collectors' binding, the other one the standard library binding. It can be shown, I believe, that neither of them is a fully satisfactory answer to the need for practical and adequate rebinding of rare and old material. The present-day collectors' binding is a somewhat unfortunate survival of the type of binding that originated in the course of the nineteenth century and reached its culminating point in the 1880's and the 1890's. One of the chief characteristics of this type of binding is its high, often exorbitant price. It owes its existence largely to the fact that a collector who has paid many hundreds or thousands of dollars for a manuscript or a printed book will find it only natural to spend a sum for binding that has at least a percentual relationship to the price of the volume. As a result, the de luxe binder catering to these needs had to find a standard of technique, materials of bindings, and a kind of decoration that would justify high prices. To be sure, books of this kind are usually sound from a technical point of view. The pages will have been repaired with the greatest of care; they will show a superior job of hand sewing, with thread of high quality and substantial cords; and the leather will be of the finest and smoothest quality, and it may even last. But it is after this stage in the binding process that so much damage is done. The entire binding will be covered, in all possible and impossible places, with gold tooling. There will be silk lining sheets and an endless sequence of specially inserted blank pages at the beginning and the end: all these things showing that no time, no effort, no material has been saved to give 'the very best.' Yet, by the time the de luxe binder has finished his work, there is very little left of the old volume. It has been locked up, as it were, in a gilded cage, and has hardly room to breathe. Its true physiognomy is hidden under an artificial coating of false splendor. There is no natural affinity between inside and outside, no pleasant relationship between covers and pages. As a matter of fact, these modern de luxe bindings all look very much alike, and if it were not for the lettering on the back, it would be impossible to say whether the sumptuous morocco covers enclose an early Venetian edition of a classic author or a volume of fashionable verses of the 1870's. This similarity is true in spite of, or perhaps even because of, the fact that the binder will have made every effort to imitate, as he knows it, an old binding to suit the old book. The result, 'a kind of refined massacre,' is usually the very opposite from what the binder really wanted to achieve.

It is this attempt to recapture the decorative spirit of an older time that marks the difference between collectors' bindings of the later nineteenth century and the rebinding methods of older centuries.

Naturally, old books have been put into new bindings for many centuries, and the methods of rebinding developed along with the general evolution of bookbinding. The mid-sixteenth century with its famous Groliers, Majolis, and the bindings for members of the royal families, marks the beginning of a specific type of collectors' binding. This was probably first used for contemporary books, but there is no reason to assume that there was any differentiation in the treatment of old and contemporary books then. So we find the same mid-sixteenth-century bindings on books of that period and on earlier printed books and on some manuscripts as well. As a matter of fact, there was no interest in the original mediaeval bindings on the part of the collectors and the librarian in secular and monastic collections of the sixteenth, the seventeenth and the eighteenth centuries.

E. P. Goldschmidt, in his splendid *Gothic and Renaissance*

*Bookbindings* gives some interesting information on this point. In discussing the comparative rarity of early monastic bindings of England and France, he mentions the devastating effect of the French Revolution upon the monastic libraries of France. 'But,' he goes on, 'an equally potent agent of destruction of the ancient bindings, operating in France as elsewhere, was the loving care of the wealthy abbeys for their fine libraries in the seventeenth and eighteenth centuries. St. Germain-des-Prés, the Benedictine houses of the Congregation de St. Maur, and other abbeys had preserved many ancient manuscripts and incunabula; but not content to build glittering baroque library rooms for them, they did not stint the expense of having them all rebound in morocco and calf with richly gilt backs. The same practice was observed by the great French collectors of the Louis XV and XVI periods, in so far as, like the Duc de Lavallière, they cared at all for mediaeval stuff; no volume was allowed to stand on their resplendent shelves before it was smoothly coated by one of the Deromes or Padeloups. Quod non delerunt Barbari delerunt Barberini, said the Romans, when in the seventeenth century Urban VIII and his family set out to modernize Rome.'

In their disregard for the original appearance of their mediaeval books these famous collectors of the past set an unfortunate example which has been followed ever since. But at least the style of decoration on their books was original as of their time; those were frankly and fully contemporary bindings, not different from the bindings applied to books that were new then and were being bound by the very same craftsmen for the first time. It was reserved for the bookbinders of the nineteenth century to invent the so-called period binding.

The standard library binding of today is undesirable on rare and old books for different reasons than those which apply to so many of the typical collectors' bindings.

The library binding, technically speaking, is not a genuine bookbinding in the traditional sense, but a revised and reinforced version of the edition binding or casing method. It originated around the beginning of this century as a perfectly legitimate means to save and protect the mass of nineteenth-century literature and the many contemporary volumes that appeared in a very unreliable format; produced by cheap, speedy methods, and using shoddy, rapidly decaying materials, such as mechanical wood pulp paper, dubious fabrics and inferior grades of leather.

The 'leather scare' in the early part of this century, when it was found that most of the sheepskins and calfs used since the end of the eighteenth century and through the nineteenth century were crumbling to dust, must have had a good deal to do with the firm establishment of library binding and with the preference for the heavy service cloths. This was all to the good, and it remains the proper method to protect the current output of every-day books which need to be circulated.

The great mistake was to adopt this standard library style without discrimination to every sort and kind of book that needed rebinding. It was, or rather still is, I fear, like trying to sew on a button with a sewing machine or to shoot sparrows with a machine gun.

In contrast to the collectors' bindings this standard library binding is technically not sound when used for the rebinding of the better kind of old books. Later on we will go into this a little more thoroughly. I have seen in libraries a great many valuable old books that have suffered severely from having had an inappropriate library binding forced on them. These bindings are straightjackets rather than fitting and pleasant clothes. I recall a copy of Dibdin, each of its three volumes trimmed to a different size, each in a different color of buckram, each with a different style of lettering on the back, and with a sewing that makes it impossible to open the books properly. The damage is not only a technical one, it is a spiritual one as well, and, last but not least, it does represent a financial loss. I think that the damage done to old books through improper binding within the last fifty years represents a very substantial amount of money. The sad thing is that the loss is usually irreparable.

# CHAPTER III

## *SUGGESTING A REMEDY*

NOTHING much would be gained in dwelling at length on the many reasons for the high number of rebinding casualties in both private and public collections. It is obvious that neither the collector or librarian nor the binder can be made separately responsible for these damages. Economic reasons, a certain helplessness due to the lack of experience and proper information, and also indifference, on the part of owners and librarians as well as of the bookbinders themselves, are the chief reasons.

The solution which I have in mind is a kind of rebinding that lies somewhere midway between the collectors' binding and the standard library binding. It is possible to develop rebinding methods that cost much less than the modern de luxe binding, and not much more than the standard library binding, and avoid the undesirable features of both.

This new approach to rebinding is not something that can be set down neatly point by point in terms of binding specifications. It is something that involves experimentation and patience, and much good will and co-operation between binders and owners and custodians of books.[1] The first thing to clarify is the nature of this new kind of 'midway-binding.' What does it consist in? In what way does it differ from existing practices? Only after these questions have been thoroughly discussed, will it be possible to show what results are obtainable by these methods and by what means they can be put into operation.

I have already mentioned the so-called period style of binding that attempts to express the character of a volume in terms of the ornamental style of a bygone period. There is an urge back of this method that would be to the good if it did not invariably choose the wrong kind of approach

[1] I know at least of one case of very successful co-operation between a well-established old collectors' binding firm and a large library.

to a problem. By being too literal and often too explicit it misses the mark. Instead of conservation of the old we get an imitation that clashes badly with the real original inside of the book. The distinction between imitation and the kind of reinterpretation, if I may call it that, that I wish to recommend is an almost invisible borderline. And yet it makes a great deal of difference in the final product on what side you finally land. The one thing from which we cannot possibly get away is that the past is the past and the present is the present. We should not today try to put a new but old-looking binding on a book. But we can save the physiognomy of the old volume by doing the new thing in terms of the old. If the period style binder manages to make a modern binding that looks like an old one, he approaches dangerously near the realm of the fake. There is, I believe, only one case where such a reproduction binding is appropriate, and that is on a facsimile of an old text. Where a whole book is put out as a close reproduction of an old publication, the binding too can be a facsimile of an old binding.

There is one other undesirable feature of the elaborately planned period binding: its cost. Naturally, a great deal of time and care is necessary to match the gilded decoration of an old binding, much more time and trouble in fact than to create a modern binding in a contemporary style of decoration which, after all, is the more creative and probably the more honest thing to do. The high price of period bindings, I fear, has done much altogether to prevent owners of old books from having their patients attended to. It certainly has made things very difficult for the hand binders today. The hand binder does need to be kept going, and anything is desirable that will help him and will encourage the preservation of his craft, which is not only noble by heritage and distinguished in age and past performance, but a necessary living link in the working methods of today.

Off and on, in lectures, magazine articles, and through exhibitions, the hand binder's plea is brought before the public. It is a pity that these appeals are often brought forth without a realization of the technical and artistic possibilities of modern handbinding. Even today many hand binders stress their ability to produce a facsimile of any given old binding rather than their interest in the contemporary possibilities of bookbinding by hand.

Of course, we do want some continuity, and we do want an expression, in the binding, of the physiognomy of the entire book. But rather than rely upon the gold tooling to perform the miracle, it is possible to find much simpler, less expensive, and really more effective means towards this goal. It is the materials of bindings and the manner of their use that one ought to observe if one wishes to determine the style of binding suitable for an old book. It has probably never occured to many owners of books that the mere choice of a certain material — of leather, cloth, or paper — is an essential part of the 'design' of a volume, or that there is a definite tradition in various places and at different periods governing this selection. The choice of material is an even more obvious part of the design where not only one material but a combination of two or three has been used. There is a large number of combinations possible among the various types of parchments, leathers, papers, and cloths. A definite law of evolution governs the way in which these materials have been applied at different times and in different localities. It is interesting to discover which are early and which come later, where a certain practice originated and how long it remained popular. Some, it will be found, are universal; they can be found almost at all times and places.

The technical processes of binding, too, have a history of their own which it is possible to trace. These processes ought to be studied carefully. In planning a new binding, it is relevant to know, for instance, whether a book was originally sewn by hand or cased by machine; whether it had a tight back or a hollow one; or whether the end-papers were added to the first and last signatures of the book, or were a part of them.

If a person has to rebind or have rebound an old book, it will be quite easy to find an appropriate and practical model, if the book is still in its original binding or shows some substantial fragments of the original binding. In that case the natural guide is on hand. The problem then is to translate the old binding into modern terms of materials and workmanship. It will be found that most of the materials used on older bindings have survived and can be found in actual use today. The same is fundamentally true of the technical binding methods. The traditional skills are not dead, they can be found if and when they are needed.

Rebinding an old book is more difficult when the original binding is gone, or when the book is found in a temporary cover or wrapper, or when the book was rebound once already. Many such second bindings have not stood up well, and it is a peculiar satisfaction to observe that it is usually the ugly, thoughtlessly utilitarian binding that after all turns out to be technically unsound.

In such cases where the book itself offers no clue for rebinding the next step is to try and find some other volume of approximately the same period and locality that still has its original binding. One may be able to find such a volume in a private library or in a public collection. Most public libraries of some size and, I believe, the majority of college libraries will own such volumes. It will be easiest to find them in collections arranged chronologically. If no such collection is available, the catalogue of a large library might be consulted under the name of a classical author. His editions are usually listed in chronological order and in many cases will yield the sample of style for which we are looking.

Some collectors and libraries have the ambition to own

as many different editions of a single book as possible. Such collections too are useful for our purposes and the older the first edition of the book the greater, naturally, the variety.

This search for a sample can, of course, be exaggerated. I am suggesting this only as a first step for the uninitiated and as a stimulus to observation and study. I cannot repeat too often that we are not after period bindings. Not imitation is recommended but sensible conservation.

It should also be said here that not the 'fine bindings' of a certain period are necessarily the best examples for which to look. We are interested more in the regular bindings found on the more ordinary books of the past centuries. Therefore, the collections of fine bindings in existence to-day are not necessarily the best source of information for re-binding purposes. I do not know now of a museum or li-brary where a permanent exhibition or collection of typi-cal bindings of all periods and localities is available. There would be considerable interest and practical use in such a collection.

The same condition prevails in the literature of book-binding. The majority of publications in the field devote themselves to a discussion of fine bindings exclusively, and in many cases they are nothing else than histories of the gold decoration of leather covers. Very little has been observed and printed about the history of bookbinding materials, their combination and the evolution of technical methods.

In its general outlines this development is a fairly simple story. The fundamental types are few, and for our purposes the finer shades and variations may be disregarded.

What makes the actual account a somewhat difficult mat-ter is the lack of definite data on the beginnings and endings of certain practices. There is a large number of interesting details observable at different places and times, but they are very hard to nail down. The following account, there-fore, cannot be considered a really reliable rehearsal of the history of binding materials and technique as such. Rather, it is a story with a moral. And the moral, as in all such cases, is more readily absorbed and recognized when the supporting facts are simple and few.

What the following pages contain is a sort of generalization of binding practices. We may call these statements the rules of a game which can be played by anyone who feels so inclined and has the interest and the patience to experiment.

# CHAPTER IV

# *THE EVIDENCE OF THE OLD BINDINGS*

## *Mediaeval Bindings*

THERE are important differences between the structure of a mediaeval volume and a book produced after 1500. The covers of the mediaeval volume are always made of wooden boards, attached to the pages with leather thongs and covered with parchment or leather; it has a flat back with no decoration or lettering on it; the covers are decorated and sometimes lettered by blind tooling. After 1500 most books have boards made of cardboard, attached with hempen cords and covered with parchment, leather, or some other material; the backs begin to be rounded and to carry decoration and lettering; gold tooling takes the place of, and supplements, blind tooling.

The heavy wooden board is in universal use from the beginnings of bookbinding to the end of the Middle Ages. It is the logical material for large and heavy volumes. Many early books were large and heavy, especially books written or printed on vellum which needed to be enclosed in substantial covers that could exercise a certain amount of pressure on the pages. The wooden boards were useful for this not only because of their own weight and firmness, but also because it was easy to apply metal clasps to them.

Wooden boards, of course, did not disappear all of a sudden at the end of the Middle Ages, they lingered on through the sixteenth century and lasted even into the seventeenth and eighteenth centuries (Fig. 56). They reappeared, in a very delicate variety, in colonial America and, again, on certain of the more ponderous volumes produced by our modern private presses.

Since the early sixteenth century boards made of paper substance have taken the place of wooden covers. They were introduced, probably by way of Italy, from the Islamic countries.

Parchment, vellum, and leather is the characteristic covering material on mediaeval manuscripts and early printed volumes. From the very beginning there is probably no time or place where these materials have not been used as a matter of course.

These materials were sometimes applied without wooden boards as plain wrappers for smaller and lighter volumes. The cords or bands of the book are fastened directly to the cover, and the first and last page of the book pasted onto the front and back cover. This is a much more lasting protection than one might suspect. The surviving examples usually show pretty flexible materials: soft, pliable leather or limp vellum, and flexible cardboard, the latter probably not much before 1500. I have sometimes wondered whether it is not the very lightness and elasticity that has made these covers survive.

Well-preserved examples are extant that appear to be of great age. But the method is so simple, allows so little variation and bears so few distinguishing marks, that it is not possible to establish a correct chronology for the practice. A wrapper of this type may have all appearance of being contemporary with the book that it contains. But only in very few cases is it possible to prove it. At any rate, we have to count with this style both as a likely early method of protecting a book and as a feasible example for modern rebinding.

Doeskin is another material used as a covering material on mediaeval books. It is usually applied in a perfectly plain manner, without any decoration or lettering, and books in this material have lasted fairly well. It is one of the few materials that were discontinued after the end of the Middle Ages.

Very extensive was the use of calf leather, usually in brown color, over wooden boards. From at least the twelfth century on, it can be found with great regularity. It is the classical binding material for the early printed book and its use in the fifteenth century in France, Germany, the Netherlands, and England is practically universal. Calf leather is the ideal medium for blind tooling.

Sheepskin is another material found on manuscripts and early printed books. Its use was more frequent than it would seem, and today quite a number of well-preserved examples are known.

Next to brown a rather brilliant red is found in early leather bound books.

All these types of binding show the use of one and the same material to cover the back of the book and the sides. This is the so-called 'full' binding, the binding in full parchment, in full calf, and even in full paper.

It will probably surprise some readers to hear that this type of binding should have begun so early. Yet, such paper-over-cardboard covers are found in certain small groups at the end of the fifteenth, and in the first half of the sixteenth century. Also, paper wrappers without cardboard covers are found occasionally. Both these types have woodcuts printed on them, usually a figure composition with a border around it.

Before leaving the fifteenth century to observe the many important innovations that came along around and after 1500, we must turn to the beginnings of the 'half binding.' The regular half binding style, where the back of the book is covered with a heavy material and the sides with a lighter one, does not come into regular use before the end of the seventeenth century. But there is one prototype that is much older and can be considered as a mediaeval ancestor: the binding in wooden boards which are left uncovered except for the back, where leather, parchment, or pigskin is applied and carried over onto the boards just far enough to make a strong, lasting connection between back and sides. It is difficult to say just when this kind of binding started and how consistently it was used. Quite likely it was one of the earliest methods of binding, in fact, it may represent a

significant stage in the origin of bookbinding. But that is a
matter of speculation.

The bindings of this type are usually quite plain, yet in
their honest, substantial workmanship, in the use of strong
natural materials, and in the unconscious emphasizing of
function in terms of materials they have a considerable
aesthetic interest. To a certain extent this binding too, like
the book bound in wooden boards and covered with leather
or pigskin, has been revived by some of our modern private
presses.

### *The Sixteenth to the Eighteenth Century*

The sixteenth century brings important innovations
both in technique and in decoration. Of the change from
wooden boards to cardboard covers I have already spoken.
This change is practically simultaneous with a trend
towards smaller books in general and pocket-sized volumes
in particular. Books are more plentiful now, and they are
carried around and accumulated in greater numbers than
ever before. They are kept in a new manner, not lying flat
as in the mediaeval library, but standing upright on their
shelves, side by side, their backs facing the reader. These
backs, hitherto flat and unadorned, now receive rounding
and backing and are given decorative treatment, and gradually lettering appears there, announcing title and author
and sometimes printer and date. By the seventeenth century
we see labels of a differently colored leather on the leather
backs, and this custom assumes greater and greater importance as time goes on.

The sixteenth century also marks the beginning of gold
tooling in the Western World after some experiments in
the fifteenth century, and many hundred years of previous
practice in the Near-Eastern, Islamic world. The technique
and style of gold tooling in the Renaissance and the succeeding periods have been more carefully observed, perhaps, than any other phase of bookbinding, with the result

that the study of the general technique of binding and the choice of materials have decidedly been neglected. It is true that some of the master craftsmen of the past have achieved some very remarkable results by gold tooling. However, as far as skilful rebinding of old volumes is concerned, it is probably better not to attempt an imitation of these patterns. They are unique products of their time and, no matter how hard we try, we cannot hope to compete with the old masters in their own unique manner.

The main thing to remember is that gold tooling, either in decoration or in lettering, does not appear as a regular practice before the beginning of the sixteenth century. The gilding of edges is approximately simultaneous, in appearance and popularity, with gold tooling. Very important is the introduction of a new kind of leather: goatskin, or morocco, as it is more generally called. Most of the morocco leather used in the sixteenth century is brown. Only gradually do we get variety in the basic hue of the leathers used. What lends such rich color and animation to many sixteenth- and seventeenth-century bindings is their decorative treatment. Gold tooling, often combined with blind tooling, is one of the most general methods of ornamentation. But there are other techniques, learned by the European binders from their Islamic masters. There is, particularly, the intricate leather inlay work of the period where characteristic patterns are cut out of the basic covering material and replaced by corresponding pieces of different leather. Similar results could be obtained by pasting down onto the leather covers thin pieces of leather in a variety of shades, and we also find bindings with differently colored patterns painted onto them. Even among the genuine examples of the Renaissance we find some that are too rich to be in very good taste. The nineteenth- and twentieth-century imitations are almost without exception artistic failures, even if some of them are remarkable examples of skill and patience.

Another binding material typical of the sixteenth century, especially in Germany, is pigskin. It is usually found over wooden boards and closely decorated with blind tooling. These bindings represent a somewhat modified continuance of late mediaeval binding practice, comparable to the continued use of Gothic type faces in the realm of German and Scandinavian printing. These pigskins occur mainly in two shades: one originally a natural brown, now slightly darkened by age; the other originally white, also usually darkened and stained by age. A careful and gentle rubbing with a slightly moist cheesecloth does wonders on these bindings, which should be oiled after they have been cleaned.

Other traditional covering materials of the Middle Ages, such as calfskin and parchment or vellum, continue to be used in the sixteenth century, occasionally still over wooden boards, but more frequently on the new type of lighter and thinner cardboard covers.

In passing along from the sixteenth to the seventeenth century, one will observe that changes are most obvious in the style and manner of decoration. In the use of materials and the technique of their application the picture remains much the same as in the sixteenth century.

In France the traditional brown of morocco leathers is gradually giving way to a very rich red which becomes the typical French material of the seventeenth and, particularly, the eighteenth century. Other colors are found as well, of course.

In England and America red morocco does not seem to come into use until about 1660.

Vellum or parchment bindings, highly polished, are still very popular in the seventeenth century, and they have by no means disappeared in the eighteenth century. With colored leather labels between raised bands on their backs and with well-executed gold tooling, they can be very fine specimens indeed.

## *The Use of Paper as a Cover Material*

Very important are the innovations which can be observed in the various papers used for bookbinding and in the manner of their application. From the seventeenth century onward, and fully developed in the eighteenth century, we find beautifully colored and patterned papers used in bookbinding. There are three main types: marbled papers, paste papers and papers decorated by woodblock printing.

There is a popular prejudice against marbled papers. 'They look like sausage and head cheese,' people often exclaim, when they are first mentioned. It is true that some of the bad ones do. To others they are objectionable for their bureaucratic appearance. True again, there are certain nineteenth-century varieties on highly polished surface, the kinds used on ledgers and other commercial diaries, which are not very attractive. As a matter of fact, many of the marbled papers one sees today are not genuine marbled papers at all, but cheap lithographic imitations, sickly in appearance and made on a bad quality of paper. But surely, no one in his right mind would object to Caruso or Lotte Lehman, because he does not happen to care for Bing Crosby or Kate Smith.

Genuine marbled papers are made by sprinkling various oil colors on the surface of water to which certain grease-repelling agents have been added These colors, skilfully stirred by the craftsman, spread, intermingle, and form patterns on the surface of the water and are transferred from there onto the paper to which they become permanently affixed.

Marbled papers seem to have been introduced into various European countries from Turkey in the course of the seventeenth century. By the eighteenth century they are certainly quite common, and various distinguishable types have developed in different countries. By constant observation and by collecting specimens it is quite possible to acquire some skill in recognizing and identifying several of the most important varieties.

Next in order of their chronological appearance one would mention paste papers, which are found, apparently somewhat later than the earliest marbled papers, from the latter part of the seventeenth century on. These decorative papers are made by first covering entire sheets with a darkly colored flour paste, this paste being laid on with broad strokes of the brush. Patterns can then be applied by various instruments and devices, by which some of the colored paste is squeezed aside or removed from the sheet, so as to let the natural light surface of the paper be exposed again to the eye.

Distinct from marble papers and paste papers are the woodblock pattern papers which are stamped or embossed from handsomely carved printing blocks in graceful all-over patterns. Woodblock-printed papers, as we have already seen, were used as early as the fifteenth and the sixteenth century, but they show one complete picture, not repeated small patterns. On the other hand, such repeated small patterns, combining into continuous decorative units, are found on woodblock-printed textiles centuries before Gutenberg. But they do not seem to appear on papers used for bookbinding purposes much before the beginning of the eighteenth century. Then they seem to be very popular indeed and used in many different ways. They include a great many varieties, from simple minutely repeated all-over patterns in two colors to elaborate pictorial arrangements, stamped with gold or silver onto the colored sheets.

The exact chronology and provenance of these various decorative papers is a difficult but fascinating study, and one of no small bibliographical importance. The collection of Mrs. Olga Hirsch, formerly in Frankfurt a.M. and now in England, is an amazingly complete record of this particular branch of the decorative arts. In this country Mrs. Rosamond B. Loring[1] has devoted years to the collecting, the study and the successful production of decorative papers.

These decorative pattern papers are first found as end-papers in the seventeenth century, and they have been used in that manner ever since. However, they do not remain confined to the inside of the volumes which they adorn. They also appear on the outside of the covers, in half-leather and half-vellum bindings and also in full-paper bindings.

We have already met the ancestor of the 'half-style' binding. It is the late mediaeval binding in strong wooden boards, with leather or parchment covered back which reaches over one or two inches onto the sides, but leaves the greater section of the board exposed to the touch and the eye of the reader. Attractive in its honest sturdiness, this type of binding was, nevertheless, doomed, when refinement of material and delicate gold tooling became fashionable. The change to cardboard covers must also have contributed to the disappearance of this prototype of the 'half binding.' There do exist some examples of books with leather or parchment backs and with raw, uncovered cardboard sides, dating from the sixteenth and, possibly, the seventeenth century. Such bindings seem to have reached a certain popularity in Germany around 1600, with cardboard covers that tried to conceal their nakedness under a coat of red or green paint. They may have been influenced by the earlier use of painted or tinted parchment covers.

The real half binding begins when the cardboard sides are covered up with plain or decorated papers. When marbled or woodblock papers are used on the outside and also inside as end-papers, invariably a differently decorated paper is used for each purpose. I do not recall a single his-

[1] In 1933 the Club of Odd Volumes in Boston published her address on "Marbled Papers" in book form. Now the Department of Printing and Graphic Arts of the Harvard University Library is publishing a comprehensive study of decorative pattern papers by Mrs. Loring.

See also Paul Kersten, 'Die Geschichte des Buntpapieres,' in *Wochenblatt für Papierfabrikation*, Jahrgang 69 (Biberach: 1938).

torical instance where the same pattern was used both on the outside of the covers and on the inside. The earlier these bindings are, the narrower is the strip of leather or parchment that reaches over from the back onto the sides. Strictly speaking, these early ones are 'quarter bindings.' Gradually, the leather areas along the spine and the corners increase. The 'half binding' shows a good balance between the two materials. The 'three quarter' binding, which leaves practically nothing but a triangle of paper, is a nineteenth-century affectation.

It is difficult to state just when the quarter-and half-binding style began. Examples are certainly found in the eighteenth century. One theory, which I have been unable to verify, is that half bindings were first introduced at the court of one of the French kings who wanted to economize on leather and ordered marbled paper sides instead. It would certainly be a worthwhile thing to study carefully the origin of these half bindings with paper-covered sides and to collect information on the earliest authentic examples known. Until such a study has been undertaken, we must be satisfied with the general knowledge that this type of binding represents good eighteenth-century practice. That it began in France is made plausible by the fact that in Germany this kind of binding is called: 'Halb-Franzband.'

Full-paper bindings over boards were first made in the fifteenth and sixteenth centuries, and they have already been described in an earlier chapter. They must be considered as isolated experiments, for at the present time there is no evidence of any connection between them and the bindings that became popular in the eighteenth century. The more recent paper-over-board bindings originated possibly about the same time as half-leather and half-vellum bindings with paper-covered sides or, more probably, somewhat later as a further step towards economy and simplification.

These paper bindings can be discovered in almost any

collection of eighteenth-century material that is approximately in its original condition. The amazing and surprising thing about them is: how well they have stood the test of time. They are usually a little frayed out at the corners, and some of the paper may have come loose from the cardboard covers; but the cords and hinges, the basic structure of the binding, are usually quite sound, much sounder than many a younger leather- or cloth-binding from the nineteenth century (Figs. 57 and 58).[2]

Along with the various ornamental papers one finds also papers in a uniform coloring, such as blue and gray. Rarely, if ever, are books with raised cords bound in paper; the backs are always smooth and quite often flat. Top and bottom of the spine, as well as the corners, are sometimes reinforced, this reinforcement sometimes concealed underneath the paper covering, sometimes partly exposed. There is gold tooling to be found on the covers as well as on the back, sometimes in a very elaborate execution.

A good sheet of paper takes gold tooling as well as any leather, cloth, or parchment.

Labels play a great part. Sometimes several of them, in different colors and with gilded lettering, are affixed to the back, simulating an elegant leather back. White labels, with black printing on them, are also frequently found.

The introduction of these paper-bound volumes coincides with the beginning of publishers' bindings.[3] We must not forget that, up to the eighteenth century, the binding of a volume was the responsibiltiy primarily of the ultimate consumer. The individual collector or institution or library would arrange for the binding of their books. Or, the

---

[2] It is amusing to find that some eighteenth-century bindings in full paper imitate the current style of half leather with paper sides. On Fig. 57, for instance, the fourth binding from the left is in mottled half leather with paper sides and its neighbor to the right is a mottled paper back with paper sides.

[3] See page 135 in Part II of this volume for a list of references on early publishers' bindings. The subject is also discussed by Donald B. McKerrow, in his *An Introduction to Bibliography for Literary Students* (Oxford: Clarendon Press, 1928), pp. 124-127.

bookseller would undertake to bind the books that he had
for sale, but not the publisher. With the rise of the novel,
of the family magazine and the almanac, with the advance
of modern publishing conditions, all this changed. Publishers sought for ways and means to put their products on
the market in a pleasant and acceptable format. They hit
upon the paper-bound volume as a good solution. They
thought of it originally as an interim-binding, a binding
that would protect and adorn the volumes until such time
as the purchasers were ready to have them rebound in a
more permanent fashion. But very soon they must have
realized that these paper-over-boards bindings could in
themselves make satisfactory permanent covers. How else
can we explain some of the very elaborate decorations on
eighteenth- and early nineteenth-century volumes bound
in paper?

Carter, in his *Binding Variants* says that 'No book in wrappers or boards was conceived of as remaining permanently
in that condition, and such examples as have survived, are
due to pure chance. Even the advent and increasing prevalence of title labels (of which an example has recently been
observed as early as 1748) merely served the convenience of
the bookseller.'

Probably, this is true for the English side of the story. But
I do not believe that it applies generally.

On the European continent various groups of almanacs
and calendars seem to have been bound quite early and
consistently in decorated, embossed papers by their publishers, who obligingly gilded the dates of these books onto
the paper covers, so that they make excellent evidence for
the practice. The *Alt- und Neuer Crakauer Schreib-Calender
auf das Jahr 1808*, reproduced on Fig. 59 from a copy in the
New York Public Library, is an amusing and charming example of the kind of lettering and decoration stamped in
gold on these colored paper covers. This particular calendar
was bound in this fashion at least as early as 1739. A copy of

the 1739 edition, in the Columbia University Library, is bound in half leather with paper sides. It shows clearly that the stamping was applied after the book was bound, because the gilded decoration reaches over from the paper area into the narrow strip of leather near the back.

Not only calendars were bound in embossed paper covers. A very attractive paper binding of 1795 can be seen, for instance, on a copy of Albrecht von Haller's famous poem 'Die Alpen' in the Faber Du Faur Library at the Germanic Museum in Yale University.

Even such a meticulous craftsman as Bodoni, the great printer-artist, sent many of his volumes into the world in pleasant yellow-brownish paper bindings with neat little white labels and crisp black printing on their backs. The early editions of the German classics, of Herder, Goethe, and Schiller, appeared in small, squarish marble-paper volumes with shining colored labels, the *Waverly Novels* in plain but pleasant looking gray paper volumes with elegant little printed white labels. Most of the eighteenth- and early nineteenth-century pocket books and gift books appeared in paper-covered boards, and in this group one finds the most elaborate examples of their kind, the ones adorned with steel-engravings and, a little later, with lithographs on the outside covers.

It is obvious that the survival of excellently preserved bindings in their original old paper covers, in full, half and quarter style, is of no small significance in rebinding. We shall return to this later on. A word remains to be said about eighteenth-century bindings in traditional full leather. For, in spite of the introduction of new styles and materials, the full-leather binding holds its own in the eighteenth century.

Almost as though they wanted to show themselves equal to the competition of the marbled papers, the leather workers now produced marbled calfskins. Mottled calf leathers had already been popular since the seventeenth century; they exhibit patterns produced by the sprinkling of the skins with various chemicals.

The so-called 'tree-calf' is only a particularly popular one of several patterns. Some of these decorating devices have proved definitely injurious to the skins to which they were applied. Many such calf bindings have come down to us, where the acid used in sprinkling has eaten holes into the leather, so badly sometimes, that the cardboard covers show through these holes. The presence of these badly damaged specimens on our shelves is largely responsible, I suspect, for a certain widespread prejudice against calf leather in general. One needs only point to the many excelently preserved calfskins on mediaeval manuscripts and incunabula, to demonstrate that it is not the nature of the skin but the manner of its treatment that has caused the damage.

The eighteenth-century goatskin, or morocco, leathers have stood up better. This is only partly due to the fact that goatskin is tougher than calfskin. It can also be accounted for by the fact that the handsome grain of morocco leather has made additional decorating by sprinkling and marbling unnecessary and, in fact, impossible. The grain itself, though, shows various new treatments. Particularly the so-called 'straight-grained' morocco becomes popular at the turn of the eighteenth to the nineteenth century. These skins are treated in such a manner as to bring out only one direction in the grain, so that all grooves in the leather appear to be running more or less parallel to each other; a first step in the direction of the artificial grains, so popular in nineteenth-century leather, cloth and even paper. The eighteenth-century morocco leathers show also a great variety of brilliant colors besides the traditional brown. One encounters red, blue, bright green, orange, and even lemon shades.

The full-vellum or parchment binding still survives in the eighteenth century.

## The Hollow Back

No consideration of eighteenth-century bookbinding would be complete without a reference to one very important change in its technique of binding, namely the introduction of the hollow back. This is a technical innovation that is viewed with very mixed feelings by modern authorities on bookbinding. Professor Ignaz Wiemeler, for many years head of the bookbinding class at the State Academy of Graphic Arts in Leipzig, has eloquently expressed himself on the subject:[4]

The volumes of the fifteenth and sixteenth centuries were stitched to genuine bands and were so made as to have a tight back. The leather was glued directly onto the back. The method of stitching in the headband was generally abandoned during the sixteenth century and replaced by the use of the silk headband. In the seventeenth century the bands were sawed in for the first time to obtain smooth backs without any raised bands. During the eighteenth century there was invented the hollow back, in order to protect and increase the durability of the gilding which, on a tight back, must follow every movement of the leather. During the nineteenth century the most far-reaching deterioration was brought about by the use of sewing two-on on sawed-in bands, by the use of false, glued-on bands and the patched-on woven headband.

The road to deterioration of binding methods went, therefore, from the tight to the hollow back. The final product of this development is the binding with sawed-in and false, superimposed bands, which even today has not entirely disappeared and is still recommended for some of our textbooks. This type of binding is the product of a long-drawn-out evolution, in the course of which an inventive spirit, bent only on destruction, was at work. Its incentive was the desire for time- and labor-saving devices, born in a time filled with falsehood and unreal values, together with the demand of the customers for bindings that looked costly, but could be acquired for less and less money. As we have pointed out, the earlier invention of the hollow back had originally different reasons. Because of the considerable

4 In an article: 'Bookbinding, Old and New,' translated from the German by Peter Mueller-Munk and Hellmut Lehmann-Haupt, and published in Number One of *The Dolphin* (New York: Limited Editions Club, 1933).

drawbacks of the tight back, in many cases the invention of the hollow back was further developed in our time. Today one frequently binds books with genuine raised bands and superimposed hollow backs. This method is much more difficult and slower than the one for the tight back. Only deliberate and well-considered reasons are responsible for it.

# CHAPTER V

# THE EVIDENCE OF THE NINETEENTH CENTURY

## Bookbinding by Machine

THE nineteenth century brings about changes of such fundamental importance, it revolutionizes the entire structure of bookbinding practice to such an extent that all previous changes, by comparison, seem like insignificant and superficial details. Even the very important developments at the end of the Middle Ages, from which there emerged the bookbinding culture of the Renaissance, have not affected the basic structure of technique and materials as deeply as has the Industrial Revolution. Nor has this process of mechanization quite spent itself. While it may appear as though the bulk of this job of transformation has been gotten over with, there is as yet no guarantee of future stability. We may yet witness surprising developments. In that sense, the nineteenth century belongs more to the present than to the past.

However, many books printed and bound in the last century already stand in need of rebinding (Fig. 58). As a matter of fact, there are probably as many, if not more nineteenth-century patients in any general collection of books than from all earlier centuries taken together. This is easily explained. More books were printed in the nineteenth century than in any single century before. Of these the percentage of volumes produced in inferior materials and by new, experimental methods is probably greater than in any previous century. Also, by the natural process of elimination by time, more books have survived from the period immediately preceding our own days than from earlier centuries.

It is obvious that the treatment of all these patients is an entirely different matter from that of books from the preceding centuries. There will be an opportunity to consider these differences more concretely in the next chapter, where we will try to put our observation of original historical methods to a practical test.

It was at this point, when I first considered these questions some years ago, that I discovered the complete absence of even the most rudimentary information about nineteenth-century machine methods in the literature of bookbinding. It hardly seemed possible, but five or six years ago there was simply nothing to be found about that in any history of bookbinding. It was fortunate that Mr. Rogers was easily persuaded, at that time, to devote himself to the difficult but promising task of filling the gap. The result of his study is fully presented in the second part of this book, and we need do no more than remind ourselves of his most important findings.

It seems to me essential to understand that 'bookbinding by machine' was not arrived at over night. Although we can definitely point to the second decade of the nineteenth century as the starting point of decisive developments, there are important and ingenious inventions and innovations all through the century. For the purposes of rebinding not all of these inventions are of equal significance. Only certain of the many innovations have a visible, permanent effect upon their product, the bound volume. For instance, it is of only secondary importance to know whether a given nineteenth-century volume was shaped by hand beating or by rolling in a press; whether it was folded and gathered by hand or by machine; or, even, if rounding and backing were performed in the old or the new way; and, also, whether the machines performing these operations were driven by man power, by steam, or by electricity. These facts are important in themselves, and in a number of other ways, as part of the history of binding. But in considering the rebinding of a volume originally created by these machines the particular operations just mentioned are of much less importance than those which we will now consider.

There is, first of all, the introduction of cloth, soon after 1820. This means a fundamental change of appearance, of the very nature and character of a book. Cloth came into existence in connection with publishers' bindings, with the popular novel, with reading by a new society. It was a democratic material. The earliest cloths used were plain and inconspicuous. With printed paper labels pasted to their backs, they looked very much like the books of that period that were bound in full paper over boards. Pretty soon, from the early thirties on, embossing presses made it possible to conceal the natural surface of bookbinding cloth by stamping decorative devices onto the covers and by applying artificial grains to the entire surfaces. It is possible to date books bound in these various cloths and to establish a definite chronology of both the patterns and the basic types of cloths used for binding purposes.

Of equal fundamental importance with the introduction and development of a radically new material is the process of casing.

This is the most significant technical feature that characterizes edition binding; it has also a decisive bearing upon rebinding problems. The difference between the traditional method of binding and casing has been fully explained in Mr. Rogers' essay. It will be sufficient to repeat here that by the old method books were sewn over cords or tapes which were then laced into or pasted onto cardboard covers that were cut and attached to the book individually and then covered. By the new method the bound pages and their covers are not connected by cords or bands but by a continuous piece of material forming a cloth hinge between the covers and the block of pages. The covers have previously been assembled together with the back strip and covered with cloth to make the case as a separate unit.

Casing started in America between 1825 and 1835, that is to say, simultaneously with the use of cloth. It started as a new type of manual process and remained a hand operation through most of the nineteenth century. Only towards the end of the century and early in the twentieth century were cases made by machine and attached to the books by machine.

It is not unimportant to emphasize this fact of casing by hand. There is a natural tendency in all of us to generalize and simplify. Not a few people think that the difference between hand sewing and machine sewing is identical with the difference between sewing through the folds of the signatures on one hand and overcasting or stabbing on the other. Actually, both types of sewing can be done both by hand and by machine. Contrary to what seems to be a not uncommon belief, the bulk of machine sewing in actual production for the trade is regular sewing through the folds, and not overcasting.

When cloths appeared on the scene, a very popular style of binding was the half-leather binding with paper sides (Fig. 64). Originally conceived as an economy, it had become established as a welcome variety and one that offered many interesting possibilities of both harmony and contrast of color and of texture. Very soon after the introduction of cloth the half-cloth binding with paper sides became popular. The element of economy in this combination was negligible; we may safely assume that people used this style of binding not because they had to but because they wanted to.

Mr. Holbrook Jackson, for one, understands this perfectly. In his volume on *The Printing of Books* he describes the interest which various authors have manifested in matters of book designing, and he speaks of Whistler and his influence upon the production of his works. 'The binding,' says Mr. Jackson, 'is perhaps the most original and satisfying contribution made by him to the design of books. The materials . . . are commonplace: brown paper and ordinary bookbinder's cloth of a dull yellow shade, but they are combined so proportionately as to produce a usable covering of subdued grace and charm. The yellow cloth just covers the spine, being gripped at the hinges by the brown paper of the boards. There is no imitation or suggestion of half- or quarter-leather binding. It is a treatment of cloth and paper without pretence. It is functional binding or casing, but it is not bleak or "mechanistic." '·

Cases can be made both by hand and by machine, and they can be attached to the bound pages both by hand and by machine. However, although machine sewing over cords or tapes is possible and even practicable, these cords or tapes cannot effectively be attached to the covers by machine. They can only be pasted down together with a cloth hinge by machine. So it can be said that in this way they are only of supplementary value. The thorough old methods of building the boards separately around the block of pages and fastening the cords or bands to these boards cannot be done by machine.

## Survival of Hand Methods

It would be a great mistake to imagine that the arrival of machine binding completely eliminated the old-time crafts-man and his methods. There were many decades of transition when the new and the old supplemented each other; to think that every mechanical solution of a certain operation automatically wiped out the corresponding step in the manual process, simply is not correct. We have with us to-day a skilful and talented group of hand binders, and there are not a few men and women who are devoting their lives, in this and other countries, to artistic bookbinding by hand. True enough, this has come about as part of the general revival of arts and crafts which, originally, can be credited to the example of William Morris and his friends and associates. But they did not create out of thin air. Rather, they instilled new ambition, new hope, and new life into the surviving elements of nineteenth-century craftsmanship.

Hand binding in the nineteenth century was, as a matter of fact, a very flourishing craft. The publishers, true enough, had assumed complete responsibility for the binding of their favored product, the contemporary trade editions. But binding for private individuals did not cease. The nineteenth century, in a sense, is one of the greatest periods of bibliophily there have ever been. This, to no small extent, was due to the arrival upon the scene of the great American bibliophile. There has hardly been a time when such rapid accumulation of so many and so tremendously important collections took place; when so much was said, written and printed about book-collecting; and when so many clubs and societies were founded.[1]

There was decidedly a demand for 'fine binding.' It can perhaps be said that the taking over, by the machine, of the complete routine of edition binding freed the hand binder and enabled him to concentrate, spend more time and energy on the individual jobs that were brought to him and, perhaps, get better prices for his better work. His taste, by and large, was not always as restrained and as immaculate as that of his best ancestors, but there is a tremendous variety and richness in the work of those decades.

One important distinction between the development in European countries and in the United States must be made. While at the beginning of the nineteenth century there could be found parallel groups of craftsmen practising hand binding on both continents, and while edition binding by machine was adopted on both continents, the craftsman in America seems to have subsided earlier and more thoroughly to the competition of the machine than the European. In the latter part of the nineteenth century this is very obvious.

One of the great American patrons of the bookbinders of his time was Samuel Putnam Avery (1822-1904), the fourth

[1] See Miss Granniss's chapters on nineteenth-century American book collecting in *The Book in America* (New York: R. R. Bowker Company, 1939).

president of The Grolier Club. He was in touch with all the well-known French binders of the period, entrusting to them the rebinding of his important new acquisitions. He encouraged them to do their very best for him and to spare no effort to decorate his volumes in the richest manner possible.

When Marius Michel, one of the prominent Parisian binders of his day, published his sumptuous *La Reliure Française* in 1880, he was asked by Mr. Avery to bind a copy for him. Mr. Avery had desired that he should make an elaborate specimen of his work. Michel answered: 'You have already the best I can do, for my own book something modest will be in better taste.' Either Mr. Avery had his way, or Mr. Michel's idea of something modest was quite different from ours. The book is now in the Columbia University Library and is a very elaborate specimen indeed.

Other members of The Grolier Club too were anxious to secure the services of good French binders. Headed by Robert Hoe, a group of them invited French craftsmen to America and thus they established the famous Club Bindery, a typical French bindery, in New York.

The great interest in bookbinding on the part of American collectors is also revealed in the number and importance of exhibitions held at The Grolier Club in the latter nineteenth and the early twentieth century.[2] The various catalogues of these exhibitions bear witness of these activities. Similar interests were pursued by other American book clubs in various parts of the country; there is, for instance, the Rowfant Bindery in Cleveland, operating for the benefit of the members of the Rowfant Club, at one time in charge of Mr. Thomas J. Holmes.

The presence of many English and French bindings on the volumes of American collectors and, particularly, the actual importation of craftsmen from France points very

[2] See for instance *An Exhibition of some of the latest artistic bindings done at the Club Bindery, New York, April 26-May 12, 1906.* (New York: The Grolier Club, 1906.)

clearly to the absence of native American craftsmanship towards the end of the nineteenth century. Careful search would probably reveal the presence, here and there, of practising hand binders. But one suspects that they were, by and large, isolated amateurs rather than the descendants of the professional hand binders that were active in this country earlier in the century.

Although not a few half-leather and even full-paper bindings were made by hand, and although much calf and sheepskin were used in the nineteenth century, the full-morocco binding is the nineteenth-century collectors' binding *par excellence*. One finds there a very faithful reflection of what was considered fashionable ornament by one generation after another. There is the noble restraint of classicist bindings at the beginning of the century, austere and simple, the inspiration for much that is good in modern binding design. Then, in the thirties, comes the so-called romantic style, based on classicist formulas, but with a new tolerance towards ornamental variety and richness, with a faint echo in it of the splendor of the bygone days of the Rococo period. And then come the painful decades of artificial historical revival, unrestrained eclecticism which uses with little taste and discrimination all the decorative ideas of the last three centuries. The materials are usually of the very best and the decoration of the very richest in these eclectic bindings. But they have, almost all, one great fault in common: they do not open easily, and they do not stay open. It is a great pity that this style of binding was used so extensively in the nineteenth and early twentieth century for the rebinding of older volumes, for it necessitated all sorts of violence. Besides the very tight sewing which makes them so difficult to open, these pages were often cropped to provide the smooth base for the highly polished gilding of the edges. Moreover, these bindings completely hide the original physiognomy of an old volume which is simply smothered in all this gold and silk and morocco.

# CHAPTER VI

## *THE PRACTICAL APPROACH*

### *To Bind or Not to Bind?*

THE first question that one should ask oneself when faced with a patient on the bookshelf is this: Should the binding of this book be touched at all? Or is this one of the cases when it is best not to try any repair or reconstruction? Would it not be better to protect this volume by placing it in a box or case? Undoubtedly, this should be done in the case of volumes originally issued in paper wrappers and where these wrappers have survived (as on the shelves of some of our leading collectors of Victorian novels). It may be necessary to do a certain amount of skilful mending to preserve these precious wrappers and prevent their tearing and fraying off; possibly a very judicious repair of the sewing may be in order. But there should certainly be no rebinding.

It might also be found wise not to try and touch books preserved in a fine old binding by some master craftsman of the past, even if, technically, the binding has ceased to function soundly. Unless the appearance of such a binding is greatly and obviously marred by the ravages of time or careless treatment in the past, it is perhaps better not to replace the old sewing, headbands, and end-papers; it is perhaps better not to disturb the original structure, even if it is now a ruin. One should remember that not only the gold tooling but also the sewing of the man who bound a book for Grolier, or of a Jakob Krause, or a Roger Payne is worth preserving.

Repair and rebinding may also destroy important bibliographical evidence. True enough, the dating of a book from the evidence of its binding is a very doubtful procedure. I have given a good deal of thought and time to this question, but have yet to be shown one really good and clearcut case where the *printing* of a book could be dated from its binding.[1] On the other hand, there can be no doubt whatsoever that the 'provenance' of an old volume, the story of its ownership through the centuries, can be of first rate importance bibliographically and in terms of literary history. It is the binding of an old volume which contains this evidence of previous ownership on the outside of the covers as well as on the end-papers inside. Anyone who has had the privilege to watch Mr. Seymour de Ricci[2] gather, in a rapid series of minute inspections of covers, end-papers, and title-page, the complete life-story of a volume through three or four centuries, will hesitate forever after to recommend repairs or rebinding likely to destroy any of this evidence!

There is no hard and fast rule by which to determine which of the old books should be left untouched, and which may safely be repaired or rebound This is a matter for individual judgement and there are, naturally, a great many borderline cases. There is also such a thing as carrying this caution too far. A fairly recent library label, carelessly pasted over the delicate gold tooling of an old master craftsman, should undoubtedly be removed. There is no reason why the label could not be carefully soaked off and preserved on the inside of the front cover, with a light pencil notation of its original location and the date of its removal. That ought to quiet the conscience of even the most scrupulous bibliographical watchdog.

The business of protecting-boxes, of slip cases and sliding cases, is well in hand There are a number of competent firms throughout the country that are willing and able to cater to this particular need of collectors and librarians. The only suggestion that I have to offer is that they be a little less pretentious, a little simpler. Why must the case be

1 These and similar questions were discussed at the second annual meeting of The English Institute at Columbia University, in September, 1940, in a series of conferences on the *Dating of Books by Bibliographical Evidence*, under the direction of James M. Osborn of Yale University.

2 See his *English Collectors of Books & Manuscripts* (1530-1930) *and their Marks of Ownership* (Cambridge: University Press, 1930).

made to look like a binding? Why must it have false raised bands on the back? After all, a case is a case, and not a binding. Why not let it be a case? The question of price is involved here. Those elaborate boxes, which seem to be the accepted thing, are fairly expensive. Quite likely, this has prevented many owners of books from using them more extensively. These boxes could be made much simpler, and it so happens that the less expensive ones would really be in much better taste.

Very often a simple case of cloth can be used which leaves the back of the book exposed. Unless the back is in very poor condition, this type of box has many advantages. It protects the book in all vital parts, it is much less expensive than the other types of cases, partly because it does not require any gilded lettering on the back. Last but not least, it does not mar the appearance of the shelves, for it shows the original back of the old volume.

## The Question of Repair

After it has been decided that a given old volume should be restored, the next question to ask is this: Should this book be repaired, or should it be rebound?

It is not quite easy to draw an exact line of demarcation between these two procedures. To a large extent, it depends on how much of the original structure is preserved and how much of the material used originally will be left after the operation is completed. A clear case of repair exists, for instance, when the original sewing is left intact, and when the original covers and most of the old back of the volume can be preserved; such as is possible in many cases of rebacking and rehinging. On the other hand, when the book has to be completely resewn, new covers and a new back have to be built, and when new lettering has to be placed on the back, there can, of course, be no doubt that this constitutes a case of rebinding.

Obviously there are borderline cases: for instance, when

all the interior structure, sewing of signatures, attachment of end-papers and the hinge have to be rebuilt, while the covers and back of the book seem sufficiently well preserved to be used again without major repair or replacement.

There can be little doubt about the desirability of preserving as much of the original binding as possible. It is not only a question of sentiment or personal preference. At the time the decision has to be made, it may seem, in many cases, as though it did not matter a great deal whether the old covers and the old back were preserved or not. It may seem like a good deal of trouble to lift off the old leather carefully, build a sound new basis and then reapply the old fragments. It would be so much simpler and perhaps cheaper to rebind the book completely. But suppose that course were adopted each time the question came up. In a very few decades, I fear, the shelves of our libraries would appear completely changed. The loss in all collections of rare and old material would be irreparable; and this loss would not merely be a sentimental one, nor purely aesthetic. It would eventually amount to the destruction of historical evidence of real importance.

In their excellent volume on *The Care and Repair of Books*[3] Harry M. Lydenberg and John Archer have brought up the question whether such a piece of reconstruction may be considered to be misleading. They have briefly and admirably settled this question.

'In such a case,' they say on page 53, 'the volume is rebacked or rebound, as much of the old cover replaced as is consistent with good work, and the vacant spots merely proclaim that a piece of restoration has been done. A good piece of craftsmanship deserves praise so long as no attempt at deception has been made. Repairing books is commendable, honest restoration is praiseworthy, work of this kind done to fool the unwary speaks for itself.'

[3] Published by R. R. Bowker Company, New York, 1931.

This book by Messrs. Lydenberg and Archer should be carefully studied by all those concerned with and responsible for the repair of old volumes. It contains a clear description of the important methods of repair, the materials necessary for this kind of work, and the tools with which to do it.[4] There is no need to repeat their advice on these pages. Also, the reader will remember that this essay is devoted mainly to the question of rebinding.

There is one rather special point of technique, however, concerning both repair and rebinding, that will bear some elaboration. Rebacking and rehinging, as currently practised and as described in the various handbooks, usually assume that the volumes thus treated were originally 'cased,' that is to say the covers, or the case, were attached to the bound signatures by a cloth hinge. Where the books were originally sewn over cords, these cords will now have to be disregarded. They are, in fact, usually cut off at the joints by the binder who is restoring the book. This is an acceptable enough method, particularly when all or most of the cords are already broken at the hinge as is so often the case. However, one should not close one's eyes to the fact that this is, after all, a compromise. Genuine, authentic restoration, in the fullest sense of the word, means a reconstruction of the original technique of a given old binding. This means that, ideally, the cords should be reconstructed and returned to their original function, namely, to secure the bound pages to the covers. But is this possible when the old leather is cracked at the hinges and the cords broken off? Figure 60 shows how it can be done. The leather back of this old volume has been carefully lifted off and laid aside, later to be replaced on the new back. The leather has also been lifted off the old covers along the hinge and turned back, exposing the joint between back and cover which used to be held together by the old cords, but is now quite

[4] See also the excellently illustrated book by Max Schweidler, *Die Instandsetzung von Kupferstichen, Zeichnungen, Büchern, usw.* (Stuttgart: Max Hettler Verlag, 1938.)

loose. To reconstruct the joint, new cords are being attached by fraying out first one end of a good new piece of cord and pasting it down on top of the old cord. This section is then stitched onto the old cord in the manner shown in the photograph. When this is completed, the loose end of the cord is frayed out and pasted to the outside of the cover, as shown on the second cord from the right. It is now possible to place a new piece of leather, carefully pared down at the turn-ins, to the back, reaching over onto the covers. The old leather of covers and back can then be safely pasted on top of this new basis.

It would be unreasonable to demand that this procedure should be followed in every case where an old volume was originally bound over cords. The process is too time-consuming and, therefore, too costly to be generally used. However, in all those cases where exceptional interest, beauty and value demand the most careful attention, this possibility of restoring the cords to their original function should be seriously considered. It is not only the satisfaction of being able to say that the greatest care has been given to the patient, it is also of undoubted technical advantage, in the long run, to restore in a manner most closely approximating the original structure. Books with tight backs (and all books originally bound in the Middle Ages and the Renaissance period have tight backs), lend themselves naturally to a reconstruction of their cords. In one particular group of volumes this method is practically the only effective means of restoration: namely in books originally bound in heavy wooden covers. Their bulk and weight and the fact that they have bevelled edges at the joint defies re-hinging and casing-in. The only really reliable way to attach these boards is by substantial cords, laced and pegged into the wooden boards. Plastic wood will perform wonders in closing wormholes and other wounds at vital points of reconstruction. If the boards are completely cracked, a thin all-over plate of aluminum is placed between the inside of the board and the end-paper which, when pasted down, will hide the metal from sight. Even razor blades have been used effectively as reinforcements for the broken wooden boards of mediaeval volumes.

The reconstruction of the cords has also distinct advantages where only one hinge stands in need of repair. In those cases the sound hinge does not need to be touched at all, and the restoration of the cords at the broken end will be the operation least disturbing to the entire structure of the old volume.

The binding on a book can be compared to a living organism, a body that derives its health and long life from the health and well-being of all its parts and from their happy and harmonious co-operation. In an old book there exists a time-honored, well played-in relationship between page and page, between signature and signature, between the bulk of the sewn signature and the covers, and between covers and back. The stress and strain of sewing, of opening and closing the covers, of turning pages and of pushing the book into the row of volumes on the shelf and of taking it out again, all these manipulations, exercised a hundred times over, have established an equilibrium of forces, an internal balance in the book. It stands to reason that when parts of this organism cease to function and have to be restored or replaced, it is best not to repair in a manner likely to bring new and different stress and strain on the old organism. The superimposition of the casing-in method on a book originally bound over cords is likely to have just that effect.

## What Not to Do

It is always undesirable to rebind by modern routine a book that was originally bound by hand in the traditional manner. The latter procedure is unavoidable on ordinary, run-of-the-mill volumes, a group which, unfortunately, does include some old volumes in traditional hand bindings. But for all volumes distinguished not merely by age but by various elements of interest, beauty, rarity, and value, it should be avoided.

This is not a piece of sentimentality, nor merely the systematic application of historical knowledge. It is simply a question of adequate conservation of values. We must not overlook that the original hand binding process has done something very definite to the shape of an old volume. A book, originally bound by hand, leads a physical existence that is mechanically determined by its binding. There is the sewing which produces a set of holes in every page at a given place. There is the smashing and the various pressings that pack the pages together in a certain, definite way. There is the backing and the rounding that give a very specific position to every single page in relation to the whole block of the book. Last, not least, there are the covers, their size and weight in a balanced proportion to the page size and the weight of the volume; there is the greater or lesser tightness of the covers, the certain amount of play at the hinges and the way in which the book opens. These are all factors that matter, both aesthetically and practically.

The thing to avoid most of all is the overcasting method of resewing, a very quick and easy way to ruin any nice old volume (Figs. 72 and 73).

The worst thing that can happen to pages, originally sewn by hand, is the breaking of the leaf at the fold and a slight enlargement of the original sewing-holes. This breaking of the leaf is largely dependent on the quality of the paper and may also be caused, originally, by too tight sewing. That, however, is the exception.[5] The usual damage, found on the various leaves, when resewing of the book makes it necessary to take it apart, consists in a slight widening of the original sewing holes, due to the working of the

---

[5] Cedric Chivers has made an ardent plea for oversewing on certain modern volumes in his essay *The Paper of Lending Library Books, with some remarks on their Bindings* (New York: The Baker & Taylor Company [1909?]). His arguments in favor of oversewing on early twentieth-century volumes can be read as equally strong arguments against oversewing on earlier books.

thread in opening and closing the book and in turning the pages.

The proper way to resew an old book is to repair the individual pages and resew through the fold, using the original holes, if possible.

The improper way to resew an old book is to disregard the original sewing and to superimpose a different new sewing by overcasting or oversewing. To do this, it is necessary to move away from the folded edge, with the result that the two inner margins are seriously narrowed. Not infrequently, due to slight irregularities in the original folding of an old volume, the needle and thread will actually hit the print. In particularly unfortunate cases, when fine old engravings that are wider than the text column have been printed onto the pages, the oversewing will cheerfully pierce holes into the very pictures that make the book a valuable reference tool, not to speak of the artistic and financial damage involved in this 'economical' operation. But that is not all. In order really to read a book bound in this manner, the student will gently but firmly press down on the fold in the vain attempt to get the book to lie flat or, at least, to stay open. Nobody can blame the gentle reader for this, although he is actually tearing practically every page in the volume. The damage done at each shove is minute, but it adds up. Figure 73 shows how the threads have worked their way from their original position in the punched holes towards the fold. In a properly sewn binding pressure on the opened pages may crack the back or affect the hinges; but it will definitely not cause the sewing thread to bite into the pages, as is the case in overcasting.

This is the chief reason why the standard library binding is so damaging to fine old volumes, from a purely technical point of view and apart from any aesthetic considerations. The fact that oversewing or overcasting is frequently done by hand rather than by machine does not help the situation in the least. The damage is just as bad.

In the attachment of end-papers and covers to the resewn pages there is probably a little more leeway. Although it is always nicer to resew an old book over cords or bands and attach these cords to the boards of the case, the reinforced hinge of the standard library binding has its advantages. It is certainly not as damaging as overcasting. One mistake frequently encountered on rebound old volumes of value is a hinge that is too heavily reinforced. The kind of life that a rare old volume is going to lead after rebinding, the care it will receive, will make it quite unnecessary to treat it like a copy of a popular novel to be circulated by the branch of a busy metropolitan library. This applies to the weight and strength of the boards and the materials chosen to cover the volume quite as much as to the selection of the end-paper, the hinge and the sewing.

In a discussion of the things that should be avoided in rebinding, the choice of covering material and of styles and types of decoration should not be neglected. How important it is to consider what was customary at the time the book was written or printed has already been emphasized. The brief survey, contained in Chapter IV and V of this essay, offers a multitude of suggestions. At the same time it should be understood that there are no hard and fast rules that we need to follow. These suggestions are offered as a help in approaching the problem of rebinding; they may not do more than help to eliminate certain undesirable procedures. For that, too, is important. For instance, I cannot help but feel that, while cloth is most suitable on books of the nineteenth and twentieth centuries, it is decidely out of place when used conspicuously on books printed before 1800, or on mediaeval manuscripts. It may not be possible to eliminate cloth altogether, particularly in the case of large and heavy old volumes that would be very expensive in leather and not strong enough in paper.

Gold tooling, for lettering and decoration, should always be used sparingly, particularly on incunabula and mediaeval manuscripts. Blind tooling should not be neglected there; it is possible and beautiful on almost all types of materials. A bookbinder who uses black ink or any other color or pigment to make blind-tooled lettering stand out more clearly does not understand that technique properly. The typefaces used for lettering should bear at least a general family resemblance to the type used inside a book. The so-called 'modern-face' family of type designs, which originated around 1800, had better not be used on books printed before 1800. More will be said about this later on.

Is it necessary to emphasize that old books should never have their edges trimmed in rebinding? This practice, the binders' 'original sin' has been denounced so thoroughly and consistently for such a long time that it has all but disappeared completely.

It would be decidedly tedious to try and draw up watertight rules for the rebinding of the books of the various periods. That is not the purpose of this essay. However, some examples of successful rebinding of various types of old books will probably be welcomed at this point.

### Some Examples for Successful Rebinding

Some years ago the Government and the people of Great Britain acquired, for the sum of £100,000, the Codex Sinaiticus, that famous fourth-century manuscript of the Bible discovered by Dr. Tischendorf in the Convent of St. Catherine, at the foot of Mount Sinai, in 1844 and 1859. This Codex, after it had been deposited at the British Museum, had to be restored. After careful study of the problem and various consultations with experts it was decided that the precious Codex should be rebound completely. The great English master binder, Douglas Cockerell, was entrusted with this task, probably the most important job of rebinding executed in this century. Mr. Cockerell took unusual precautions before he began actually to work on the manuscript. After he had assembled all necessary tools and equipment, taking the utmost care to secure only the most reliable materials, some of which were prepared under his personal supervision, he made a trial binding on blank paper which is here reproduced on Figs. 61 and 62.[6]

He devised a very ingenious method of sewing the pages which would avoid all possible stress and strain of the precious vellum leaves at the inner margin and would allow the Codex to be opened flat at any place. Figure 62 shows how this was achieved by 'throwing out' the sections from the back on guards.

The binding itself is an admirable example of contemporary design, materials and workmanship, co-ordinated in a manner reminiscent, but not imitative, of a typical mediaeval binding. Mr. Cockerell used Spanish mahogany boards, taking care to blend the beautiful natural grain of the wood into the composition of the entire volume. He used white pigskin for the back, designing a simple blind-tooled decoration which emphasizes and graphically combines the raised bands with each other. Silver clasps, designed as crosses with a little decoration, were mounted on the boards to hold the covers in place.

The rebinding of mediaeval manuscripts and of incunabula, in uncovered wooden boards with a leather back is a most appropriate solution. It is not only authentic in style, but of great technical advantage in the case of heavy volumes with vellum or parchment leaves. The strong wooden boards, held together by metal clasps, greatly help to keep the old pages pressed flat against each other. With the unavoidable succession of excessive summer humidity and excessive dryness of winter steam heat, the warping and buckling up of old parchment is almost inevitable. When firmly enclosed in well-seasoned wooden boards, they are at least partially protected from such damage.

[6] The original photographs were shown, together with various examples of Mr. Cockerell's work, at the exhibition of 'Modern Bookbinding, New Design in an Old Craft,' held in the spring of 1935 at Columbia University. Mr. Cockerell has described his rebinding of the Codex Sinaiticus in an article in *The British Museum Quarterly*, Vol. X, No. 4.

Another authentic style for the binding of mediaeval manuscripts and early printed volumes is the full-leather binding. Figure 63 shows three early printed books in the Newberry Library in Chicago, all bound by Douglas Cockerell in beautiful morocco leather over binders board, and decorated simply and appropriately in a combination of blind and gold tooling. It could perhaps be argued that neither gold tooling nor morocco leather are typical features of fifteenth-century binding, representing more nearly sixteenth- and seventeenth-century practice. That, however, would mean carrying observance of historical precedent a little too far. What matters is that Mr. Cockerell's bindings are well-fitting clothes which do not conflict in any way with the character of the pages that they enclose. Also, their design conveys a general impression of dignity and tradition.

Half-leather bindings with decorated paper sides, the reader will remember, became popular from the end of the seventeenth century on, and they stayed popular through the nineteenth century. These bindings, by and large, have stood up remarkably well, much better, in fact, than many volumes bound in presumably more reliable materials. Figures 57 and 58 show, above, a row of well-preserved eighteenth-century bindings in paper-over-board covers, and, below, a group of nineteenth-century volumes in leather and cloth, all of the latter in pretty bad shape. It would, of course, be possible to find well-preserved examples of nineteenth-century leather and cloth. However, that is not quite the point. What matters is that a piece of high-grade paper has better lasting qualities and is far more attractive than a piece of low-grade cloth or leather. I would go even farther and venture to guess that the proportion of well-preserved eighteenth-century paper covers to those in not so good condition is much more favorable than the proportion of well- and badly preserved nineteenth-century bindings in full cloth or leather. At any rate, I feel safe in recommending the use of well-made decorative papers in rebinding.

Figure 64 shows a group of early nineteenth-century volumes, well preserved in their paper sides and leather backs and corners. All of them are examples from Miss Isadore G. Mudge's collection of Early English and American juvenile periodicals. Below, on Fig. 65, are shown volumes from the same collection, all of which have been rebound within the last five years. To match their appearance with the well-preserved colleagues on the shelves of Miss Mudge's collection, they were bound in old papers, salvaged and collected over a number of years from discarded old covers and end-papers. They were bound in pieces of used, but well-preserved leather, taken, for instance, from ladies' discarded handbags.

Not all old papers fit equally well on all old books; there are national differences and distinctions of periods. However, it is surprising how soon one can acquire the knack of fitting things together appropriately and with pleasant effects. Miss Mudge had an interesting experience in rebinding the little volume reproduced in the center of Fig. 65 which came to her sadly in need of repair. She picked from her portfolio of old papers one that seemed particularly suitable for the book. When the binder went to work, she found, hidden from sight under the white end-paper, a fragment of the old marble paper which, to everybody's amusement and delight, turned out to be of exactly the same pattern and color as the one selected by the owner, a century later, for its rebinding !

It is by no means necessary to limit the use of decorative papers to such instances where original old papers are available for rebinding, nor need one insist that only volumes printed after 1650 should be thus bound. On Fig. 66 is shown a group of one eighteenth- and three sixteenth-century volumes in the Newberry Library, all bound in half leather with modern marble paper sides. These particular marble papers were made by Douglas Cockerell, and were skilfully fitted onto the new covers of the old volumes.

There are several reasons why this type of half-leather binding with paper sides is recommendable for old volumes. It was originally devised to take the place of full-leather bindings, offering a more economical, yet pleasing alternative. Today such bindings continue to represent a pleasant and economical substitute in all cases where rebinding in full leather would be desirable, but impractical for various reasons. The paper-over-board binding, provided a high-grade quality of paper is being used, has excellent lasting qualities. There is, in fact, no reason why light and small volumes should not occasionally be bound entirely in paper-over-boards. More will be said about this in Chapter VII.

There is yet another reason why the bindings exhibited on Fig. 66 represent a fortunate solution of the rebinding problem. These marble papers by Mr. Cockerell, and the same is true of decorated pattern papers made by other experienced and talented designers, are traditional in their technique and general appearance. Yet, no future expert will have difficulty in identifying them as the product of our own twentieth century. Within the realm of decorative papers they are fresh and original contributions, distinct from the earlier patterns. Their use on old bindings, it seems to me, represents a blending of regard for tradition with contemporary expression that is very desirable. It is certainly a far cry from the slavish imitation of old binding styles that makes the laboriously executed 'period bindings' so tiresome and so unsuitable for fine old volumes.

## The Contemporary Fine Binding

It has been pointed out earlier in this essay that the 'period binding' is a product of nineteenth-century eclecticism. It was after the middle of the last century that leading bookbinders in various countries began deliberately to imitate the fine old bindings of the Renaissance and the Baroque periods. In the rebinding of old volumes they usually defeated their own aims. The more care and patience they employed to reproduce every technical feature and, particularly, every detail of gold tooling found on the old masterpieces, the greater was the discrepancy between the old original pages and their glittering modern covers.

This entire approach to rebinding contrasts sharply with the methods employed by master binders of earlier centuries. When a bookbinder of the sixteenth, the seventeenth, or eighteenth century had to rebind a mediaeval manuscript or an early printed volume, he invariably designed what was then a 'modern' binding. He approached his job in much the spirit of an architect of those centuries who was commissioned to add a chapel or rebuild a destroyed portion of a mediaeval cathedral. Almost all the Romanesque and Gothic cathedrals of Europe have additions frankly executed in Renaissance, Baroque or Rococo styles. These additions often have great architectural charm, just as many eighteenth-century bindings on mediaeval volumes are often beautiful examples of craftsmanship and decoration. We would perhaps prefer that many of these volumes had not been rebound at all, but we cannot say today how badly they stood in need of restoration. At any rate, the men who rebound them dealt with them as they would with a newly printed volume; they bound them in their best contemporary manner.

This is an interesting point which raises a very important question. Should we not extend to our own contemporary binders the same privilege which the master craftsmen of the past enjoyed? Is there any reason why we should not allow a fine binding in contemporary style to be placed on a fine old volume? The fact that, so far, this has not been done to any great extent would seem to make it all the more desirable to try the experiment. Fine old furniture is by no means out of place in a well-planned modern interior, and it looks well even in the company of good furniture of contemporary design. It has long been discovered that the best work of almost any period or country can, with some tact and skill, be made to live harmoniously with the best of any other period or country. Why should that not apply to modern fine bindings on old volumes?

To those who think of modern design as synonymous with eccentricity and with 'being different for difference's sake,' this suggestion will, undoubtedly, be disturbing. There are probably a great many collectors who would object very seriously to submitting any of their fine old volumes to such treatment. In answer to objections of this kind, I would say that there is widespread ignorance of the nature of contemporary fine binding as well as of the extent to which the art has been practised in the last few decades.

The Columbia University Exhibition of Modern Bookbinding in the spring of 1935 was the first exhibition held in this country since the beginning of the first World War, to show a representative selection of the work of living craftsmen from many countries! [7] Further opportunities for the study of modern bindings were offered in the various national exhibits at the New York World's Fair of 1939 and 1940 and at the San Francisco World's Fair,[8] which brought to many people their first acquaintance with this form of applied art.

Apart from individual early forerunners, there are in the main two sources of what we might call the contemporary style in bookbinding. Historical eclecticism was perhaps more regularly practised in Paris than anywhere else

[7] A catalogue was published, containing names and addresses of some eighty bookbinders in the United States and eight European countries. It is entitled *Modern Bookbinding, New Design in an Old Craft. Columbia University, Low Memorial Library, April 15 to May 6, 1935.*

[8] See the catalogue *Fine Bindings Exhibited at the Golden Gate International Exposition, San Francisco, 1939,* with a foreword by Morgan A. Gunst. Privately printed by the Grabhorn Press in San Francisco.

in the nineteenth century, and it was only natural that in Paris first a movement for greater simplicity and purity arose. There are astonishing early examples in France of a simple linear style which, thirty years ago, anticipated much of what is being done today. Subsequent developments in France have led on to a more brilliant and intricate style than the beginnings of French modernism. This later phase has had an influence in Italy and other Latin countries as well as in England and America.

In England contemporary work has its own independent roots which go back as far as the latter part of the eighteenth century, where the figure of Roger Payne stands out as a monumental, if isolated, exponent of new ideas. His work was in the minds and possibly before the eyes of such men as Cobden-Sanderson and Douglas Cockerell, in those days an enthusiastic young disciple of the English revival of the arts and crafts. The rich experience of a devoted life has gone not only into his own work, but has also inspired groups of promising students at the London County Central School of Arts and Crafts. Another interesting group of contemporary craftsmen has centered around the First Edition Club in London whose secretary, Mr. A. J. A. Symons, has organized exhibitions of modern bindings and has done much to recommend the best work of English hand binders to collectors.

On the continent, outside of France and the Latin countries, the influence of the English revival was paramount in the early years of the century. Scandinavia felt its refreshing breath, and in these Northern countries, with valuable traditions of their own, an interesting blend of the old and the new came about. Mr. Anker Kyster of Copenhagen is an exponent of this school and, like Cockerell, his influence on the younger master binders of his country has been considerable. In Sweden, Mr. Akke Kumlien of Stockholm is responsible for some of the finest modern bindings designed and executed anywhere.

Germany, Austria, and Switzerland, like Scandinavia, learned a thorough lesson from the English movement early in this century. Since then there has been a steady growth of interest and of competence, due in no small degree to the encouragement which public institutions and schools have given to the craft. One of the most productive of these schools, the binding class of the State Academy of Graphic Arts in Leipzig, is headed by Professor Ignaz Wiemeler. Outstanding examples of his work were shown in a one-man show at the Museum of Modern Art, held in New York in the fall of 1935.[9]

Interesting examples in the revival of the folk traditions were reflected in the binding of the countries that had gained independence after the first World War, such as Poland, Hungary, and Czechoslovakia. Czechoslovakia had an interesting decade of such work between 1920 and 1930, and many good examples of this movement were deposited at the Industrial Arts Museum of the Chamber of Commerce in Prague. In the thirties a new trend made itself felt, centering around the work of the State Graphic School in Prague, which testified to the blending of national elements with a distinct influence of the post-war French school of binding.

It is impossible, at this moment, to estimate the effect of the second World War upon the arts and crafts of the various European countries. It would seem not improbable that they survive. At the same time, one looks instinctively to the United States for some assurance of continued devotion to such valuable traditions of craftsmanship. Contemporary hand binding in this country reflects a variety of influences. The style and workmanship of the late nineteenth century have survived here perhaps more fully than in any other country; but there are promising signs of freer and more independent expression. Some of the best work

[9] See the catalogue of that exhibition, entitled *Ignaz Wiemeler, Modern Bookbinder. October 2nd to October 24th, 1935.* With an introduction by Monroe Wheeler (New York: Museum of Modern Art, 1935).

done in this country was shown in the 1935 exhibit of 'Modern Bookbinding.' A large number of representative American bindings was included in the San Francisco World's Fair exhibit of 'Fine Bookbinding.' [10]

Opportunities for training in the art of hand binding have been considerably broadened by the establishment, in 1934, of bookbinding classes at Columbia University, under the direction of Gerhard and Kathryn Gerlach who both received their training at the Leipzig Academy with Professor Wiemeler. Their efforts supplement much valuable and patient work by individual instructors, such as Gertrude Stiles in East Cleveland, Ohio; Beatrice A. Wilson in Philadelphia, and, along with others in New York, Edith Diehl. Previous to the establishment of her New York bindery Miss Diehl[11] studied for five years in European binderies, working at the bench continuously. Her New York bindery was enlarged in 1912 to acommodate students. At that time she employed two of the Frenchmen formerly working at the Club Bindery of The Grolier Club (see page 227). Miss Diehl was later in charge of a binding department at William Edwin Rudge and for about two years pro-

[10] See the catalog of that exhibition, listed in footnote 8 on page 245, for a complete list of the binders and their books. Another valuable source of information about hand binders in America is an annual publication about its members and their activities by the Guild of Book Workers in New York, Mrs. Sinclair Hamilton being the secretary of that organization.

The work of Curtis Walters, whose mosaic bindings are most unusual examples of fine binding in this country, is discussed by Azalea Clisbee in an article entitled 'Curtis Walters, American binder, an appreciation,' in *The American Book Collector*, II (1932), 124-134.

American hand binding early in this century is described in Louis H. Kinder's *Formulas for Bookbinders*. (East Aurora, N. Y.: The Roycrofters, 1905.)

*Arthur Eggeling and his Associates* was published by the Eggeling Bookbindery in New York in 1925 to describe their establishment and services.

*A Rod for the Back of the Binder, Some Considerations of Binding with Reference to the Ideals of The Lakeside Press* tells of the efforts of a large industrial printing plant to encourage fine hand binding. It was published by The Lakeside Press, R. R. Donnelley and Sons, in Chicago, in 1928.

*Bookbinding & Book Production, The Official Business Paper of the Industry* (until August, 1936, entitled *Bookbinding Magazine, the Official Business Paper of the Industry*), under the editorship of David M. Glixon, has done its share to help the cause of individual craftsmanship.

[11] Letter to author, Jan. 18, 1941.

duced the bindings of books designed by Bruce Rogers. Her place at Rudge's was later occupied by Peter Franck, now of Gaylordsville, Conn.

## A Plea for Hand Binding

Collectors of books and libraries cannot dispense with the work of the hand binders, particularly in rebinding. There exists now, I feel, a sort of no-man's-land which is cultivated neither by the binding firms catering to collectors, nor by commercial library binders. Much of the work recommended in the foregoing pages lies in this no-man's-land. The situation seems to me to offer distinct opportunities to young people who are willing, for a period, to work hard and be content with comparatively modest earnings. A great many books are now not being attended to because the customary charges of the hand binder do not allow more than an occasional job of repair, and because the standard library binding, while economical, is unsuitable for this type of work. Large libraries, particularly, are confronted with almost unsolvable problems, where large-scale repairs and restoration are necessary, but only limited funds available. Some sort of reorganization is obviously highly desirable. A great deal would be gained if it were possible to make individual hand-work more readily available and at lower prices, where a steady amount of work is assured.

Some libraries have begun to experiment with their own little departments for the repair, the restoration, and a good deal of the rebinding of their rare and valuable material. These experiments, so far, have been successful, not so much because these libraries preferred to work in this manner, but because it was the only economical way of getting the work done properly. There is no reason why professional binders should not take a share in this work and greatly increase their usefulness to the libraries in their localities. Is it utterly fantastic to suggest to commercial

binders the organization of departments specifically designed to take care of work that has to be done individually
and by hand, at prices reasonable enough to enable their
customers to send them the many books that cannot now
be taken care of?

# CHAPTER VII

## *ABOUT PAMPHLET BINDINGS*

THE problem of quantity is particularly pressing in the binding and rebinding of rare and valuable pamphlet material. An occasional pamphlet can be taken care of in one way or another; but when large groups of these slender volumes stand in need of attention the difficulties are almost insurmountable. There exists here exactly the same no-man's-land that we found in the rebinding of full-sized volumes. On one side, there is the conventional collector's pamphlet binding, technically adequate but over-elaborate and quite expensive. The purely utilitarian library pamphlet, on the other hand, is inexpensive and adequate enough for run-of-the-mill material; but it is hardly suitable for old and rare material.

The collector's pamphlet binding is really nothing else but a very slender variation of the customary de luxe binding. It usually employs full leather or three-quarter leather with cloth-covered sides. It has tiny, elegant gold lettering on its slender spine, gilt edges, doublures, silk lining sheets, and often entire signatures of empty pages at the beginning and the back. These bindings are often very charming in themselves but, like full-grown de luxe bindings on old books, they tend to obliterate completely the physiognomy of the volumes which they enclose. Always keeping in mind that we are dealing with material that will enjoy the protection of a private library or a reserve collection, it is fairly easy to find models suggestive of a more appropriate style of binding. We will discover that, in former days, many pamphlets have been bound in full paper-over-boards with little labels on the back or in paper-over-board sides with a narrow back strip of cloth or leather and with cloth or leather corners. These pamphlets, sewn by hand through the fold, have stood up very well indeed. There is no reason, I think, why this style cannot be adopted in such cases where the number of patients in need of treatment is large. The substitution of paper for leather will help to cut expenses considerably. Hand sewing through the folds, on the other side, is not so very difficult on pamphlets which, after all, have but a very few signatures. The difference in price between proper sewing and overcasting is not really so very great here.

Figure 67 shows, on the left, the routine library pamphlet as found in many a small and large library. It is unsuitable for valuable old publications first of all on account of the sewing which — the photograph shows this clearly — prevents the volume from being properly opened and read and which will eventually tear the pages very badly (see Fig. 73). This style is also impractical because, in its standard combination of brown paper and brown cloth, the pamphlet will be indistinguishable from hundreds of similar pamphlets on the library shelves. The back is particularly unattractive, and, altogether, the binding lacks any sort of distinction or grace.

On the right, and in front, is shown a pamphlet sewn through the fold. Behind it is a similar example which shows an improved cover treatment. The main difference lies in the kind of cloth chosen for the back strip and in the paper used for the covering of the sides. Also, the insertion of a narrow flat black strip greatly improves appearances and provides the basis for a much neater workmanship at the spine. The fact that the original printed label could, in this particular instance, be cut out and saved from the original paper covers is one of these fortunate coincidences which are not so rare as it might seem.

The difference in cost that exists between hand sewing through the fold and oversewing, while not large enough to prevent hand sewing on rare and valuable pamphlets, will, nevertheless, make it impossible to dispense altogether with the cheaper type of pamphlet sewing; as a matter of fact, there are a great many pamphlets that do not need a different treatment. However, the difference in price between unattractive papers and pleasant ones is negligible, and it costs nothing at all to match various colors of cloth with various types of papers. I am dwelling on this merely to point out that there is room for improvement and for pleasant variation in all types of pamphlet bindings.

Variation in the patterns and colors of paper covers is not only pleasing to the eye but of real value in locating a volume. No matter what system may be devised to arrange books on shelves and to find them there, once we know a book, we look for it not primarily by its number or class-mark but by what we remember of its appearance.

One technical error found particularly often in pamphlet binding is the use of too heavy boards. I have seen cases when these covers, applied with all good intentions, have literally torn the sewing apart and have done great damage to the old pages.

There are exhibited, on Fig. 68, some pamphlet bindings done a few years ago by Mr. Charles M. Adams. They were hand sewn through the fold over tapes which were fastened to the covers and bound in cloth back with decorative or plain paper sides. The little labels were printed in black on white or tinted papers which match the color of back and sides. The type was set up on a little toy press. (A decent piece of hand-lettering would also have been quite satisfactory.) These bindings show what pleasing and satisfactory results are possible with economical yet reliable materials, with careful workmanship, with taste and a little patience.

CHAPTER VIII

## THE STANDARD LIBRARY BINDING

IT has been pointed out earlier on these pages that no worthwhile old volume originally bound by hand in traditional manner should be rebound by oversewing and casing-in. Does this also apply the other way around? Does this also mean that no volume originally issued in a publisher's edition binding should be rebound in the traditional hand method? The answer to this, it seems to me, must be that a good, traditional hand binding never does any harm anywhere,[1] but that in a great many cases it should be unnecessary to employ this rather expensive method. A volume originally enclosed in a case could very well be rebound by casing-in. Well then, would not the standard library binding be the ideal solution for all volumes originally issued in publisher's bindings? To answer this fairly, one should consider the differences that exist between edition binding and library binding.

The standard library binding owes its very existence to the weaknesses of the average edition binding. It originated in response to an urgent demand for economical and lasting protection of books in circulation, books exposed to continued and heavy use and abuse. The standard library binding is the result, by and large, of the tremendous and rapid expansion of public library service towards the end of the last century. It was designed specifically to take care of problems created by the deficiencies of contemporary publisher's bindings when put to heavy use. In a sense, the library binding can be said to be a more solid, reinforced version of the edition binding. It employs, first of all, a much more lasting covering material, it uses stout end-papers and a heavy reinforced hinge. In these features it does not differ, in basic structure, from edition binding, even if it

[1] Except possibly on books printed on certain particularly poor types of papers, intended for heavy circulation. See Cedric Chivers, op. cit.

can be said that the manner of affixing the reinforced end-papers to the covers and signatures goes a good deal beyond the edition binding. The main structural difference, however, lies in the sewing: the standard library binding usually employs overcasting. This feature constitutes the chief economical advantage of library binding. It is, in fact, the very thing that makes it feasible. To insist upon sewing through the fold in quantity rebinding would be quite unreasonable. Overcasting is never an ideal solution, of that there can be no doubt; but it is an entirely practical and feasible one in a great many cases. The chief and general mistake has been to put this standard library binding to a use for which it was never intended, namely as a cure-all, indiscriminately applied for all types of material in need of rebinding. This brings us straight back to the question whether the standard library binding can be recommended for all books originally bound in a pubisher's edition binding. The answer is no. We have to discriminate, and segregate within that group in exactly the same manner as among other types and groups of old books. Again, as in the case of volumes published before 1830, there is no hard and fast rule by which to determine what nineteenth-century volumes ought to be singled out for preferred treatment and which ones can safely be treated as routine cases. That depends entirely on the individual library or collection; what is possible in one place may not be practical in another. Also, there are a great many borderline cases. However, the first edition of an important author, to be preserved as part of a collection of Victorian literature, for instance, obviously belongs in the 'preferred treatment' group; a contemporary novel or textbook, easily replaced and intended for circulation and eventual discarding, obviously not.

What type of rebinding, then, ought we to use on the better kinds of nineteenth- or early twentieth-century volumes that were originally bound in publisher's bindings; on books that we would like to save from the stigma of thoughtless standardization? We come to an important and somewhat surprising point there, the fact, namely, that comparatively small adjustments are necessary to adapt the standard library binding to the rebinding of the better type of nineteenth- and early twentieth-century volume. It is very largely a matter of organization, of making it possible to give these books the individual attention which they deserve and not to treat them as so many numbers in a job lot.

At the risk of being reprimanded as a stickler to inessential details I would like to show at what specific points adjustments are possible. I agree, that taken separately and by themselves, they mean very little. But in the aggregate they do amount to something. Patiently studied and consistently applied, they could help tremendously to 'take the curse out of library binding' without unduly increasing the cost.

The sewing presents the biggest problem. Complete resewing of the entire volume is often necessary. The one thing to be avoided by both the custodian or owner of the volume and his binder is an automatic agreement that resewing through the fold is out of the question in every case. There may be many instances where overcasting is the only way that is economically feasible. Yet, the possibility of sewing through the fold should always be explored, and it should be done whenever possible. It is only fair to state at this point that the 'Minimum Specifications for Class "A" Library Binding' [2] rule that 'Books unsuited for oversewing shall be repaired and reinforced by sewing through their folded sections.' But we need a more thoroughgoing discussion and a more general understanding among both librarians and library binders as to what books are 'unsuited for oversewing.' These 'Minimum Specifications' do not contain any reference to rare and old volumes and to

[2] As reprinted from the *Proceedings of the Sixtieth Annual Conference of the American Library Association*, October 15, 1938.

the problems which their rebinding presents. They speak of 'Special Volumes' which are defined as 'Any undersized, oversized and odd-sized volumes or any volume that requires special handling.' That is far too vague. In another place, under 'Sewing' we find the following ruling: 'Exceptional books such as little folks' picture books, music, certain art books, and some reference books, shall be sewed through their folded sections.' This definition does not even approach the realm of old and rare volumes. It is very much hoped that the discussion of the problem on these pages will help to bring the question to a head.

In many volumes originally issued in publisher's edition bindings it will be found that the old sewing is still intact, but that the old casing is gone to pieces and the original hinge is damaged beyond repair. In routine library binding sturdy new end-papers with reinforced hinges are used, and they are affixed by one of various ways to the volume. They are usually attached by overcasting. Would it not be possible to vary this procedure and avoid overcasting on books that belong to the preferred-treatment group? It would be highly desirable carefully to explore this possibility. Quite likely, the added time and care necessary to accomplish this would more than pay for itself in added attractiveness, preservation of original structure, and in ultimate lasting quality.

The appearance of most standard library bindings today is unnecessarily dreary and unappetizing. Particularly when the book is not intended for heavy circulation duty, is it possible to improve the appearance without materially increasing the price. How can this be done?

There have been various attempts in recent years to dispel the gloom that is likely to be cast over a reading room full of dreary buckram volumes, by 'brightening up the shelves.' These extremely well-meaning experiments usually have failed, because they tried to solve a problem from without rather than from within. There have been those attempts to eliminate all dark cloths and concentrate on brilliant light colors, or to express the contents of a volume by the nature of the cloth chosen, flower patterns for garden books, anchors and sailing ships for voyages and so forth. Nothing looks quite so depressing as one of these once valiantly gay volumes after a number of readers have left their imprint on the covers. In one instance, at Christmas time, a librarian tried to express the spirit of the season by arranging alternating shelves of red and green volumes near her door. These are all ephemeral ideas, interior decorating instead of bookbinding. The only way to 'brighten up the shelves' is to forget about the shelves and concentrate upon each individual volume. Do the best you can for each book, as it deserves it, and the shelves will look after themselves.

It is not always necessary to use the heaviest types of service cloth on all books that are to be rebound. The weight and strength of the cloth should be in proportion to the size and weight of the volume and to the kind of use to which the book will be put. Within the same category of strength and weight there are many variations of texture and a great choice of colors. Some of the colors found in the various binding cloth sample books are so atrocious that one has a hard time to imagine why they were ever included, particularly the purples and some of the greens.

There are a number of ways in which the cloth can be folded around the boards at the corners. It is not always necessary to use rounded corners which make every volume look like a cross between a hymn-book and a domestic ledger. Nor does the cloth need always to be folded at the corners into that heavy clump which makes a dent in the pages which are next to it.

There is only one kind of end-paper which matches cloth of all colors, and that is white; but white end-papers are impractical, and they rarely match the white paper of the book itself. A good rule is to use an end-paper that is midway in shade between cover and pages, lighter than the covers, but darker than the pages. Everyone has seen certain dirty greyish-green-pinkish types of end-papers. This variety is supposed to go well with cloth of every color, because it has particles of every color somewhere in its pattern. That is, of course, a fallacy, because small specks of color run together in the human eye and are seen as one dominant shade. There is no one color for an end-paper that will fit every color of cloth, but with only two colors it can be done. With one shade of grey and one of light buff a fairly good match is always possible.

The same rule applies to the sprinkling or staining of the edges, if and when that is desirable. No one color of sprinkling or staining can be found that will go well with cloths of all colors, but with two to choose from it can be done.

These remarks should not be interpreted to mean that not more than two colors should be used for end-papers and for the sprinkling of edges. What I want to emphasize is the fact that with only one color a satisfactory match is impossible. There is no limitation to the number of colors and the varieties of patterns that can be used successfully for end-paper in library bindings.[3]

A harmonious color scheme for cloth covers, edges and the end-papers can go a long way to make a binding attractive without adding a cent to its cost.

One of the ugliest features of many library bindings is the visible cloth hinge on reinforced end-papers. There is a tradition that this strip of reinforcement must be exposed so that the librarian can see, at a glance, that the binder has really put it in. If that is the real reason for its existence, the exposed hinge, besides being ugly to behold, is an appalling monument to librarians' ignorance and to the untrustworthiness of library binders. The librarian who cannot feel with a touch of his finger if the hinge is reinforced or not, should not have anything to do with book-

[3] See Geza Schütz's article 'Individual Endpapers,' in *The Library Journal* (Nov. 15, 1934), p. 868.

binding; and the library binder who is liable to cheat at this vital point of structure does not deserve to stay in business. So why not cover up this symbol of bad taste which has now lost all meaning if, indeed, it ever had any?

Another difficulty on library bindings is the lettering. This is such an important problem that a somewhat detailed discussion is necessary, and this the reader will find in the next chapter.

There is one more suggestion I would like to offer about the making of the cases of library bindings. The possibilities of the 'half-style' should not be entirely neglected in this connection. Half-cloth bindings with paper sides were as popular in the nineteenth century as were half-leather bindings with paper sides in the eighteenth. It is not without significance that the earliest example of an American book bound in cloth which came to Mr. J. W. Rogers' attention, namely Harper's 1829 edition of *Rome in the Nineteenth Century*, was bound in half purple cloth with paper-covered boards.

It is true that today there is no technical advantage in a case that is made by combining cloth and paper; it is neither cheaper than a case made of full cloth, nor more lasting. The advantage is an aesthetic one. Very attractive combinations of cloth backs and paper sides are possible. In instances where a nineteenth-century volume was originally bound in this fashion, and where this book belongs to the 'preferred treatment group,' this style can be recommended without reservation.

Perhaps it will be helpful briefly to sum up the most important points discussed in this chapter:

1. The standard library binding, as commonly practised, is not recommended for the rebinding of old and rare volumes, nor for various other types of special material.

2. The chief objections to the use of standard library bindings for rare and old books are (a) oversewing, (b) appearance.

3. Elimination of total and partial oversewing is recommended whenever possible, and sewing through the folded signatures recommended instead.

4. The appearance of library bindings can be materially improved without increase of cost by (a) careful selection of materials to fit each individual volume, (b) carefully matching the materials and colors of covers, end-papers, edges, inside pages, (c) more attractive and more suitable lettering.

5. With the improvements suggested under (3) and (4), library bindings can be used for certain old and rare books and for various special material. They are particularly suited for volumes originally issued in publisher's edition bindings of the nineteenth and early twentieth century.

# CHAPTER IX

## *LETTERING*

IF all binders, or all those who have to put the lettering on rebound volumes, were trained typographers, there would be no difficulty about gilding. The trouble is that those who do this lettering often know nothing at all about typography, or they know only certain isolated, special rules which they have learned as part of their trade. An inspection of Fig. 69 will prove this point. The four volumes on the left, representing typical lettering on typical library bindings, are faulty in their gilding. They are faulty not because of adherence to or violation of any special rules governing gilded lettering on bindings, but simply because they are in poor typographic taste. In other words, the mistakes made in these four titles would be mistakes anywhere, on a title-page, a tombstone, or in a newspaper advertisement.

The gilded lettering on these four volumes exhibits the following mistakes: combination of type faces of different fonts; unnecessary variations of sizes of type; poor arrangement of spacing between the lines ('leading'); variations of letter spacing within different lines of the same title; and poor relationship of type sizes to size of volumes.

The three volumes on the right of Fig. 69 show what pleasing results are possible by avoiding these basic typographic mistakes. They are perhaps not perfect examples of lettering, but they do show a marked improvement achieved without increasing the cost of lettering by one cent.

One special problem is that of the long title on a narrow back, which does present particular difficulties. To solve this problem, various fonts of specially tall and narrow gilding types have been placed on the market. The curious thing is that these types, as they are normally used, rarely do solve the problem. They are almost always less legible

# A SPECIMEN OF THE NEWBERRY LIBRARY BINDERY TYPE

**24 POINT**

# THE NEWBERRY LIBRARY

**14 POINT**

## THE NEWBERRY LIBRARY ·

**12 POINT**

### THE NEWBERRY LIBRARY ·

**10 POINT**

THE NEWBERRY LIBRARY ·

**8 POINT**

THE NEWBERRY LIBRARY ·

71. *A specimen of the Newberry Library bindery type.*

and less attractive than a smaller type of normal design, but with ample space between the lines. A glance at Fig. 70 will serve to illustrate this point.

There is a general tendency to overestimate the value of size in making titling on book backs legible. Design of the type face used and proper arrangement on the back of the book are at least as important for legibility as is the size of the type.

Suitable and attractive designs are extremely hard to find among the various fonts of brass type offered to book-binders by their supply houses. Specimen books have been issued which do not contain a single acceptable type face.

This problem is particularly acute for the rebinding of rare and old volumes. It is interesting to learn how Mr. Ernst Detterer, Librarian of the Wing Foundation at the Newberry Library in Chicago, solved the problem. After continued disappointments with the brass types offered on the market, he designed his own binding type which is here reproduced on Fig. 71. To do full justice to this type one should, of course, see it not in black on white but im-pressed in gold or blind tooling upon leather, pigskin, or cloth. The type is well rounded without running too wide, and vigorous without being coarse. It retains its character-istics through all the five sizes in which it was cut. The type is neither decidedly 'old-style,' nor yet an outspoken 'mod-ern-face' design. In other words, it stands midway between the types based on traditional Renaissance models and those following the classicist emancipation of Bodoni and Didot. In this the expert will recognize an almost shrewdly suc-cessful designing of a type for universal application, a type that will not be out of place on any of the volumes for which it is intended.

The number of possible designs of universal usefulness is distinctly limited. As a general recommendation I would suggest that two families of gilding type be selected for a given library or by a binding firm. One of them should be a good, well-rounded old-style face, and the other one a crisp modern-face type. Each of these families should be available in a full range of sizes. There is practically no text that is not printed in a type belonging roughly in either the old-style or the modern-face group. Therefore, these two families of gilding types should always make it possible roughly to match the letters on the outside of a book with those used in the inside. That the two styles should never be used together on the back of the same book is perhaps a superfluous warning.

Where difficulties are encountered with the locating and purchasing of really acceptable brass type, an interim solution is suggested. For a limited number of impressions, such as, for instance, in the lettering of rebound old and rare material in a given collection, ordinary foundry types, the kind sold for hand composition purposes, can be used. An unlimited choice of type families in all conceivable designs and sizes is available in foundry type, which, carefully used, can very well be made to serve until the time when permanently satisfactory brass types can be purchased.

This brings up the whole question of materials, of what to choose and where to purchase them.

CHAPTER X

## *MATERIALS*

THROUGHOUT these pages it has been taken for granted that all the various materials needed for the rebinding of old volumes are available to those who need them and who want them. It is my belief that, in the long run, this is true — in spite of many serious obstacles. It could be argued that the foreign sources of supply have been closed to us for the duration of the present war. What is more, there are those who will predict that the present world crisis will altogether wipe out what has remained of the old traditions of craftsmanship; that the making of parchment, the tanning of leather without injurious chemicals, the making of fine rag paper by hand, and the production of decorative pattern papers, all these crafts and skills that flourished in England, Holland and France, in Germany and Italy, will be swept off the map. Others will agree that, even if they are available, these materials should not be used because they are not suited to our climate. On the other hand, native American production of leather and parchment, of decorative pattern papers, and the like will be said by some to be in a state too tentative and precarious to supply any kind of steady demand. Last but not least, it could be pointed out that even the purest and most lasting materials are doomed in modern steam-heated apartments and libraries and in air that is polluted by injurious chemical agents.

It would be unduly optimistic to deny that there is some truth in these arguments. But they are not altogether true, and that is the thing that really matters.

Supplies from abroad, as a matter of fact, are not completely exhausted, nor have they altogether ceased to reach these shores. Even if this should come to be the case, there is no reason to expect that the war will last forever and that there will not be a return to some sort of normality. Is it altogether immodest to hope that these pages will be of some interest and help after the war?

We do not know now what sort of world we will be living in and what will happen to our economic and industrial system. However, the various crafts and skills have survived a great many violent storms before now; in particular, they have stood the impact of industrialization and show many promising signs of vigorous new life. People still like to do things with their hands, in spite of, or even we begin to suspect, because of the machine. This is true of the United States as of any other country in the world. The experiences of the last decades have shown this to those who are able to see such things without prejudice.

Our climate will not change, that is true. Much of the country will continue to suffer from moist, hot summers and will, in wintertime, continue to be so cold that steam-heat is indispensable. However, we are learning more and more about air-conditioning and, particularly, humidification, both in our homes and in public buildings. We are also making progress in eliminating industrial pollution of air and of water. There is good reason for a dose of healthy optimism in these regards.

There is another aspect of this question of materials. Counter arguments are always voiced the loudest by those who do not want to experiment and to change, by those who follow the law of least resistance and of inertia. Those who do see possibilities for improvement and change would rather do something about it than argue. As far as the rebinding of old books, along the lines here suggested, is concerned, no one need feel that the question of materials is unduly difficult. It is not any more difficult than any of the other problems and questions involved. Those opposed to the entire approach will, undoubtedly, seize upon this question of materials as an excuse to veto these suggestions altogether. But the collector and librarian and bookbinder who sees that these suggestions are sound and possible and the obtainable results desirable, will not be discouraged by the problem of getting the proper materials. The location of reliable sources of supply, the hunting up of importers and native craftsmen, the collection of fragments of old materials, will be a source of pleasure rather than a drudgery.

The last word about the comparative lasting qualities of various domestic and imported materials has not been said. Experiments and tests of one kind or another are continuously going on. It would serve no practical purpose to tabulate on these pages the various findings. Such information would be enough to fill a volume all by itself, nor would such an effort produce results that could be considered final in any sense.

The best way to serve the reader is perhaps to list the various materials, mention some of the printed discussions about them and indicate possible sources of supply. Although it is always a little risky to mention names of dealers and firms in a book, it would hardly be fair to leave the reader without at least some indication of where to start his efforts. The following suggestions, then, are to be understood as just that, and as nothing more. They make no claim of listing all, or even most of the makers, or dealers, or importers of bookbinding materials.

## Parchment and Vellum

The best parchment and vellum is made in England and is imported from England. A very good grade comes from Holland.

St. John Hornby in *The Ashendene Press*, published in this country in Meriden in 1939, has this to say about his experiences:

From the year 1902, when I first began to print copies of my books on vellum, down to the present day, the skins have been supplied continuously by Messrs. H. Band & Co. of Brentford. The art of preparing vellum of the quality used for manuscript books up to the middle of the XVIth century would seem to have been entirely lost. But the fact that I have dealt with Messrs. Band for over thirty years may, I hope, be taken as a testimony to their comparative excellence in their craft.

The Stevens-Nelson Paper Corporation, 109 East 31 Street, New York City, imports this and other vellum and parchment. Another importer of vellum is Garo Keshishian of 432 Fourth Avenue, New York City.

The nearest to parchment and vellum that is made in this country is the material used for drum-heads. Some of this could, if importations should cease, be used when sandpapered and properly seized.

George A. Hathaway, of New York City, has been experimenting with white and colored parchment and vellum for twenty-five years and has probably come nearer to the English vellum than anyone else in this country.

### Leather

Although this is the most problematic of all materials used in the rebinding of old volumes, it is nevertheless quite indispensable. Unusual efforts have therefore been made by various experts and institutions to detect the causes of its deterioration and to select suitable and lasting skins which will stand up in the future  Extensive tests have recently been conducted by the Harvard College Library. The March 1940 issue (No. 30) of *Harvard Library Notes* contains, on pages 334-340, a most instructive article, entitled 'Bookbinding Leather,' by Robert F. Fiske, describing a series of tests together with a bibliography of recent articles published on the subject in this country.

In England too, various agencies have concerned themselves with these problems. Within the last decade there have appeared two reports, entitled: *The Causes and Prevention of the Decay of Bookbinding Leather*, Interim Report of the Bookbinding Leather Committee, issued by Printing Industry Research Association and British Leather Manufacturers' Research Association, London, St. Bride Institute, 1933; and Second Interim Report, 1936.[1]

The New York Public Library has conducted many experiments with leather in the past twenty-five years.[2] Several years ago, on the advice of the Bureau of Standards in Washington, D. C., they started working with chrome tanned leathers, used originally for making shoes. From this they have developed suitable bookbinding leathers of high durability, in co-operation with two firms, namely R. Neumann & Co., Hoboken, New Jersey, and the Steinhardt Leather Company in Newark, New Jersey.

In England Douglas Cockerell in Letchworth, Herts., has developed unusually beautiful bookbinding leathers in co-operation with G. W. Russell & Son, Ltd., in Hitchin, Herts. Both natural grain calf and fine goatskins have been produced which are remarkable for the beauty of their textures and the unusual, subdued colors which blend admirably with the various shades of old leather. These leathers supplement the excellent Richardson leathers, which are deservedly famous in this country.

Several firms have handled and are handling bookbinding skins imported from England and the European continent. There are, for instance, Edward Assenheim, of 1215 East 37 Street, Brooklyn, New York; Post & Floto, of 14 Read Street, New York City, and Louis De Jonge & Co., of 161 Sixth Avenue, New York City.

## Decorated Pattern Papers

The use of decorative papers has been recommended, for various good reasons, throughout the pages of this essay. It

[1] The work of R. Farady Innes, F. I. C., is also of importance. See *Journal of the International Society of the Leather Trades Chemists*, 1933, page 725; and *Library Association Record*, March 1934, Sept. 1934, Nov. 1934.

Earlier English investigations and experiments are described in the *Report of the Committee on Leather for Bookbinding*, edited by The Rt. Hon. Viscount Cobham and Sir Henry Trueman Wood, M.A. (London: Published for the Society of Arts by George Bell & Sons, 1905.)

[2] See John Archer's article 'A Ten-Year Test of Bindings,' in *New York Public Library Bulletin* (February, 1936), Vol. XL, No. 2, pp. 97-100.

is particularly important that the reader be guided to reliable sources of supply for this important material. The choice of suitable colors and patterns to fit each individual volume in need of rebinding is a matter of personal taste and experience. There is unlimited room here for experimentation and variation, provided always that one basic caution be observed under all circumstances, namely that a sheet of really good quality is chosen. Fortunately, most papers decorated by hand, that is to say, genuine marble papers (not the cheap lithographic imitations), paste papers and woodblock pattern papers are reliable. They are made by people who understand quality in paper, who know that their efforts would be wasted on sheets of inferior grades. Those who decide to decorate their own papers should, of course, get expert advice as to the kind of paper to use.[3] It should be understood that neither marbling, nor paste paper making, nor the impression of woodblock patterns affect the lasting quality of a sheet of paper. If certain papers fail to endure, it is not the fault of the decorating process but of the paper stock itself.

The most reliable source of supply is a library of old books. It is surprising how quickly a store of decorative papers can be built up, if a systematic effort is made to save every old end-paper, every paper-covered board from any volume that is too far gone to be repaired. In a good many instances, the sewing, cords, boards, corners, leather and cloth may be gone, but the old paper is still in good condition. It is always worthwhile to save it. Its very existence, the fact of its survival, is a testimony to its quality.

The librarian who can draw on the yield of large numbers of old volumes is not obliged to use these old materials on the very same volumes from where they were gathered in the first place. By saving the decorated papers from all

[3] See *Permanence and Durability of Paper. An Annotated Bibliography of the Technical Literature from* 1885 A.D., *to* 1939 A.D. By Morris S. Kantrowitz, Ernest W. Spencer and Robert H. Simmons (Washington: U. S. Government Printing Office, 1940). (Technical Bulletin No. 22.)

old volumes that have come apart, and by re-using them only in the rebinding of the 'preferred treatment group,' he can build up a surplus reservoir that will give him choice and variety. In this regard he has a distinct advantage over the individual collector. The private owner of a library will either have to rely on his bookbinder for this type of supply or, if he is so inclined, he can start his own collection of end-papers. Most dealers of rare and old books are glad to be on the lookout for old papers, if they know that their customers are interested in them.

Among the modern decorative pattern papers one can readily distinguish between those that are traditional in method of production and in patterns and those that represent independent, original efforts. Contemporary Italian woodblock papers, for instance, are often indistinguishable, in their patterns, from those printed in the eighteenth and early nineteenth century. However, the quality of the basic stock in this group differs considerably. Printed pattern papers in attractive modern designs, produced by the woodblock method as well as by various modern printing processes, have been made in Czechoslovakia and in Great Britain.[4]

Marble papers in conventional patterns have come particularly from France and Germany. Interesting modern marble papers have been made in Germany and in England, notably by Mr. Douglas Cockerell and his son Sydney Morris Cockerell.[5] (See Fig. 56.)

Far Eastern decorated papers, from China and Japan, are often very attractive and reliable in quality. Their use in rebinding, however, is somewhat limited. The colors and patterns usually found on them do not correspond very readily to the traditional European models. However, where a somewhat freer interpretation of an old pattern or

[4] See *A Specimen Book of Pattern Papers, designed for and in use at the Curwen Press* (London: *The Fleuron*, 1928).

[5] See Sydney M. Cockerell, *Marbling Paper as a School Subject* (Hitchin: G. W. Russell & Son, 1934).

a completely independent design is the aim, Far Eastern papers offer many interesting possibilities, both as end-paper and as covering material.

The best way to procure foreign decorative papers of various types and patterns is through paper importing houses in this country. For many years both Thomas N. Fairbanks, of 373 Fourth Avenue, New York City, and the Stevens-Nelson Paper Company (see page 268) have made every effort to make attractive and enduring types of European and Far Eastern papers available in this country. They also handle domestic papers of unusual quality.

Outstanding among domestic producers of decorative papers is Mrs. Augustus P. Loring, associated with the Club of Odd Volumes in Boston, Massachusetts. Mrs. Loring, starting as a collector of old papers and an amateur producer of marble and paste papers, is rapidly approaching professional status. For instance, her paste papers have been used in the binding of entire editions by the Merrymount Press in Boston and the Limited Editions Club in New York.[6]

Miss Veronica Ruzicka, the daughter of Rudolf Ruzicka, noted wood-engraver and type-designer, has recently entered the field with her 'Proteus' papers, a group of charmingly designed paste papers which should do well for rebinding purposes as well as for various other uses.

The making of the different kinds of decorated papers is being taught in not a few schools and classes throughout the country.[7] It is very much hoped that from the many that take it up as a pleasant pastime and amiable hobby, at least a few will graduate into genuine amateurs and will, eventually, become real craftsmen. There is a definite need for their services.

[6] See page 213, footnote 1.

[7] An excellent brief guide to the various processes is Geoffrey Peach's *Hand decorated pattern papers for book craft* (London: Dryad Press, 1931).

## Book cloth

The introduction of cloth into this country, the rise of a native industry of cloth manufacturing and finishing and the structure of the industry have been dealt with so thoroughly by Mr. Rogers in Part II of this volume, that it would be superfluous to add to that information. Moreover, samples of their products are being distributed throughout the libraries of this country so liberally and so continuously by the various manufacturers, that there is really no need for further amplification.

# CHAPTER XI

## *ON THE CARE OF OLD VOLUMES*

NOT the most prudent choice of materials, nor the most meticulous workmanship can ensure lasting protection, if books are not given healthy living conditions after they have been repaired or rebound. The best long-range rebinding policy, in fact, is to make rebinding unnecessary and to eliminate as much as possible the causes for decay. There is nothing much we can do with books originally bound, or rebound, by inferior methods and unreliable materials. They will have to be repaired or rebound for a second time. There are, however, certain factors that affect even books in the most durable and carefully executed bindings, and no matter whether old or new.

Our climate is one of the permanently threatening factors that have to be taken into account. Books, like human beings, thrive under moderate conditions of temperature and humidity. The change of heat and cold alone is not the source of decay. It is the change from excessively humid heat in the summertime to the excessively dry heat of steam-heated buildings in the winter that does the harm. The same thing that affects our mucous membranes, causes headaches and sinus trouble shortens the lives of our bindings.

A less obvious but equally injurious source of deterioration is the presence, in practically all industrial and metropolitan areas, of dangerous chemical agents in the very air that surrounds the owner of books and his cherished volumes. 'If he lives near a laundry or smelter or power house,' say Messrs. Lydenberg and Archer,[1] 'or any one of a dozen lethal instruments developed by our advanced civilization, he may be sure that day by day and hour by hour their chimneys and smoke stacks belch forth gases that pollute the air and are certain to take their toll of anything in his

[1] Op. cit., pp. 24, 25.

house composed wholly or partly of leather or paper.'

There are two weapons with which to fight these various enemies, lubrication and air-conditioning.

## Lubrication

There can be no doubt that a regular oiling of all leather bindings does much to lengthen the lives of bookbindings and makes them resistant to various harmful influences.[2] Anyone who has seen how a dried-out leather cover will simply lap up the oil, as though it were both thirsty and starved, will not need to be convinced of the desirability of this treatment. To be effective, it should be done about once a year. The best time would seem to be the late summer and the early fall, when the excessive humidity of midsummer days has departed, and before the excessive dryness of steam-heating exacts its annual toll of victims. The early fall is not a bad time for such things on the calendar of the average library. In a private collection, a rainy Labor Day weekend would provide the ideal setting for this charitable action.

Not only books bound in full leather but also those with leather backs and corners, in short, all exposed leather parts should be oiled. With a little practice it is quite easy to prevent the oil from getting onto the paper or cloth sections of the covers. Be careful not to return the volumes to the shelves before they have absorbed all the oil. If necessary, a final rubbing-off with clean cheese-cloth, gently applied, will take care of any excess lubricating material.

Various formulas for the preparation of book-oil are in circulation, and various dealers in rare and old books are prepared to furnish their customers with suitable preparations.

[2] See Louis N. Feipel and William R. Thurman's article 'Preserving Leather Binding,' in *The Library Journal* (September 15, 1938), 63:706. Also 'Protective Steps recommended in Prevention of Leather Decay,' in *Bookbinding and Book Production* (July, 1936), 24:20.

For collectors and librarians who prefer to mix their own, two formulas in current library use are hereby communicated.

### Book Oil as Used by Columbia University Library

For twenty pounds use:

| | |
|---|---|
| Castile soap | 0.6 lb. (10 oz) |
| Neat's-foot oil | 5.0 lb. |
| Tallow | 2.0 lb. |
| Double rectified turpentine | 2.4 lb. (1/3 gal.) |
| Distilled water | 10.0 lb. |

Add two ounces of oil of cedar.

Dissolve the soap in water on a steam bath. Melt the neat's-foot oil and tallow together by heating in the same way. While both solutions are hot pour the soap solution in a thin stream into the melted tallow and oil mixture while stirring thoroughly. Continue to stir until an emulsion is obtained. Let the emulsion cool to room temperature and add the turpentine and oil of cedar. Keep in well-stoppered bottle and shake before using. Apply with fingers or cloth. After ten or fifteen minutes rub with clean cloth.

### Book Oil as Used by The University of Pittsburgh

Dr. W. A. Gruse of the Mellon Institute of Industrial Research recommends the formula presented in Leaflet No. 69, Bureau of Chemistry and Soils, by R. W. Frey and F. P. Veitch, with certain slight modifications.

| | | |
|---|---|---|
| Neat's-foot-oil | 25 | parts by weight |
| Anhydrous Lanolin | 17.5 | parts by weight |
| Pure Japan Wax | 10.00 | parts by weight |
| Ivory Soap Flakes | 2.5 | parts by weight |
| Distilled Water | 45.0 | parts by weight [3] |

Ivory soap which has been in storage for a while and has become hard and dry is more satisfactory than fresh soap. Alternatively, the outer layers of partially aged cakes could be used.

[3] The University of Pittsburgh's Department of Chemistry increased the distilled water to 50.0 in making up the above recipe.

This gives a dressing which assumes a satisfactorily pasty consistency at once.

All ingredients except the soap and the water should be melted together in one container without overheating. The soap and the water should be mixed in another container; the mixture should be warmed and stirred until the soap is dissolved. The soap solution should then be poured in a thin stream into the melted grease mixture, stirring vigorously. A thin milk-like emulsion will result which should be allowed to cool. When about cold it will be much stiffer, and should then be stirred constantly and thoroughly until uniform in appearance. The preparation should be rubbed into the leather binding with the hands, and the book then set in a warm place for a few hours.

## Air-Conditioning

It is not easy to make recommendations for air-conditioning. The best procedure will depend on conditions prevailing in a given library or collection, on the available funds and technical facilities and on the good will and understanding of all those concerned. The only thing that can be stated with emphasis is that something should be done to counteract the effects of excessive dryness, excessive humidity and of air pollution.

A complete system of air-conditioning through an entire building is obviously the most desirable solution. The fact that such a generous scheme is rarely, if ever, possible should, however, not prevent the installation of individual humidifiers.[4] There are various types of air-conditioning units on the market which can very well be installed in individual vaults, treasure rooms and exhibition rooms.

In the private library the problem is equally acute, but its solution has the added advantage of benefitting not only the books but also the people who live in those rooms. Again, as in public institutions, it is a question of the pocketbook. However, there are many types of inexpensive

[4] The Treasure Room and the Department of Printing and Graphic Arts at the Harvard University Library have made successful installations of individual humidifiers in specific rooms.

radiator pans and simple humidifiers on the market which everybody could afford. They are sometimes scorned by the experts as ineffective and superfluous. They probably cannot solve the problem completely, but undoubtedly they do some good

A partial solution of the problem of humidification and air-control is, undoubtedly, better than none at all.

Excessive dryness, as a matter of fact, is more easily coped with than excessive humidity, which tends to develop mildew or mold. 'The best remedy,' to quote once again Messrs. Lydenberg and Archer,[5] is prevention, and the best method of prevention is storage in light, well ventilated rooms where the books are kept dry. All easy enough to say, to be sure, but what help has any owner of books against the humid heat that occasionally swoops down on hapless residents of the southern and eastern seaboard of this continent? Well, for one thing, he can shut the windows and turn on artificial heat, no matter what the thermometer says as to outside temperature. He must first drive away the humidity. Heat may be uncomfortable, but if it is dry the mold will not spread. Then rub the books with clean, dry cloths, and keep careful watch to see that no advance takes place.'

The recommendations in this chapter are obviously neither new or original. These things have been discussed very thoroughly by experts in these matters on various occasions and in several publications.[6] However, their advice cannot

[5] Op. cit., p. 28.

[6] Questions of care and preservation are discussed in the following publications not previously cited in this essay:

A. E. Kimberly and B. W. Scribner, *Summary Report of Bureau of Standards Research on Preservation of Records*, Bureau of Standards Miscellaneous Publication No. 144 (Washington: United States Government Printing Office, 1934).

Thomas M. Iiams, 'Preservation of Rare Books and Manuscripts in the Huntington Library,' *The Library Quarterly* (October, 1932), Vol. II, No. 4.

E. Zaehnsdorf and C. J. Hutchins, 'The Care and Preservation of Books,' *The American Book Collector* (January, 1932), Vol. I, No. 1.

E. Zaehnsdorf, 'The Preservation and Care of Books,' *The American Book Collector* (June, 1932), Vol. I, No. 6.

Lloyd S. Brown, *Notes on the Care and Cataloguing of Old Maps* (Windham, Connecticut: Hawthorne House, 1941).

be repeated often enough. What is the use of careful repair and rebinding, if living quarters are provided which will, sooner or later, defeat all efforts of preservation?

## CHAPTER XII

## *CONCLUSIONS AND*
## *RECOMMENDATIONS*

T HE most important conclusion that forces itself on anyone concerned with the physical future of the old and rare volumes in our private and public libraries is this — that the most satisfactory way to rebind an old book is not the most expensive one but the one most difficult to obtain. The methods which are both technically soundest and aesthetically most satisfying do not necessarily require the most costly materials nor always the most expensive workmanship. But these methods are not regularly practiced today. They are in a binder's no-man's-land, lying as they do somewhere between the territories covered by the collectors' binders and the library binders. The need for "intermediate" binding has long been recognized but not directly in connection with the rebinding of old and rare volumes. Yet it is this very group which would benefit most materially from an effective reorganization of bookbinding establishments. Both the quality and the quantity of material in need of treatment throughout the country is so considerable that the demand for "intermediate binding" can be said to present a distinct opportunity.

The reasons why there is, at the present, no adequate supply of suitable binderies and binders for this kind of work are, briefly, the following:

1. Increasing pressure on most binders to turn out durable bindings for heavy circulation books at as low a price as possible. Inevitably, this has led to standardization, mechanization, division of labor, disappearance of the old type of all-round craftsmen and insufficient supply of skilled labor to replace them.

    Proper treatment of old and rare material is particularly difficult where state laws or municipal statutes require libraries to give their binding to the lowest bidder. The libraries of certain State Univeristies, for instance, have found it difficult or impossible to explain the need for discrimination in rebinding and repair.

2. The isolation of the fine binder; his tendency to cater to the wealthy collector exclusively; a tradition which emphasizes external appearance, expensive materials and decoration rather than solid and aesthetically satisfying craftsmanship throughout.

What then are the fundamental requirements in developing the right kind of binderies for this type of work?

1. Organization of groups of craftsmen thoroughly familiar with the traditional methods of hand binding and with traditional materials; of men and women who love their work, who bring to it sympathy and patience, and who would be willing to forego large profits in return for a congenial and interesting occupation.

2. Such an organization could be (a) a separate workshop, (b) the department of an established firm of either collectors' or library binders, (c) a department in a library or subdivision of a library bindery.

3. Such an organization would have to be assured of a steady volume of this type of work, so that a permanent group of the right kind of craftsmen could be given security. This means that the proper economic territories would have to be worked out which could support such binderies or departments. A large university could offer such conditions; so could a group of public libraries; so could a metropolitan center having a number of collectors.

4. Close co-operation of the libraries and collectors would be essential. They would have to estimate potential volume of work from their collections and, provided always that reasonable prices are guaranteed, give assurance of continued support.

5. Last, not least, the successful operation of such a scheme would depend on a systematic education of collectors and libraries on the one hand, and the training of suitable craftsmen on the other.

Existing opportunities for the training of bookbinding craftsmen should be enlarged and additional facilities developed. Directors and teachers of bookbinding courses throughout the country would have to consider the need for craftsmen competent to rebind and repair old and rare volumes. Their training would have to include, in addition to a thorough mastery of technique, a knowledge of the history of binding and of the binding techniques of the various periods, the nature of book materials both old and new, and something of the evaluation of contents and values of books.

Hospitals have been endowed for the study of special diseases and for the training of doctors and nurses to treat these patients. Would it not be a worth-while thing to endow a book hospital?

Collectors and particularly librarians should learn above everything else to differentiate between run-of-the-mill books and material that deserves individual treatment. Library School courses in the history and technique of bookbinding would have to be developed. On the staff of even the smallest library there could be at least one person with such a background. Larger libraries, with their own binding departments, would benefit greatly if they appointed at least one staff member to the permanent duty of segregating the 'preferred treatment' material from routine job lots and to hold him — or herself personally responsible for the prevention of rebinding casualities.

There is hardly a single one among these suggestions that has not been separately attempted somewhere within the last decade or so, and many isolated experiments are undoubtedly being made at the present time. These pages, we hope, may help to unite these efforts and show along what lines a solution of the many difficult problems might be sought.

## SUPPLEMENT TO PART III

I T will be well to remember that this part of *Bookbinding in America* deals primarily with basic principles. It does contain a number of technical suggestions, and mentions methods and materials, but the main emphasis is on the ethics and aesthetics of the rebinding of old volumes.

In these matters, and they take up by far the major portion of its total contents, *On the Rebinding of Old Books* has not been superseded by the many new publications on bookbinding. In many regards these pages still represent the only serious discussion of basic principles and alternatives concerning the rebinding of old and rare volumes.

The last twenty-five years have seen a heightened pace in the publication of literature on bookbinding in general, and on conservation in particular. As far as the United States is concerned, this reflects very clearly the phenomenon commonly known as the "cultural explosion." It is quite natural that the spectacular growth of library resources during these years, the forming of numerous rare book collections in academic institutions and in private libraries, the amazing increase in the number of rare book curators and of "Friends of the Library" associations, should have sharpened concern over the proper conservation of rare books and manuscripts, and related materials.

HISTORY OF BINDING TECHNIQUES

*On the Rebinding of Old Books* strongly recommends the much neglected study of the history of binding techniques as an important guide to the solution of current problems. At least two important publications have appeared since 1941:

CLOUGH, E. A. *Bookbinding for Librarians*. With illustrations and diagrams. London, Association of Assistant Librarians, 1957.
The book discusses the practical problems of the librarian who has to deal with bookbinding. "The chapter on the history of bookbinding concerns itself not with the development of decoration, but with the changing techniques and materials used in bookbinding over the centuries." There is a brief chapter on "The Repair and Care of Books and Bookbinding" and a "Select Bibliography."

MIDDLETON, BERNARD C. *A History of English Craft Bookbinding Techniques*. With foreword by Howard M. Nixon. New York and London, Hafner, 1963.
This is an important pioneer work in tracing the history of the technique rather than merely of the decoration of bookbinding in England. Chapter IV deals specifically with "Book Repairs and Restoration."

Although by no means especially concerned with binding technique, the following publication is so comprehensive in scope and so beautifully and amply illustrated, that it deserves to be recommended here:

WALTERS ART GALLERY. *The History of Bookbinding 525–1950 A. D.* An Exhibition held at the Baltimore Museum of Art, November 12, 1957 to January 12, 1958. Baltimore, Maryland, 1957.
The material is arranged strictly in chronological groups and includes sections on American seventeenth to nineteenth century trade bindings.

CARE AND REPAIR    The following publications, previously mentioned here, have been reissued in new editions:

COCKERELL, DOUGLAS. *Bookbinding and the Care of Books: A Textbook for Bookbinders and Librarians*. With drawings by Noel Rooke and other illustrations. 5th edition. London, Pitman, 1953.

The book "is intended to supplement and not to supplant workshop training for bookbinders." Part II deals with "Care of Books When Bound."

LYDENBERG, HARRY M. and JOHN ARCHER. *The Care and Repair of Books.* Revised by JOHN ALDEN. New York, R. R. Bowker, 1960.

"In preparing this new edition of a work whose usefulness has been so amply manifested, an effort has been made to retain its established virtues, and to supplement them with reports on developments in preservation in recent years of which the library administrator and the technician should be aware. . . ." (from John Alden's "Introduction"). With an excellent annotated bibliography.

SCHWEIDLER, MAX. *Die Instandsetzung von Kupferstichen, Zeichnungen, Büchern usw.* 2nd edition. Stuttgart, Max Hettler, 1950.

The late Max Schweidler is internationally recognized as a past master of the art of restoration of papers and bindings. The book is especially valuable for the detailed descriptions of secret, often jealously guarded, paper-manipulating techniques.

The following books, published since 1941, belong on the recommended list of readings:

DUEHMERT, ANNELIESE. *Buchpflege.* Stuttgart, Max Hettler, 1964.

The first comprehensive bibliography of the literature on the care and repair of bindings. Over 200 pages list 2,000 entries of works published in several languages, arranged strictly by subjects and indexed by subject and author. The index is hard to use, however, since one has to refer back to the contents page to locate the section under which entries are listed.

COCKERELL, SYDNEY M. *The Repairing of Books.* Illustrations by Joan Rix Tebbutt. London, Sheppard Press, 1958.

"The purpose of this work," by the son of the late Douglas Cockerell, "is to explain some of the ways that damaged books can be repaired, so that librarians, archivists, collectors and others who are concerned with the care of books can do simple repairs themselves, and be able to give clear instructions when sending items to the binder. . . ."

LANGWELL, W. H. *The Conservation of Books and Documents.* London, Pitman, 1957 and 1958.

The author is concerned mainly with the lasting qualities of papers, adhesives, inks and binding materials, especially when manufactured under modern conditions and involving new chemical and physical processing. He defines the elements of quality and durability in simple language, and goes on to explain how physical deterioration of existing books and documents may be prevented.

From among numerous periodical articles, the following are listed here:

BAUGHMAN, ROLAND. "Conservation of Old and Rare Books" in: *Library Trends,* vol. IV (Conservation of Library Materials), January, 1956.

TRIBOLET, HAROLD W. "Binding and Related Problems" in: *American Archivist,* vol. 16, April, 1953, pp. 115–126.

———. "Protect Those Documents" in: *Autograph Collector's Journal,* January, 1950.

———. "Trends in Preservation" in: *Library Trends,* vol. XIII, no. 2, October, 1964. See also *Midwest Museums Conference Quarterly,* Spring, 1966.

There is an important Italian periodical entirely devoted to all questions and aspects of care and repair:

ISTITUTO DI PATHOLOGIA DEL LIBRO. *Bulletin.* Rome, 1939. (Publication was suspended from 1943 to 1945.)

The editor from 1939–1952 was Alfonso Gallo, who is also the author of several publications in the field. An article describing the Institute appeared in German in a Danish publication:

GALLO, MICHELANGELO. "Das Institut für Buchpflege 'Alfonso Gallo' in Rome" in: *Libri,* vol. 5, no. 1, Copenhagen, 1954, pp. (35)–40.


A great amount of experimentation and work has been carried on in Russia. The results of these efforts are available in the following publications:

ACADEMIA NAUK SSSR. — N. YA. SOLECHNIK (Ed.). *New Methods for the Restoration and Preservation of Documents and Books.* Translated from the Russian. Published for the National Science Foundation, Washington, D. C. and the Council on Library Resources by the Israel Program for Scientific Translations.

GOSUDARSTVENNAYA ORDENA LENINA. BIBLIOTEKA SSR im. *Collection of Materials on the Preservation of Library Resources.* Two numbers in one. Translated from the Russian. No. 2 edited by L. G. PETROVA. Moskau, 1953. No. 3 edited by L. A. BELYAKOVA and O. V. KOZULINA. Moskau, 1958. Published for the National Science Foundation, Washington, D. C. and the Council on Library Resources by the Israel Program for Scientific Translations.

Both publications are available from the Office of Technical Services, U. S. Department of Commerce, Washington, D. C. 20540.


An official publication on standard library bindings has been prepared under the direction of the Joint Committee of the American Library Association and the Library Binding Institute:

THE STANDARD LIBRARY BINDING

FEIPEL, L. N. and E. W. BROWNING. *Library Binding Manual*. Chicago, American Library Association, 1951.
    ". . . an elementary book on the binding and, to a lesser extent, the care and preservation of printed materials . . . It does not go in deeply for special bindings for library collections or for extra bindings for individual volumes. It is confined to minimum requirements for the ordinary run of books . . ."

LETTERING    It is still difficult to find good brass or other metal type for lettering on rebound old volumes. A Swiss firm produces and markets a line of types for these purposes which are cast in a suitable and durable metal and in attractive designs. These are the "Haas Hard Alloy Types" furnished by the Haas'sche Schriftgiesserei A. G., 4142 Muenchenstein, Switzerland.

MATERIALS    In the reprinting of an out-of-print volume its discussion of historical conditions is far safer from the danger of obsolescence than the sections devoted to current matters. In the case of Part III of this book it has already been pointed out that the discussion of basic principles and procedures, which takes up a major portion of its contents, seems to have stood the test of time. This includes the pages dealing with the historical use of the various bookbinding materials and the corresponding suitability of modern materials in rebinding. However, the recommendations of certain specific services, methods of conservation and sources of supply for leather, paper, etc. are obviously to some extent out-of-date. Moreover, they were written under the pressure of wartime uncertainties.

There is no reason to assume that some of the following references and recommendations may not likewise become outdated some day. Nevertheless, they are included in the hope that they will be useful to the reader for some years ahead.

The following book, although a general manual on the

conservation of many kinds of artefacts, is listed here because of its excellent section on materials:

PLENDERLEITH, H. J. *The Conservation of Antiquities and Works of Art: Treatment, Repair and Restoration.* London, Oxford University Press, 1956 (reprinted 1957).
 A comprehensive manual by the Keeper of the British Museum's Research Laboratory. Part I, Organic Materials, contains chapters on: 1) animal skins and products; 2) papyrus, parchments and paper; and 3) prints, drawings, and manuscripts—all relevant to bookbinding. The appendices contain valuable information on chemicals, acidity, humidity, leather tests, leather dressings, etc.

A monograph on bookbinding materials in current use, which should prove useful to the students of rebinding methods, is the following publication:

THUMA, MAX. *Die Werkstoffe des Buchbinders: Ihre Herstellung und Verarbeitung.* 4th edition. Stuttgart, Max Hettler, 1960.
 This well-illustrated, standard training manual deals with all currently used materials: paper, leather, cloth, plastics, pigments, adhesives, etc.

Of the many important investigations and reports on PAPER the lasting qualities of book paper, the following is among the most useful for the student of rebinding:

BARROW, WILLIAM J. *Deterioration of Book Stocks: Causes and Remedies.* Two studies on the permanence of book papers. Edited by Randolph W. Church. (Virginia State Library Publications, No. 10.) Richmond, Virginia State Library, 1959.

Decorated pattern papers are of great importance in rebinding. Two major studies of their history have appeared since 1941:

LORING, ROSAMOND B. *Decorated Book Papers: Being an Account of Their Design and Fashions.* Cambridge, Department of Printing and Graphic Arts, Harvard College Library, 1942.

The first serious attempt to collect into a continuous, reasoned account technical and historical information on the many different kinds of pattern papers known to have been produced. The author also shows, by instruction and through some fine original examples and facsimile reproductions, how marble papers, paste papers, and printed pattern papers can be made today.

HAEMMERLE, ALBERT and OLGA HIRSCH (coll.). *Buntpapier: Herkommen, Geschichte, Techniken, Beziehungen zur Kunst.* Munich, Georg D. W. Callwey, 1961.

Published on the occasion of the 150th anniversary of the Buntpapierfabrik A. G. Aschaffenburg, who subsidized the lavish production of this, the finest history of decorated pattern papers, mainly European and Near Eastern, since the Middle Ages. Magnificently illustrated and containing many original specimens and color reproductions.

The importance of handmade papers from the Far East has been mentioned on pages 271–272. A splendid publication published a few years ago in Tokyo deserves to be mentioned here:

TINDALE, THOMAS KEITH and HARRIET RAMSAY TINDALE. *The Handmade Papers of Japan.* Four volumes in Japanese cloth portfolio: I. The Handmade Papers of Japan; with a Foreword by Dard Hunter; II. The Seki Collection; III. The Contemporary Collection; IV. The Watermark Collection. With an envelope of original papermaking fibers. Rutland, Vermont and Tokyo, Charles E. Tuttle, 1952.

The Stevens-Nelson Paper Company (formerly the Japan Paper Company), mentioned on pages 268 and 272, is still a major source of supply for handmade papers, as well as for parchment and leather. It should be noted that the

firm's name has changed to Andrews/Nelson/Whitehead
(a division of Boise Cascade Corporation), and its address
to 7 Laight Street, New York, N. Y. The company published a sample book of unusual splendor:

> *Specimens: Good Paper, a Few Scratches in Black Ink,*
> *Some Red* ... New York, Stevens-Nelson Paper Company,
> 1963.
> Described in its introduction as "a catalogue of the
> finest printing and art papers in the world," the volume
> is made up of signatures of papers imported from Western
> Europe and Japan, and each designed, illustrated and
> printed by teams of outstanding graphic artists and
> typographers.

As far as other sources of supply are concerned, it can
be mentioned that Sydney M. Cockerell, the son of the late
Douglas Cockerell, continues to make fine marble paper
in Cambridge, England. Brigitte Cramer, Hulgårdsvej 12,
Copenhagen, Denmark, makes and sells a rich assortment
of paste papers in many colors and patterns. In this country, Mrs. Nancy Storm of Sedona, Arizona, designs and
produces unusual paste papers which can be purchased
from her stock or made to order.

As a source of supply for parchment, the firm of Messrs.    PARCHMENT
H. Band and Company of Brentford, England, is still foremost in the business. The firm is represented in this
country by Andrews/Nelson/Whitehead in New York (see
above under PAPER).
A scholarly and carefully documented and illustrated
article on parchment and vellum, dealing first with its
production, then with its conservation and restoration, is:

> FACKELMANN, ANTON. "Das Pergament: Seine Herstellung
> und Seine Betreuung in den Bibliotheken" in: *Biblos,*
> *Oesterreichische Zeitschrift fuer Buch-und Bibliotheks-*
> *wesen.* Vienna, 1961, vol. X, no. 3, pp. 118–130.

LEATHER    Regarding chrome tanned leathers discussed on page 269, Mr. Harold Tribolet, Manager of the Extra Bindery at the Lakeside Press, Chicago, comments as follows: "The chrome tanned skins are difficult to fabricate and hand tool, in comparison to those tanned by the traditional vegetable process." H. Band and Company (see above) has been tanning goatskins by a combination vegetable and chrome process in an effort to incorporate the advantages of each.

The oasis niger goatskin tanned by G. W. Russell and Son, Ltd. in Hitchin, England, retailed by Andrews/ Nelson/Whitehead, Inc. in our country, is excellent leather for binding books of permanent value.

The question of leather deterioration and its prevention continues to occupy the serious attention of the experts. An important monograph on the subject is the following:

PLENDERLEITH, H. J. *The Preservation of Leather Book-bindings*. London, The British Museum, 1946 (reprinted 1947 and 1950).
". . . The treatment of leather that has already deteriorated will always remain an important problem for the librarian and book-collector . . . it has been found necessary, in the light of modern research, to cover a wider field and deal with the causes and prevention of binding leather deterioration."

Mr. Tribolet has volunteered the following important recommendations (not quoted verbatim):

Plenderleith's work states that the application of a protective salt to leather will retard chemical action. He recommends a seven percent aqueous solution of potassium lactate, to which one-quarter percent of paranitrophenol is added as a protection against mould. I use and recommend the potassium lactate solution, followed (the next day) by an application of the time-tested mixture of neat's-foot oil, pure, 20° C., cold test (60.0 percent) plus lanolin, anhydrous

(40.0 percent). Technical Library Service, 261 Broadway, New York, N. Y. 10017, supplies these solutions.

Concerning various oils used as leather dressings, Mr. Plenderleith is of the opinion that they are almost entirely non-effective in arresting chemical decay, but that they are useful in keeping leather supple. On this point Mr. Tribolet points out that many of the leather preparations (including the "British Museum Dressing") containing beeswax have caused serious problems because, in some instances, the wax remains tacky, causing books to stick together; in other cases the wax has been known to harden the leather. Apparently the variable difficulties are caused by the uncertain quality of the beeswax used.

Many of the leather dressings containing soap, sodium stearate, and certain unknown ingredients in proprietary preparations appear to be beneficial when they are applied; then upon drying, a semi-opaque film appears, together with a white substance in the deeper crevices of grainy leather. Obviously, leather dressings of this kind should be avoided.

Mrs. Polly Lada-Mocarski, experienced master binder and teacher of the craft at Yale University, recommends a special wax with insecticide qualities, made in France. It comes in small metal tubes, like oil paints, in six different colors to blend with the color of the leather to be treated. The preparation is called "CIRE 212," and can be ordered from Madame Flieder, Attachée de Recherches au C.N.R.S., Musée National d'Histoire Naturelle, Laboratoire de Cryptogamie, 12 Rue Buffon, Paris 5, France.

While this preparation is commendable for its insecticidal properties, its wax content appears to cause the same difficulties as some of the preparations described above.

Concerning the cleaning of pigskin bindings, page 210, saddle soap applied with a slightly moist cheesecloth is an effective treatment for discolored bindings.

Air-conditioning is now almost universally recognized as the most important single factor in long range conservation. A word of warning must, however, be said against its use in old and leaky structures. When a building is not well sealed off from the outside atmosphere, the intrusion of air that is not filtered and temperature and humidity controlled, can cause conditions injurious to old bindings.

FLEX
BINDING A word should be said about Flex Binding, a radically new method of binding, and its possible uses in care and repair. Flex Binding, briefly, is a method of holding single sheets or folded sheets, or both, together with polyvinyl glue (paste). This glue, differing from other adhesives which become brittle when dry, remains plastic, and being chemically inert will not migrate to or affect other materials. Mrs. Lada-Mocarski has experimented thoroughly with Flex Binding and has reached the conclusion that valuable and rare books should never be repaired with polyvinyl acetate glue, which is very hard to remove when an old and rare book has to be repaired again. This applies to any rare materials, such as maps, prints, manuscripts or anything written, printed, or printed on vellum. However, it has the following specific uses in hand bookbinding:

— Rebinding any contemporary, machine-made book, for binding the pages as well as making the case.

— Inserting single sheets into an already bound book.

— Rebinding pamphlets or just holding together fragile pamphlets printed on bad pulp paper.

— Binding music, as the plasticity of the adhesive permits the pages to lie quite flat.

— Binding two-page spreads. It will lie fully open thus avoiding an interruption in the center of the page.

— Attaching covers that have come loose, provided the leather has not disintegrated and become powdery. This procedure takes great skill and requires much practice on inferior books before attempting valuable ones.

— Repairing damaged corners before covering with leather again. This, too, requires considerable skill.

— Repairing all types of cloth bindings that are coming apart.

— Making all types of book boxes and cases.

In addition to Mrs. Polly Lada-Mocarski and Mr. Harold Tribolet, whose valuable assistance is amply evident in the above pages, I owe a word of thanks to Mr. E. A. Thompson, Book Restorer, at 430 West Arbor Vitae, Inglewood, California 90301. He has supplied a valuable list of references which, for the most part, are included in the above pages.

ACKNOWLEDG-
MENTS

Hellmut Lehmann-Haupt

# INDEX

NOTE: This index lists the names of bookbinders discussed in the text of the book. Additional names are listed in Appendix A, pages 99-116.

The names of private and institutional owners of early American bindings are listed in Appendix B, pages 117-127.